KINSALE

HARBOUR

St Germans

Old map

WATERFORD

COUNTY

Ringrone

Sandy Cove I.

Sandy Cove

Sandy Cove pt.

Lwr Fort

Iron at Low Water

Nohavel pt.

Dungar

Slewglin

Kinsman Pt.

Frowerd point

New Fort

Plummers Cove

Rincoran Cove

Ruddocks Cove

Money point

Gillingchac point

Oyster haven

THE

SOUTH-WEST

COAST OF

IRELAND

from Dungarvan

to River Shannon

Cork

Youghill

Ardmore head

Downdaniel

Monks Creek

Leagues 20 in a Degree

CORK

COUNTY

Dingle

COUNTY

IRELAND'S
PIRATE
TRAIL

Praise for *The Stolen Village*:

'A harrowing tale that sheds light on the little-known trade in white slaves ...'
BBC History Magazine

'An enthralling read ...' *The Irish Times*

'Do yourself a favour and read it' *The Arab Irish Journal*

Praise for *Hell or Some Worse Place*
(previously published as *The Last Armada*):

'Entertaining, chatty, and superbly researched, replete with fascinating anecdotes and tragicomic relief, this is popular history at its finest.' *Library Journal*

'Fascinating ... lively and enthralling ... Ekin is a wonderful guide through this engrossing tale.' *Sunday Times*

'What an extraordinary story' The Pat Kenny Show

DES EKIN is a journalist and the author of five books. Born in County Down, Northern Ireland, he began his career as a reporter at age sixteen and rose to become Deputy Editor of the Belfast *Sunday News* before moving to his current home in Dublin. He worked as a journalist, columnist, Assistant Editor and finally a Political Correspondent for the *Sunday World* from 1982 until 2012. He has written two crime novels, *Stone Heart* and *Single Obsession*. His first true-life history book, *The Stolen Village* (2006), was shortlisted for the Argosy Irish Nonfiction Book of the Year Award and Book of the Decade in the Bord Gáis Energy Irish Book Awards 2010. His book on the 1601 Spanish invasion of Kinsale, *Hell or Some Worse Place* (previously published as *The Last Armada*), was shortlisted for the National Book Tokens Nonfiction Book of the Year in the 2014 Irish Book Awards. He is married with a son and two daughters.

IRELAND'S PIRATE TRAIL

A Quest to Uncover our Swashbuckling Past

DES EKIN

THE O'BRIEN PRESS
DUBLIN

First published 2021 by The O'Brien Press Ltd,
Originally published 2018 by The O'Brien Press Ltd,
12 Terenure Road East, Rathgar, Dublin 6, D06 HD27, Ireland.
Tel: +353 1 4923333; Fax: +353 1 4922777
E-mail: books@obrien.ie; Website: www.obrien.ie
The O'Brien Press is a member of Publishing Ireland.

ISBN: 978-1-78849-245-4

PICTURE CREDITS

Early 1600s map of Ireland: From *Pacata Hibernia Vol. II*. Mutiny on deck: By Howard Pyle (1853-1911) from (1903) *Howard Pyle's Book of Pirates*. Mrs Glass: From *The Newgate Calendar* December 1765. Pirate Hanging in Chains: from *Thames Pirate Hanged in Chains* in Albert Hartshorne (1893) *Hanging in Chains*. Map of the Caribbean *A Map of the Middle Part of America* (used in two illustrations) and figure of Captain Henry Avery: Both from Charles Johnson (1742) *A General and True History of the Lives of the Most Famous Highwaymen, Murderers, Street Robbers &c*. Cusack book: *The Grand Pyrate, or The Life and Death of Capt. George Cusack, the Great Sea-Robber (1676) by 'Impartial Hand'*. Benjamin Franklin: From *Memoirs of Benjamin Franklin* v1 (1834). Duel Between French and English ships; Boston Harbour; William Monson at Broad Haven; seascape of Henry Avery attacking the Emperor's ship; John Paul Jones (hatless); duel between British and Spanish ships ('Admiral Anson taking a Spanish Galleon'); and massed Viking fleet: all from Frederick Whymper (1880) *The Sea, Its Stirring Story of Adventure and Heroism* v1, v2 and v3. Luke Ryan: from *Hibernia Magazine* 1782. Anne Bonny, Jack Rackham, and Mary Read: all from Charles Johnson (1724) *A General History of the Pirates*. Quelch/Roach newssheet: From *The Arraignment, Tryal and Condemnation of Captain John Quelch*, a broadside published in London, 1704. Joseph Dudley: From *Historical Pamphlet No. 1: Governor Joseph Dudley (1903) Thomas Dudley Family Association*. Marsh's execution: Thirteenth Century drawing by Matthew Paris in his manuscript *Chronica Majora*. Henry III: From *Cassell's Illustrated History of England (1902)*. Marisco Castle, Lundy: From sketch by J. L.W. Page in Page (1835) *The Coasts of Devon and Lundy Island*. Tomb of Burke warrior: from Hubert Knox (1908) *History of County of Mayo*. Richard Bingham: From *Memoirs of the Binghams* (1935) by Rose Elizabeth McCalmont. 'Ye Sanctuary of Grany O Male': simplified version of detail from John Speed (1610) *Map of Ireland*. Granuaile and Elizabeth: From *Anthologia Hibernica* July 1793. Compaen fleet and book: from Anon (1659), *Claes G Compaen of Oostzanen*. John Paul Jones (in hat): from John Sherburne (1851) *The Life and Character of John Paul Jones*. Norsemen in longboat: from H.A. Guerber (1909) *Myths of the Norsemen*. Ouzel Galley painting: from W.H.G. Kingston (1875), *The Missing Ship, or The Log of the Ouzel Galley*. Early 1700s map of Ireland: Reproduced by kind permission of Lionel Pincus and Princess Firyal Map Division, the New York Public Library, *A New and Correct Chart of the Coast of Ireland (1702-1707)* The New York Public Library Digital Collections.

Published in

DUBLIN

UNESCO
City of Literature

Printed and bound by ScandBook UAB, Lithuania.
The paper in this book is produced using pulp from managed forests.

MIX
Paper from
responsible sources
FSC® C021394

For Sally

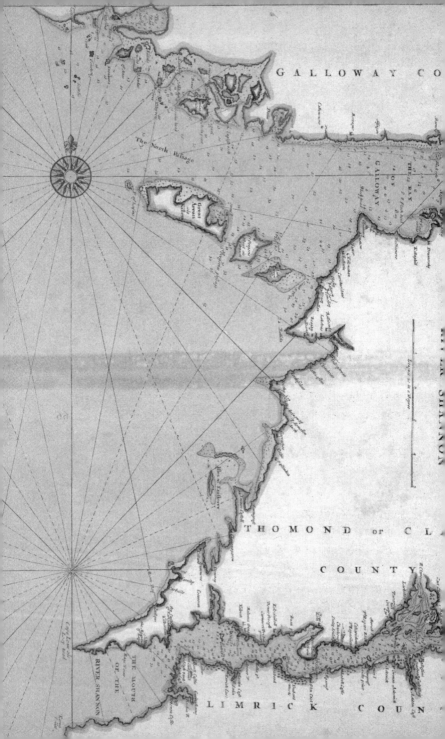

CONTENTS

Ireland in the early 1600s, as charted in *Pacata Hibernia*: pirate clans controlled the west coast, and the labyrinth of islands and inlets of the southwest made an ideal base for freebooters from all over Europe.

PREFACE

In the dead of night, four pirates haul their longboat on to a deserted beach after hijacking a ship and killing almost everyone on board. On their way to shore they have left a trail of silver treasure across the seabed: their longboat was so laden down with pieces of eight that they were forced to jettison purseloads of the coins just to stay afloat. Now, watched only by the stars, they dig a deep trench in the sand and bury the remainder of their plunder.

At another beach, in a different century, a band of buccaneers steals ashore from a Caribbean ship on a midsummer evening. Witnesses say they are carrying so much stolen treasure in sacks and casks that they are bowed down under the weight. They divide up their spoil and vanish into the night.

Another harbour, another era. A pirate ship pulls in to a remote haven, its captain desperate to sell off his cargo. The local Admiralty official is duty bound to arrest them, but they offer him a bribe of a female African slave so, instead, he decides to look the other way.

Are these pirate tales from exotic Jamaica or Hispaniola? Sweat-stained Government reports from tropical Nassau or the Mosquito Coast? Or flights of fancy from modern Disney scriptwriters?

No, all these true-life episodes happened in Ireland. They are part of the little-known buccaneering history of the greatest 'pirate island' of all.

Ever since I was a child, I have been fascinated by pirates. But I'd always assumed that those colourful freebooters and privateers flourished only in torrid, overheated climates, in faraway places like Port Royal or Tortuga Bay.

When I was a youngster, eagerly devouring stories about Blackbeard and Capt'n Morgan, I always felt a little cheated that we didn't have any pirates in the grey, cold, misty and unromantic seas around Ireland and Britain.

It was only years later, when I began research for my book *The Stolen Village*, that I discovered the astonishing truth. Not only did Ireland have a plenitude of pirates, and buccaneers by the boatload ... but, for a period in history, Ireland was Pirate Central. It was one of the two bases in the western world where sea robbers operated with defiant impunity.

At one stage, the frustrated English authorities complained that there were two areas where pirates effectively ruled unchallenged. One was the notorious Barbary Coast of North Africa, and the other was the southwest coast of Ireland.

They complained that the latter area was effectively a pirate economy. English and Irish money was rarely seen in the district – the main currencies were pieces of eight and Barbary ducats.

The more I found out about Ireland's forgotten pirate heritage, the more I longed to write a book about the subject. When the newspaper where I worked as political correspondent was hit by large-scale job cutbacks, I was suddenly free to take up the challenge. Like many people who find themselves unexpectedly adrift after many years of continuous employment, I felt rootless, terrified and yet, at the same time, liberated and exhilarated. Embarking on the 'pirate trail' seemed like a good metaphor for a scary new freedom and a new life.

I didn't want to write a conventional history of piracy. Because pirates cover such a wide range, they have little in common. Like flotsam from a scuttled prize-ship, they are scattered randomly throughout history: scattered geographically; scattered chronologically; disconnected in their motives and in their methods. The great 1600s pirate admirals who menaced the southern Irish coast with thousands of men, and who seriously challenged the English King's authority, had little in common with the opportunistic local coastal raiders of the 1400s and 1500s. The Viking raiders who founded entire cities were on a different scale to the small-time sea-muggers who lurked outside harbours to hijack fishing smacks. And men like America's John Paul Jones, who fought for the liberty of nations, do not sit easily beside the Barbary corsairs of Baltimore fame, who captured women and children for sale on the slave markets.

This posed a predicament. All I knew for sure was that I wanted to select some of Ireland's biggest, most badass pirates, to summon their spirits up from the deep, and to bring them to life without letting clichés get in the way.

I decided to take to the road on my quest. My aim was to visit their birthplaces, their centres of operation and the scenes of their greatest triumphs and defeats. I hoped to assimilate the atmosphere, in order to better understand their lives. I drew up a plan to tour the Irish coast from north to south, from Rathlin Island and Dunfanaghy to the Wexford Saltees and Roaring Water Bay; and from east to west, from Dalkey Island near Dublin to Clare Island and Broad Haven in Mayo, seeking out the pirates' stomping grounds, talking to those who knew their stories best, and trying my best to separate the myth from the reality.

As a former motorcyclist, my first instinct was to do the trip on a Harley Davidson with a Jolly Roger flag – somehow it seemed appropriate – but I abandoned that idea because (a) it was a bit too theatrical; (b) it might have been misinterpreted as a mid-life crisis, which of course it obviously, definitely, was not; but mostly because (c) The O'Brien Press did not take up my repeated hints and buy me the €25,000 Harley Heritage Softail Special I felt was necessary for the job. So mostly I travelled by car and on foot, but where it was necessary or just more appropriate, I went by ferry or sailboat.

This was also a journey in search of Ireland's pirate 'soul'. I can't think of any other country outside Africa's Barbary Coast where pirates have loomed so large in the national psyche. According to ancient annals, a race of pirates called the Fomorians played a major role in the island's early history – that's pure mythology, of course, but myths speak volumes about a nation. Legend also claims that our patron saint, St Patrick, was brought here by Irish pirates. Ireland's capital, Dublin, was settled and shaped into a city by those most successful of all sea-raiders, the Vikings, who also founded Waterford and Wexford. For centuries, much of our coastline was controlled by four great pirate families – the O'Driscolls, O'Sullivans, O'Flahertys and O'Malleys. And for large chunks of our history, piracy became a valid form of political protest.

Yet this rich and varied historical landscape is in danger of disappearing under an avalanche of well-intentioned glamorising and myth-making. Take, for instance, the famous Grace O'Malley, or 'Granuaile'. She was indeed a remarkable woman, but her towering status in legend tends to overshadow many other, more successful, pirates. In this book, I question some of the myths and try to put her extraordinary life into some perspective. And talking of women pirates … for such a small country, Ireland has supplied perhaps one-third of the world's greatest female freebooters. Another, Anne Bonny from Kinsale, is celebrated in Pirate Pilgrimage the Sixth.

While those two names are reasonably familiar, there are other pirates, like George Cusack, William Marsh and Peter McKinley, who evoked terror in their own age but are little known today. Others, like William Lamport, are more celebrated in the Americas than they are at home.

Buccaneers know no boundaries, so this book will feature not only the Irish pirates who terrorised their homeland (Black Tom, Edward Macatter, Fineen O'Driscoll) and the Irish-born pirates who flourished abroad (Cusack, Marsh, Peter Roach), but also the overseas corsairs and buccaneers who were drawn to these shores – the likes of Henry Avery, Peter Easton and Claes Compaen.

This trip was a journey of discovery for me, too. I was quite surprised to learn that pirates weren't always unwelcome when they sailed into Irish harbours. These freebooters had the power to transform the economies of places they visited, within hours. They often sold exotic goods for half-nothing, and then spent much of the money they earned, locally, on over-priced supplies, on drink and on tavern women. I found that some local chieftains, like Michael Cormick of Broad Haven, actually sought to lure pirates into their harbours with promises of feasting and dancing, and what we might now call 'honey traps'. In other centres, like Killybegs and Baltimore, local officials looked on benevolently while freebooters ram-paged and caroused around the streets like the buccaneers in a *Pirates of the Caribbean* theme ride.

When you discover that your local Admiralty officer, your lawyers and even your jurymen are actually pirate collaborators, all bets are off. At one stage, southwest Ireland had its own version of the expression 'the law west of the Pecos', naming the village of Leap as the frontier: 'Beyond the Leap, beyond the law'. They weren't joking.

I was also surprised to learn about the wide variety of pirate car-goes. True, they would bring ashore vast hoards of gold and silver coins, but they also made their fortunes from such unexpected items as goats' gallstones (known as 'bezoar stones' and taken medicinally) and crushed beetles (cochineal, used as a dye). These were a fraction of the weight and every bit as valuable as coin, but don't feature in any pirate shanty I've ever heard.

I've often wondered how much of the idiosyncratic character of the Irish has been moulded by our experiences of living alongside pirates. In small coastal villages, the approach of a strange sail could herald either death and destruction, or unimaginable prosperity, depending on the community's reaction. These villagers were on their own, far from help, and ruled by corrupt officials. They had to live on their wits, their instincts, and – above all – their tradition of unquestioning hospitality. Perhaps the most recognisable Irish character traits of today – exceptional hospitality at a moment's notice, friendliness with a core of steel, and the ability to strip a newly arrived stranger bare of all secrets within ten minutes while appearing to be nothing more than casually chatty – are actually legacies of many centuries of successful adaptation to this impossible situation.

So please, grab your canvas kit-bag, sign your X on the parchment, and join me for this exciting journey into a fascinating aspect of our history. This is not a travel book, and it's not an academic history book either. It's more like a wandering odyssey, providing a series of glimpses into an intriguing and colourful world that has largely been forgotten.

And if you think I've omitted some pirates and some locations, you're absolutely right. We have to leave some for the next expedition!

A quick note about the text: This is a work of non-fiction. Everything is sourced, and nothing has been made up. Phrases in standard quotation marks are an accurate quotation from a source. Where I use a Continental-style quotation dash, it signifies an indirect quote: that is, an honest reflection of what was said, but not the exact words. I use the term 'piracy' to mean robbery at sea, whether attacking another ship or stealing the ship you're already on. While words like 'freebooters' and 'buccaneers' once had separate and specific historical meanings, I use such terms interchangeably, in the popular modern sense, to mean pirates.

PART I

East by Sou'-East

1

PIRATE PILGRIMAGE THE FIRST

Dalkey, Tramore, New Ross, Dublin

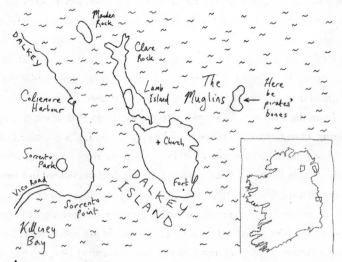

A journey of a thousand sea-miles begins with a single step.

Just a few minutes' stroll from my home in south Dublin lies a beach of grey, black and brown shingle. It's unimpressive in itself, but it commands one of Ireland's most spectacular views. A couple of miles away, the craggy outcrop of Killiney Hill, dark green and vibrant yellow with wild gorse, is set against a sky that, on this sunny afternoon, is as startlingly blue as a Chinese porcelain vase. The hill rolls chaotically down towards the sea, where, just across a narrow sound, you can see two distant rocky islets inhabited only by seabirds, rabbits and feral goats. The inner one is Dalkey Island. The outer one is known as The Muglins, and it has a special place in pirate history.

It's a fine day for a walk: breezy and cool, yet blessed with brilliant sunshine that gifts the everyday colours with an unnatural sparkle and glow. I amble along Killiney strand and up a punishingly steep stone stairway from Whiterock beach to the Vico Road. Here, surrounded by road-names rich with the resonance of Italy, I sit on a stone wall to catch my breath. Bramble, heather and furze tumble down the rocks towards Killiney Bay, a sweeping, mezzaluna-shaped inlet that has been compared to the Bay of Naples.

Nearly everyone in Dublin wants to live here. Only the richest do. Nicknamed 'Bel Eire', it is home to such stars such as Bono and Enya, people so famous they don't even have to use two names.

From the Vico Road, I wander into tiny Sorrento Park, a rocky crag offering a fine view over Dalkey Sound and its islets. The sun is now low in the sky behind, but while everything around me is in deep shade, the islands remain brilliantly lit up, as though deliberately spotlighted in a *son-et-lumière* display. Behind the main island lies the low-slung Muglins islet, with its red-and-white, torpedo-shaped lighthouse. Three centuries ago, however, this island was used for another, more grisly, form of warning. The hanged corpses of two notorious pirates were suspended here, in chains, as a chilling reminder to passing seamen that piracy would not pay. These buccaneers – Peter McKinley and George Gidley – will feature in my first true-life story.

I wander along the coastal road to Coliemore Harbour, a tiny port facing Dalkey Island. It is petite but disarmingly pretty, with brightly-painted rowboats scattered along an ancient stone slipway to a harbour not much larger than a sizeable room. It's hard to imagine that this once served as Dublin's main harbour, with merchant ships anchoring in the bay and ferrying their cargoes in by boat. Now, on sunny days, the sailors are outnumbered by the tourists, the anglers and the amateur painters.

Right now, with the little Dalkey Island archipelago vividly illuminated by what seems like its own internal glow, the colours are almost hyper-real: the island's granite rocks, covered by millennia of moss and lichen, blaze bright in a vibrant honey-mustard colour; the grass varies from a shimmering lime-green to a deep, rich emerald; and the stonework of a ruined church provides its own solemn bass chorus of grey and brown.

Dalkey Island has a long and strange history. Archaeologists once dug up a Bronze Age skull that, on burial, had been ritually filled with shellfish – no-one knows why. In the Viking era, a Christian bishop held prisoner on the island tried to swim across the sound to freedom, but drowned in the attempt.

I find a viewing-telescope and scan its shoreline. Half-a-dozen grey seals lie on the island's rocks, dozing and stretching as lazily as Sunday afternoon teenagers. Two feral goats stand on the horizon, their shaggy beards and warped, gnarled horns giving them a Pan-like aura. Gulls fight for space, occasionally flying up in an angry flurry to chase away a rabbit, and in the shallows, terns with vivid orange beaks forage for dinner.

For a moment I am blinded by a blast of pure white as a yacht sails by. It passes, and I tilt the telescope towards the separate Muglins islet, where the two grotesque cages containing the pirates' bodies once swung and creaked dismally in the wind, day and night, night and day, until eventually the metal rusted into powder. Some part of them must remain there, dust of men intermingled with rust of metal, in the earth of this island.

As the afternoon sun disappears, the islet loses its sunny glow and becomes dark, shadowy and melancholy. Two black cormorants stand motionlessly on the rock, their wings grotesquely outstretched, seeming to stare directly at me.

It's a good thing that I'm not superstitious.

On the Trail of
McKinley's Gold

6 December 1765. Tramore, off the southeast coast of Ireland.

The vessel that shimmered eerily in the sea-mists might have been a ghost ship.

Half floating, half submerged, she wallowed so deep in the water that the waves touched her deck-rails and only her sails were visible to the approaching merchant trader.

The master, a Canadian named Captain Honeywell, later reported that he would have smashed straight into her if he hadn't spotted her and changed course at the very last minute.

Honeywell, who was on his way to Waterford, hove-to and inspected the mystery vessel. He noted in his log – dated 6 December 1765 – that the stricken ship had three masts and that her top sails were still billowing in the wind, as though straining to free her from the shackles of the immense weight of seawater that filled her hold. Honeywell was also struck by the fact that all her deck-boats were missing and 'not a living creature could be seen'. Yet the ship remained intact. She had not been wrecked.

A day or so later, eight boats left Wexford to investigate, but the mystery only deepened. The unfortunate ship – the *Earl of Sandwich* – was already breaking up, and the rescuers were unable to board safely. The vessel was 'a very rich ship', they concluded, and had carried not only a valuable cargo of wine but also some well-off passengers. Yet there was not a soul to be seen, alive or dead.

The boatsmen caught their breath when they spotted a black, corpse-like object floating on the waves nearby. When they rowed around to reclaim the 'body', they found that it was merely a capuchin – a long, hooded cloak of the type worn by women of quality. It was clear that the victims of this mystifying disaster included at least one affluent female passenger.

It would be another hundred years before the name *Mary Celeste* became notorious as a symbol of a ship that had been inexplicably forsaken. In the meantime, for those few days in December 1765, the baffling case of the *Earl of Sandwich* was on everyone's lips.

As time passed, the sea yielded up some of *Sandwich's* cargo. The wine from the dozens of casks that washed up on shore was identified as Madeira, which meant that the vessel had probably sailed from the mid-Atlantic. But what had happened to the women on board? Or the captain? Or her crew?

The investigation took on an even grimmer aspect when an embroidered sampler turned up amid the flotsam. 'Kathleen Glass,' it was signed. 'Her work, finished in the tenth year of her age.'

As exhaustive inquiries continued, the authorities reached their grim conclusion: someone had 'murdered the crew, and afterwards scuttled her'.

Sandwich disintegrated a few months afterwards, and told its secrets only to the sea. Only four crewmen knew what had happened on board that ill-fated vessel. Their names were Peter McKinley, George Gidley, Richard St Quintin and Andres Zekerman. These men were very much alive – and they were carrying a fortune in stolen pirate silver and gold.

Three days earlier – 3 December 1765

The four pirates had so much treasure stowed in the rowboat, it almost dragged them to a watery death. As they rowed away from the sinking and bloodstained hulk of the *Sandwich*, its dead weight was like the hand of a dead man, a ghostly avenger pulling them deeper and deeper into the grey-green waves. It seemed to draw and suck the very ocean over their gunwales, into the bilge of their boat, until the ice-cold seawater was rising around their feet faster than they could bail it out.

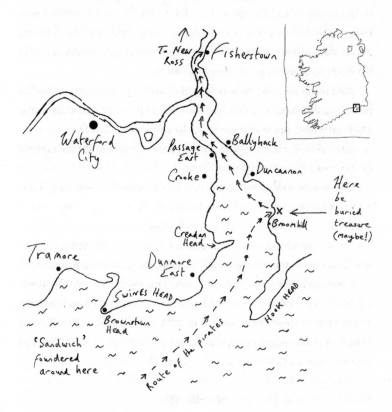

The shore was still far away. McKinley, Gidley, St Quintin and Zekerman looked at each other. All seasoned seamen, they did not need to do the calculations. Unless they jettisoned some of the treasure, their corpses would join it all on the seabed, so deep down into the grim bladder of the ocean that no light would ever glint off the precious coins scattered uselessly among their bones.

With hearts as heavy as the purses they lifted, they began to scoop out handfuls of coins and hurl them into the sea: Spanish silver dollars, the legendary 'pieces of eight' of pirate lore. These casually-tossed handfuls were worth more than they could earn honestly in years, and they were chucking out dozens of them, scores of them, each blighted coin tainted with the blood of the innocent people they had murdered.

Eventually the boat lightened until it rode over the waves instead of ploughing through them. They had lost much of their money, but the trade-off was that they just might survive to spend the remainder.

The coast of the Waterford estuary, at first grey and miasmic in the winter mist, began to resolve and assume a shape. Rocks and trees. Greyish-brown sand. Grey-green grass. It looked grim in the winter night, and yet never had any land seemed so welcoming.

Straining at their oars, they pulled hard against the current until they felt the first rough kiss of the shingly sand against the sea-beaten wooden bow. They hauled the craft up to safety and looked at each other in disbelief. They were exhausted and soaked to the skin. Two of them were bleeding from sword wounds. Yet they had done it. They had stolen a fortune, a king's ransom, a Midas's hoard. Bags and bags of milled Spanish silver dollars, of golden ingots, of gold-dust. They had stolen so much that they couldn't even carry it all away.

Their landfall was merely a temporary stop. They knew there was an English fortress at Duncannon, a little further into the estuary, and they had no wish to be stopped and searched by a naval patrol while carrying two tons of pirate silver. Under a canopy of stars, the four men hauled 249 sacks of coins further up the beach, beyond the high-water mark, and buried the bulk of the treasure – not too deeply, but just enough to hide it for a few days. They took careful note of the location – a lonely cove near Broomhill Point on the eastern shore. Then they combed the sand across until it seemed as though the beach had lain undisturbed forever.

The four pirates took the remaining bag of treasure and launched their boat. They headed north towards Waterford, but ultimately had their sights set on Dublin and a new life.

For a few years in the late 1700s, the name of Irishman Peter McKinley ranked alongside those of the world's most infamous pirates. Today, he is almost unknown, although every year, thousands of day-trippers gaze across the rushing waters of Dublin's Dalkey Sound towards the island known as The Muglins, where his body was hanged in chains as a grisly *memento mori*.

Little is known about McKinley's background. He was reportedly a northern Irishman, and his name certainly suggests links with Donegal's prominent McGinley clan. He began as a mariner, and by the 1760s rose to the rank of boatswain, or deck foreman. As bo'sun, McKinley would plan the day's work schedule, sending some seamen aloft to the rigging and despatching others to clean the decks or crank the windlass. Each piercing note from his bo'sun's pipe, rising high above the roar of wind and crashing sea, was a coded order that would send men leaping to their tasks.

As he sailed across the world's sea routes, McKinley must have watched with envy as vast fortunes were made by the wealthy merchants, sitting comfortably in their Dublin or Liverpool mansions, while the seamen risked their lives and their freedom. Not for *them*, the risk of losing a leg in a terrifying plunge from the yardarm, or the sickening fear of ending up as a Barbary slave. The seamen sweated blood, and the rich took all the rewards.

In the course of many long and muttered conversations, McKinley discovered that he had a kindred spirit in a Yorkshire seaman called George Gidley. As a ship's cook, Gidley must have seen how the crew's food was often tainted and inedible on delivery. Crooked suppliers would cut corners to maximise profits, and the men sickened and suffered as a result. The whole system was every bit as rotten as the supplies. In this corrupt world, it was every man for himself.

In the summer of 1765, McKinley and Gidley joined the crew of a brigantine that was due to sail from London to Santa Cruz in Tenerife with a cargo of baled goods, hardware and hats. It seemed like a standard journey, with a very ordinary cargo. They had no way of knowing that under the blazing sun of the Canaries, the *Earl of Sandwich* would be caught up in a dramatic rescue mission, and that she would sail towards home rich with treasure. Their moment was about to come.

Summer, 1765
As the *Sandwich* sailed away from England, heading southwards through the Atlantic swell, a Scots adventurer named George Glass languished in a Tenerife prison cell, accused by the Spanish of being a spy. Perhaps he *was* a spy, because his seafaring career up to that point was reminiscent of a rip-roaring novel by John Buchan or Patrick O'Brian. Certainly, Glass was a pirate – or at least one of the State-sponsored variety known as privateers.

Glass had begun life as a ship's surgeon, but had swapped his scalpel for a cutlass to become a freebooter, licensed to attack his country's enemies. The war between England and France brought him both good fortune and bad luck. He had taken a French merchantman, but was sub-sequently captured by a French naval vessel and thrown into some West Indies hellhole. Freed in a diplomatic transfer, he returned to privateering and reportedly amassed a fortune valued in the thousands of pounds. It hadn't been easy: the irrepressible Glass had survived a mutiny and seven spells in jail, each time emerging more fired-up than ever. This was a Glass-half-full kind of man.

It all went wrong when he decided to join an early version of the scramble for Africa. He tried to develop trade on the Guinea Coast, but was rebuffed by the locals and soon ran out of provisions. He left his ship lying offshore and sailed in an open boat to the Canaries to restock. How-ever, the Spanish authorities didn't buy his story. This *hombre* was clearly an English spy. They decided he belonged in prison. Glass was not the sort of man to languish in prison, however, or indeed anywhere. He wrote a plea for help on a hard biscuit, using charcoal as a pencil, and tossed it blindly into the street. He was in luck: the message was picked up by a foreign seaman and passed on to the commander of an English vessel.

The visiting English captain demanded Glass's release, only to be thrown in prison himself as a suspected accomplice. When word reached London, the English diplomats protested vigorously to the Spanish. Sepa-rately, Glass's distressed wife sold her possessions and set off from London to the Canaries with her twelve-year-old daughter Kathleen.

Meanwhile, McKinley and Gidley were sailing around the mid-Atlan-tic on the *Sandwich*. The captain, John Cochrane, delivered his goods in Santa Cruz de Tenerife and collected a cargo of Madeira wine, silk and a dye named cochineal (made from crushed beetles) that was much in demand. When Mrs Glass arrived, she sought Cochrane out and tearfully pleaded for his help. Cochrane pledged to do everything he could to bring her husband home.

Exactly how Glass made his exit from prison is not clear. Was it a jailbreak? Bribery? Or a diplomatic fudge, with Spanish eyes deliberately averted to enable an escape and get everyone off the hook? Whatever the circumstance, Glass ended up on board the *Sandwich* as a free man.

The *Sandwich* left the Canaries with a truly remarkable cargo. Somehow, together with all the silk and wine and powdered beetles, the ship had manage to acquire 'a large quantity of Spanish milled dollars, some ingots of gold, some jewels, and a small quantity of gold dust'. The milled Spanish dollar – with its edges mechanically patterned to prevent illicit trimming – was the trusted currency of the mainly Hispanic New World. These silver coins were the equivalent of eight smaller money units ('*reales*'), and were known to the English as 'pieces of eight' because they were literally cut up into eight 'pieces' or 'bits' to provide change. (Even today, Americans sometimes call a quarter dollar 'two bits'.)

The *Sandwich* carried at least 250 sacks of these Spanish dollars, and possibly more. All told, the ship's treasure was worth £100,000 in 1765 money – in modern terms, anywhere upwards of €12.2 million.

How, exactly, had the *Sandwich* obtained such a breathtaking fortune? This is one of the great mysteries of the saga. It couldn't all have come from trading goods. It was almost certainly part of the fortune that Glass had amassed during his buccaneering career. One contemporary source says the *Sandwich's* treasure included 'what Captain Glass had shipped on behalf of himself and his partners'.

Perhaps recent experience had persuaded Glass to cash in his assets and return home to a life of respectability. Or possibly the treasure had been released from its bank vaults and hidey-holes by Mrs Glass in a bid to buy his freedom, and only part of it was needed. One theory, although never proven, is that Cochrane and Glass had been partners in an earlier privateering business. Whatever the truth, there was undoubtedly some-thing unusual about the *Sandwich* and her cargo.

None of this bothered George Glass and his wife as they set out on their long voyage to London in November 1765. Even less so, their daugh-ter Kathleen – she of the embroidery sampler – who was described as a very winsome child, and rapidly charmed everyone with 'her beauty and fine accomplishments'. As far as they were concerned, the *Sandwich* was their salvation, and its crew were their shining knights. All their problems were over – or so it must have seemed to the rose-tinted Glasses.

McKinley and Gidley had other ideas. Even before the ship had left the Canaries, the bo'sun and the sea cook were already plotting to steal the treasure. Cold-blooded murder was being planned and plotted in McKin-ley's nasal northern drone and Gidley's gruff Yorkshire accent. Two other crewmen agreed to join the conspiracy: a Dutchman named Andres Zeker-man, and another Yorkshireman called Richard St Quintin. After heated discussion, they decided they needed to go to the most extreme lengths to secure the fortune that lay so enticingly in the hold. They 'entered into a conspiracy to murder all the persons on board'. That meant a death sen-tence on eight innocent people: Captain Cochrane; the ship's mate Charles Pinchent; the mate's brother James; the cabin boy Benjamin Gallipsey; and all four passengers – Captain Glass, Mrs Glass, their daughter Kathleen, and their unnamed servant boy.

It was planned as the perfect crime. With everyone dead, there would be no risk of a witness turning up years later. The *Sandwich* would simply disappear, scuttled to the bottom of the ocean. Her cargo would be written off, and everyone would assume that the cruel sea had claimed yet another ship with no survivors.

They struck one hour before midnight on the last day of November. The timing was careful and deliberate: the *Sandwich* had left the open sea and was preparing to pass the southern coast of Ireland, McKinley's homeland. As bo'sun, he had altered the schedule to ensure that all four conspirators were on night-watch.

McKinley knew that Captain Cochrane made his last rounds at 11pm. As Cochrane paced the deck, absorbed in his inspections, the two ringleaders pounced. McKinley seized the captain and pinned him down. Gidley

'Gidley grabbed an iron spike, raised it high and stove in his skull': a typical pirate mutiny on board ship, as depicted by an artist in 1903.

grabbed a heavy iron spike, raised it high and stove in his skull. They hefted him on to the gunwale and tossed his body into the sea.

One of eight dead.

The noise alerted two loyal crewmen – the mate Charles Pinchent and his brother James – who sprang out of their bunks and rushed up on deck. We can imagine the surprise and horror on the brothers' faces as they recognised the attackers as their own shipmates. They didn't have a chance. The iron bars rose high and plunged down on their unprotected heads.

Three of eight dead.

By this stage, it was impossible to ignore the noise. George Glass ran up from his cabin, took one look at the carnage, and bounded back to get his sword. Glass – described as 'a very powerful man' – posed the greatest threat. He was an expert swordsman, and had once quelled a mutiny single-handed simply by facing down the rebel crewmen and asking who wanted to be first to be skewered on his blade. McKinley knew that a frontal attack would be fatal. Instead, he lurked in the shadows by the companionway and grabbed Glass from behind, pinning his arms.

– Kill him, he yelled at Zekerman.

The Dutchman circled cautiously, his eyes on Glass's sword. Somehow, Glass managed to free his arm from McKinley's grip and thrust his blade toward Zekerman, slashing his arm and drawing blood. Gidley and St Quintin dived in to help, and as McKinley held on grimly, the three others managed to wrestle Glass on to the deck. In the process, Glass stabbed McKinley in his left arm. Finally they used his own sword to run him through, not just once but several times. His body was tossed into the increasingly bloody sea.

Four of eight dead.

The captain's wife and daughter were hauled out on deck.

—Have mercy, Mrs Glass implored, falling to her knees. Please don't kill us.

Zekerman was unmoved.

—Prepare to die, the Dutchman growled.

Mrs Glass pointed to her daughter.

—Kill me if you must, she pleaded. But this child has done you no harm.

—To the devil with you, snarled McKinley.

Sobbing helplessly, mother and daughter hugged in a last embrace. Impatient at the display of affection, McKinley and Zekerman lifted the two and threw them overboard, still alive and still locked together. They would not survive for long in the icy winter sea.

Six of eight dead.

Held captive during the *Sandwich* mutiny, Mrs Glass pleads with the pirates to spare the life of her little daughter. 'To the devil with you,' snarled Peter McKinley, throwing them both overboard.

The servant and cabin-boy weren't attacked, but if they thought they were being shown mercy, they were wrong. The mutineers ignored them only because they had to correct a ship that was wallowing out of control. They hauled on the wheel and adjusted the sails, pointing the *Sandwich's* bow towards the southeast coast of Ireland.

The attack had begun just before midnight on Saturday, 30 November, and ended in the early hours of Sunday, 1 December. Thwarted by contrary winds, they had to tack back and forth all through Sunday, Monday and Tuesday morning, before finally approaching the sea estuary leading towards Waterford, some thirty miles away, early that afternoon. At this point, the four men decided to abandon the ship.

The conspirators launched the ship's longboat and loaded it with the sacks of Spanish dollars, the gold ingots and the gold dust. They didn't want to leave any behind, but yet they must have felt uneasy as they watched the two tons of metal push the longboat deeper and deeper into the water.

The last of the thugs smashed the *Sandwich's* seacocks, allowing the seawater to pour into the ship, before leaping into the longboat. The men rowed off frantically, aware that their boat might be sucked under by the downward force of the sinking brigantine.

—Help! Bring us with you!

The plaintive cry came from Benjamin Gallipsey, the cabin boy. Along with the Glasses' servant, he had been callously left to drown on the sinking ship.

The four men ignored him and concentrated on their oars.

The cabin boy hurled himself into the grey winter sea. He was a strong swimmer and, with vigorous strokes, soon managed to catch up with the pirates. He clung to the boat's transom and held on for dear life. His courage didn't impress the four pirates. Grabbing one of the oars, they battered the boy mercilessly until he was forced to let go. He soon went under, and 'was immediately drowned'.

Seven of eight dead.

That left only one witness alive – Captain Glass's servant boy, who was still on board the sinking ship. There are conflicting accounts of his fate. The pirates, testifying later, claimed to have seen him washed overboard by a wave and 'soon drowned'. Another version maintains that, as they rowed off, the pirates watched him climb up the mast until at last he faded from view. This version maintains the boy survived – because the *Sandwich* obstinately refused to sink. The combined force of a landward sea-current and a brisk wind shunted her closer towards land until she became wedged on a sandbank just off Tramore, County Waterford. The story goes that the boy shouted for help until he was rescued. A few days later, as he was recovering on land, Captain Honeywell sailed past in his Canadian ship and almost struck the *Sandwich*. By a miracle of wind and current, a vital element of McKinley's plan – that the ship should sink without trace – had failed to materialise. The crime was revealed. And the manhunt for the murderers began.

They still might have got away with it. If they had handled things right, they could have lain low, negotiated a midnight crossing to England, and lived quietly and unostentatiously until the heat died down and they could reclaim their haul.

But delayed gratification was not a concept these men embraced to any great degree. After burying their treasure, they rowed further up the estuary with one simple plan in mind. They wanted to get dry, get fed and get drunk, in that order. Eventually, after they'd sobered up, they would travel to Dublin and enjoy all the delights that awaited newly rich men in the big city.

When they sailed unchallenged past the English naval fort at Duncannon, they relaxed. This region was renowned as a haven for pirates.

Wherever men could be bought with gold and could be trusted to keep a secret, the murderers felt they would be safe. Their vast riches would make them invulnerable.

They landed near Fisherstown, just south of the bustling river port of New Ross. After securing their longboat, they headed straight for the welcoming lights of the Ballybrazil village inn. The locals must have spluttered into their tankards of ale as these strangers burst in, filthy, wild-eyed, blood-spattered, two of them suffering from recent arm-wounds and all four smelling rankly of sweat and seawater. But when they threw some silver dollars on the counter, they became the most welcome customers in the world.

The night of Tuesday, 3 December, passed in a blur as the pirates enthusiastically fulfilled their immediate ambitions. They 'refreshed them-selves at the alehouse', says one account. They became so refreshed that one opportunist relieved them of a purse containing 1,200 silver dollars, and they didn't even notice until the next morning.

On Wednesday, the four hungover fugitives packed up what remained of their treasure and set off towards Dublin. They made it as far as New Ross, just four miles away, where they did just about everything they could to arouse suspicion. When a landlady turned them away from her inn, McKinley solved the problem by giving her a handful of Mrs Glass's jewel-lery. They were later to give even more lavish gifts to the maid – she got a necklace, gold earrings and thirty-six Spanish dollars.

A local moneychanger was able to change 1,250 of their pieces of eight – but only by pulling in all the gold available in town. McKinley and Gidley were decidedly annoyed that he couldn't change more. Within a few hours, they were the talk of the entire area.

On Thursday, they set off for Dublin with six hired horses and two guides. Their obliging landlady had sewn them separate purses to carry their coins. After another overnight stop, they arrived on Friday.

By this time, local authorities were starting to connect the *Sandwich* murders with the reports of the four newly rich revellers. They located their abandoned longboat at Fisherstown, and found a few pieces of eight in nooks and crannies. Sloppily, the four men had neglected to clean up. They had left damning evidence, directly linking them to the *Sandwich*.

Questioned, the guides who had taken the four men to Dublin revealed the pirates' whereabouts in the city. They had moved into lodgings on the western fringe of Dublin – on Thomas Street, in an inn known as the Black Bull.

The area around Thomas Street was, at that time, a place close to a pirate's heart. It was the first stop for the draymen hauling grain from the countryside. This raw material, combined with fresh water from a local river, had made the district the beer production centre of Ireland. Just six years beforehand, a young upstart named Arthur Guinness had opened a new brewery at No. 1 Thomas Street. Meanwhile, a distillery pumped out the hard stuff, and there were plenty of pubs where a thirsty man could enjoy both products to his heart's content. The name of one street – 'Cut Purse Row' – spoke volumes about its reputation in that era.

McKinley, Gidley, St Quintin and Zekerman must have felt that they were home and dry as they settled in to their new lives. Within a day, they had exhausted the New Ross cash and needed to change more. A visit to a nearby goldsmith earned them another £500 and – as it turned out – also sealed their fates.

On Sunday, two days after the pirates' arrival, investigating officers arrived in Dublin with arrest warrants. The two lesser conspirators, Zekerman and St Quintin, were the first to be seized. Interrogated separately, they identified the goldsmith who had changed the money. He in turn told them McKinley's whereabouts and warned the investigators that they were about to lose Gidley – the ship's cook was at that moment frantically bouncing along the rocky road to Cork in a fast carriage behind four horses, with plans to flee to England on the first available ship.

The officers quickly nabbed Peter McKinley, but when they searched all three prisoners, the only items they found were 'a few guineas, an ingot of gold, and a small parcel of gold dust'. Creepily, the three men had also retained 'some toys', which they must have taken from Glass's daughter. Undeterred, the investigators scoured the area and confiscated all the pieces of eight they had spent.

Meanwhile, mounted officers were riding flat-out to intercept Gidley. They caught up with his carriage in the midlands, and threw him into Carlow jail. The cook proved to be wealthier than his colleagues – a search revealed fifty-three guineas, some silver and a valuable Portuguese coin, a *moeda de ouro*.

The manhunt was over. It was time for retribution.

The pirates didn't have to travel far from the Black Bull Inn to their less salubrious quarters in the city's notorious jail at Newgate, just off the same street. Early in March 1766, all four appeared in court, charged with multiple murder. By this time, there was public outrage over the thugs' merciless treatment of Mrs Glass and her child. The fact that the killings had taken place within hours of Kathleen's birthday somehow made the story more personal and tragic. The trial provided a focus for the citizens' fury and the streets were thronged with an angry baying mob.

The guilty verdict was as unsurprising as the sentence of death was inevitable. After the trial, the authorities' main worry was that the men would be torn apart, limb from limb, before they reached the gallows at

St Stephen's Green. They had to provide a formidable army escort of cavalry and infantry to protect the men they were about to kill.

On Monday, 3 March, the four ragged and chastened figures were taken on their last journey to the Green, where the gentry in the newly fashionable houses around the perimeter could get a prime view of the execution of the decade. The four pirates mounted the scaffold, and eight feet kicked empty air. The executioners announced to the cheering crowd that the McKinley gang's reign of terror was over.

❋ ❋ ❋

The body of an executed eighteenth-century pirate is hung in chains by the harbour as a deterrent to others. The bodies of the *Sandwich* pirates McKinley and Gidley were displayed in more elaborate metal cages, first on the Liffey's South Wall and later on the Muglins at Dalkey.

Even after their deaths, McKinley and Gidley continued to shock and revolt the good citizens of Dublin. Their dead bodies remained a cause of offence for weeks after the execution, almost as though the pirates were exacting a grisly, post-mortem revenge. They were, metaphorically, the world's first zombie pirates.

Those of you with a queasy disposition should perhaps skip the next few paragraphs. Following a long tradition, the authorities decreed that all four bodies should be exhibited along the banks of Dublin's River Liffey as a warning to passing seamen.

Metal-and-chain cages were constructed – not very well, as it turned out – to allow the corpses to be suspended at the port entrance. Zekerman and St Quintin were displayed at the shoreward end of the newly-created embankment linking Ringsend with the South Bull sandbank. The instigators, McKinley and Gidley, had pride of place on the South Wall – then, as now, a favourite spot for promenaders seeking fresh air and natural beauty.

Fresh air and natural beauty was exactly what Dubliners didn't get. They were disgusted by what one English writer, portraying a similar scene in London, described as 'the dingy, dead, iron-bound bodies', and 'the horrid grating sound as the body in the iron frame swung creaking to and fro'. Before long, the novelty began to wear thin, and so did the metal. Within a few weeks, there were complaints about decomposing flesh falling through the cages. On 1 April, seaside strollers were shocked when – in a grisly episode more redolent of Hallowe'en than April Fools' – Peter McKinley's remains completely escaped his cage and landed splat in front of their feet on the path.

The solution? Not a decent burial, but better cages. Zekerman and St Quintin remained where they were, on the embankment, while the two instigators (or what was left of them) were removed to Dalkey, further south on Dublin Bay.

There, on the little-visited island known as The Muglins, they were suspended on the south-facing rocks as a gruesome admonition to sailors negotiating Dalkey Sound towards the busy little harbour of Coliemore.

The story of the *Sandwich*, almost forgotten today, was a major talking point in the late 1700s, and was certainly still a familiar story a century or so later, when a young Scottish writer calling himself Captain George North wrote a novel under the working title of *The Sea Cook*. It was a tale of piracy, mutiny and buried treasure. The villain of the piece was a sea cook, who plots with a small number of shipmates to murder his captain and officers as they sail home laden with booty.

The fictional sea-cook warns that the officers cannot be cast adrift or marooned. Only death will do. 'Cut 'em down like so much pork ... I give my vote to death.'

The sea-cook warns his accomplices not to let drink interfere with good judgement: 'If you would only lay your course a point to windward, you'd ride in carriages, you would. But not you. I know you. You'll have your mouthful of rum tomorrow, and go hang.'

Although written long after the event, it was a warning that seems almost tailor-made for the drunken mutineers on the *Sandwich*.

The writer was Robert Louis Stevenson. The novel was renamed *Treasure Island*. The question is: was he inspired by the eerily similar story of the *Sandwich* plot? Were Stevenson's conspirators based on the McKinley gang? And was George Gidley, the cook aboard the *Sandwich*, the inspiration for the mutinous sea cook who became the most famous fictional pirate of all time – Long John Silver?

A week after my visit to Dalkey, I decided to retrace the pirates' journey from their first landing at the beach near Broomhill Point in Wexford, through Fisherstown and New Ross, to Dublin.

Driving through Wexford's charming Hook Peninsula, I saw a sign to the beach I was looking for. I walked down a steep, rocky decline to find an almost perfect sandy strand, shaped in a curve and sheltered by a natural embrace of high rocks.

Children splashed happily in the water and families picnicked on the same golden sand where the pirates of the *Sandwich* buried their silver dollars.

What happened to McKinley's hoard? That's the twelve-million-dollar question.

The wreck of the *Sandwich* itself was to yield at least some of the treasure – coins that the pirates had either missed or left behind. One year after the tragedy, a diver explored the seabed and recovered over 1,000 silver dollars. There may be more. Finding it would be a difficult task – but not nearly as difficult as finding the trail of coins that the pirates jettisoned from their longboat.

The buried treasure on the beach proved easier to find (at least, some of it did). After confessions from the convicts, the Revenue men sent diggers to the spot. A local man helped with the logistics, and received a valuable snuff-box for his trouble. By January, they had excavated enough coins to fill eleven barrels, and two companies of dragoons were drafted in to escort the treasure to Dublin.

Yet it was whispered at the time that the Collector had not collected it all. After the diggers had disappeared, a local aristocrat issued a warning that any more treasure found there was his. Today, the legend persists that beneath these sands, and perhaps scattered on the seabed under the tides, McKinley's treasure still lies undiscovered on a beach that was renamed to reflect its reputation.

They don't call it 'Dollar Bay' for nothing.

2

PIRATE PILGRIMAGE THE SECOND

County Meath

There are times of year when travelling through County Meath is like running your fingers through a pirate's chest of gold and silver. The exuberant yellow of the rapeseed crops; the faded old gold of the grain fields and the harvested hay; and sometimes, glimpsed between a copse of trees, a glint of silver from the rippling River Boyne.

But that colour palette will come later in the season. As I drive through the county on this cool and sunny spring morning, its landscape is still bright with fresh growth and promise. The new leaves still have that translucent green that shimmers with the wind and the light, as though each leaf is a circle of lime-fruit, sliced surgically thin and held up to the sun. The grassland glows emerald in the sunshine, avocado-green in the shade.

Meath has always been a treasure trove of stories. Poetic placenames like Slane, Kells, Trim and Tara feature repeatedly in the Irish annals as targets of the Viking sea-raiders who sailed right up the Boyne with an enormous fleet of sixty ships to spoil and enslave. From their base at Kells, they captured 'three thousand men or more' for sale as slaves. Among their many atrocities here was the burning alive of 150 worshippers in a church. The Vikings were followed by later generations of pirates, who regularly plagued the county's seaports.

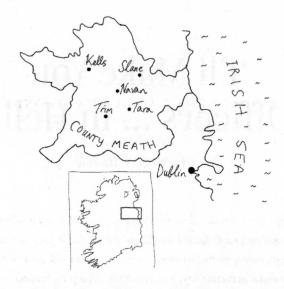

Meath is known as 'the royal county', and that's appropriate since it was the birthplace of a man who was known – at least for a short time in the late 1600s – as the king of all corsairs. His contemporaries called him simply '*The* Great Pirate', because he was 'the most signal [that is, outstanding] robber in history', a man who was 'superlatively wicked' and 'guilty of unparalleled crimes'.

Yet this man had trained as a religious friar, until his life dramatically changed – in a sort of reverse Damascus Road experience – and he went over to the dark side somewhere on the road from County Meath into Dublin. Following his probable route, I wonder exactly where it was. 'Within two miles of Dublin', says one historian, placing it somewhere between today's Royal Canal and the Liffey.

Although the exact location is a mystery, the result was a turning point in history. From that point on, George Cusack's life went to hell.

'I'll Make You Officers ... in Hell.'

– *George Cusack*

The bell shall ring, the clerk shall sing
The good old wife shall wind us.
The sexton shall lay
Our bodies in the clay
Where the Devil in Hell shall find us.
— George Cusack's sea shanty

Of all the buccaneers featured in this book, the Irish Captain George Cusack comes closest to the popular notion of a pirate. No parrot or wooden leg, unfortunately, but all the other elements are there. He roared curses like a poet and blasphemed like a man who'd sold his soul to the Devil.

Originally groomed as a friar, he ricocheted to the opposite extreme, reasoning that, if he were Hell-bent anyway, he might as well act as outrageously as he wanted. During the quarter-century that he ruled the waves, he stole from relatives, betrayed his comrades, faked shipwrecks in order to rob his benign rescuers, and – allegedly – slept with his own sister. He candidly admitted that his two weaknesses were 'loose women and riches'. His motive in life was simple – to make himself an enormous pile of pieces of eight – and yet he was capable of arguing theology and the finer points of law with the best of them. His sharp and acerbic wit turned even his own trial into a comedy show. When he wasn't indulging in piracy, he took on an equally stage-romantic role as a jolly highwayman.

Cusack did all the clichéd things that Disney pirates do – berating his lily-livered shipmates, callously setting his victims adrift in the ocean in small boats, and forcing mariners who annoyed him to 'walk the plank' from the ship into the sea. However, Cusack was such a badass that he even went one stage further and dispensed with the plank.

We know this last bit from the evidence of one of his victims, a fellow Irishman named Edward Creswell, whose encounter with Cusack in July 1674 was pretty typical. Creswell, from Derry, was on board the ship *Robert*, on a journey from Amsterdam to Newcastle, when he noticed suspicious activity among a group of men led by a 'Mr Smith' who'd been taken on as passengers in Holland. Smith and his cronies were whispering and conspiring together, to the extent that Creswell became convinced that they were plotting to take over the ship. Cusack, alias Mr Smith, must have noticed this, because he singled Creswell out for special attention after he surprised the crew and seized the *Robert*.

Creswell, who had been asleep at the time, awoke to find a ferocious figure standing over him with drawn sword.

'[He] did attack me, striking me over the face with the flat of his sword,' Creswell testified later, 'calling me dog, swearing several oaths, using me in a very ill manner.'

While the *Robert* was being seized, other members of Cusack's pirate gang were elsewhere, capturing three other merchant vessels from Sweden and Denmark. When the four ships rendezvoused, the pirates ordered the crewmen of the *Robert* into an open boat with only one sail and enough food for twenty-four hours, 'leaving us to the mercy of the sea'. In a further display of cruelty, Cusack 'let the water go out of our casks, which was more dear to us than victuals'. When the crewmen protested, Cusack snarled, 'Go. The Devil will furnish you with sails and anchors.'

Creswell alone stood up to the pirate. Stripped to his underwear by the robbers, he asked Cusack to give him some outer clothes to ensure his survival in the bitter North Sea winds. Instead, the enraged pirate captain drew his sabre and forced Creswell up on to the gunwale at the very edge of the ship. He prodded him with the blade until he went over. 'Cusack, with his sword drawn, caused me to leap overboard,' he testified.

Wallowing helplessly in the water – no doubt to the great amusement of the pirate gang – Creswell would have drowned if one of the Danish sailors had not intervened to save him. Cusack did not bother to stop him, possibly because one of the pirates searching the Swedish ship had just discovered a hidden hoard of one thousand pieces of eight. He had hit the jackpot – but, as things turned out, he was not destined to enjoy it for long.

George Cusack was uncontrollably 'wild' even as a young man. Unlike many pirates, he was not forced into the trade by political upheaval, persecution or hard times. Born around 1630 into a respectable middle-class family in the eastern part of County Meath, he trained to become a religious friar before deciding, coldly and of his own volition, to enter a life of crime.

'The wildness of his youth not agreeing with a religious life,' says his contemporary biographer, 'made him rob his nearest kinsman, Mr Benedict Arthur, of £60 and his watch within two miles of Dublin.'

It was a decisive moment. Cusack fled Ireland for Flanders, where a spell of soldiering convinced him that he would never be happy taking orders from superiors. Later, as a gunner's mate on a ship bound for Africa, he was habitually mutinous. As his biographer writes, 'all the usual punishments' – that is, whippings and worse – failed to break his spirit. Cusack found a more comfortable role as a 'pressmaster' in charge of gathering recruits by fair means or foul, but he went too far when he spirited away a condemned criminal. The sheriffs pursued him and Cusack spent several months in the Marshalsea Prison.

In jail, Cusack made a solemn resolution: he would never serve under any man again. He would 'run away with the first good ship he could get employment in'. That turned out to be the *Hopewell*, a merchant ship heading from Cadiz to Virginia. Halfway across the ocean, Cusack and his followers overwhelmed the watches in the dead of night. He forced the captain, the ship's officers and the injured seamen into a small boat, and set them adrift in the wild Atlantic. The captives begged for the *Hopewell's* longboat, which would give them a chance of survival. Cusack's reply was to blast small-shot at them until they had rowed clear.

The new captain announced that, in future, the rules would be simple. They would capture any vessels they met, except those from England; they would use the captured ships to seize other vessels; and they would divide future spoils equally.

—If you agree, Cusack said, you must take an oath to live and die together.

After receiving their pledges, Cusack rifled the ship and threw away any incriminating papers or logs. He also grabbed a large Bible from the captain's cabin and moved to hurl it into the waves. When the mutineers begged him to spare the good book, Cusack snarled a reply that was later to become legendary.

'You cowards!' he thundered as he threw the Bible away. 'Do you think to go to Heaven and do such actions as these? No – I will make you officers in Hell, under me.'

This all-or-nothing approach was to be Cusack's philosophy. The ship's song, possibly composed by Cusack himself, was cheerily fatalistic:

Hang sorrow, let's cast away care,
The world is bound to find us.
Thou and I and all must die,
And leave this world behind us.
The bell shall ring, the clerk shall sing,
The good old wife shall wind us.
The sexton shall lay
Our bodies in the clay
Where the Devil in Hell shall find us.

The *Hopewell* was reinvented as the *Valiant Prince*, with a forged log-book identifying it as a Dublin ship bound for Jamaica. However, Cusack arrived in the Caribbean to find that the crew he'd cast adrift had arrived before him. His cover was blown and he was a wanted man. After several close shaves, in December 1668, he went ashore in the Leeward Islands to find the English military waiting for him. He fled into the woods, where he found conditions unbearable:

'Being dry with such insatiable thirst,' Cusack wrote in his journal, 'I found a puddle of rainwater to the value of a pint betwixt two rocks. Sharing to everyone his portion, we marched further.' Two intermediaries met him and suggested an unarmed truce. Cusack agreed, 'being unable to live in those solitary and rather venomous woods, where [insects] sting'd us as bad as wasps'. He added, presumably with a straight face: 'Honour was forced to yield to unworthiness.' But once he'd been disarmed, the Governor's men immediately clapped him in irons in an airless hold, 'as if I had perpetrated the greatest murder in the world … with great courage, [I] overcame this villainous action'.

The pirates were taken to Barbados, where they managed to escape, grab an empty boat, and return to sea. At a nearby French island, their luck changed for the better when the captain of a richly laden frigate, the *Saint*

Joseph, innocently recruited the entire bunch to protect him against privateers. All Cusack's birthdays had come at once: the *Saint Joseph* not only held a valuable cargo of wood and tobacco bound for Lisbon, but bristled with twenty-eight guns *and* carried 20,000 pieces of eight in hard cash.

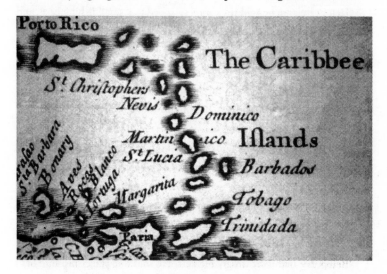

George Cusack, labelled 'The Grand Pirate', terrorised the Caribbean in the 1660s. Hunted by the English navy, he fled to the Leeward Islands (top, centre), where he was captured, but escaped in Barbados (right). He hit it lucky when a captain unwittingly hired his crew of buccaneers … to protect him against pirates.

They were only two nights out of port when Cusack took over the ship. He re-christened it *The Flying Devil* and sailed it to New England, where he sold the cargo and burned out the hull. He bought new ships and loaded them with tobacco, informing his men that, next morning, they would head back across the Atlantic to Ireland.

—Here's some spending money in advance of your share, he told his crewmen. Go ashore and make merry.

While his grateful mariners were living it up in the local pub in expectation of their fortune, Cusack cynically abandoned them. He sneaked out of port with a few fellow-plotters, 'leaving their fellows as empty of their hopes as full of their liquor'.

Back in Ireland, he sold the cargo, swapped to a small fishing boat, and sailed into St George's Channel. He waited until a Glasgow-bound frigate sailed past before signalling distress.

—We've been shipwrecked, he hailed his victim. Help us, or we'll starve.

Once aboard the frigate, they seized control and set the captain and crew adrift on the fishing boat. The pirates sailed to Galway, where they sold the stolen ship and its cargo.

Forced to lie low in Ireland, Cusack bought some horses and joined a gang of highwaymen, but after a series of robberies he ended up in jail in Dublin. Somehow, Cusack managed to convince his jailers that he was awaiting a pardon in England. He skipped bail and fled to Holland, where he soon resumed his former piratical life with the capture of Creswell and his shipmates on the *Robert* in 1674.

Cusack became increasingly reckless. He sold one prize ship in Aberdeen for around £250, even though it was worth £3,000. He sailed up the Thames and moored at Gravesend for nine days, in full view of two forts. It was almost as though he were tempting fate.

Fate was, indeed, closing in on him. Later that year, a navy ship pursued Cusack off the Essex coast.

'When Cusack saw the King's yacht and colours, he would have engaged,' writes his biographer, 'but his men would not. He being on the deck with a pistol in each hand, swore: "God damn me that I should be hanged".'

The navy men easily overwhelmed the pirates, and Cusack was thrown into jail. On Thursday, 7 January 1675, he and six of his comrades were due to appear before the Admiralty Court at the Old Bailey on a range of piracy charges.

Incredibly, he escaped yet again. From his cell, he crawled down a chimney into a less secure area, and then scrambled down a rope into a garden. He didn't take the opportunity to flee London, but instead lay low in Holborn. When officials located him, they found him in bed with a woman whom some identified as his own sister. It was Thursday morning, and the court was just about to sit.

The Admiralty Court assembled in high solemnity. A ceremonial silver oar was borne before the Judge as he took his seat to swear in the jury.

However, Cusack was determined to take centre stage. He objected to the jury, on the grounds that they were landlubbers who had no knowledge of the sea. 'We will be tried, my Lord, by men of our own trade!' he shouted.

Since his own trade was piracy, the court collapsed in laughter. Even his fellow prisoners, who were staring death in the face, chuckled 'heartily' at the sheer cheek of the proposal.

—Overruled, spluttered the Judge.

Undaunted, Cusack took another tack. He did not deny seizing the *Robert*, but claimed he had been acting as a legitimate privateer for France. As proof, he presented his commission.

—This is in a completely different name, the Judge protested in bewilderment.

—That's not my fault, Cusack replied indignantly. I can't read French.

—In any case, said the Judge, such a commission would not have given you the legal right to attack a British ship.

—True, Cusack conceded. But the owners were Dutch. They lived in Rotterdam.

And so it continued, Cusack arguing the finer points of law with humour, but also with adroit skill. 'Mr Cusack appeared to be a person of a clear courage and good understanding,' a court reporter observed. 'He pleaded very well for his life, but the matter was too foul to be washed off with good words.'

The jury obviously agreed. They found all eight men guilty. Desperate to avoid the hangman, Cusack made one last plea. Since he was a skilled mariner, he argued, he could 'wash off the stains' of his crimes by serving a life sentence on a navy ship.

But the Judge had heard enough. The sentence for piracy and robbery was clearly laid out in law, he said. The pirates should be taken to Execution Dock and 'hanged till they were dead'.

By now, Cusack had become something of a popular anti-hero. As he was taken to Execution Dock at Wapping Stairs, a 'vast multitude' massed along the docks and 'thousands' of small boats bobbed in the Thames, all vying for the best viewpoint to see the worst sea-robber in history meet his end.

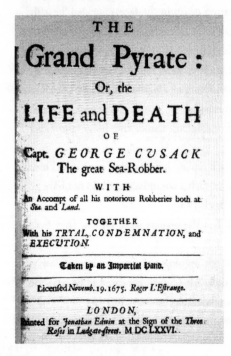

THE
Grand Pyrate :
Or, the
LIFE and DEATH
OF
Capt. *GEORGE CUSACK*
The great Sea-Robber.

WITH
An Accompt of all his notorious Robberies both at *Sea* and *Land*.

TOGETHER
With his *TRYAL, CONDEMNATION,* and *EXECUTION.*

Taken by an Impartial Hand.

Licensed *Novemb.* 19. 1675. *Roger L'Estrange.*

LONDON,
Printed for *Jonathan Edwin* at the Sign of the *Three Roses* in *Ludgate-street.* M DC LXXVI.

'Notorious robberies both at sea and land': this account of his sensational trial turned the County Meath pirate George Cusack into a legend in 1676. Unfortunately for him, it was posthumously.

When the tide retreated, exposing the Admiralty's zone of jurisdiction, the condemned man was readied for the rope. In the 1600s, the system of hanging was still crude: no sharp drop from a falling platform to break the neck and give a merciful swift death; simply the removal of a low stepladder to leave the victim kicking and slowly strangling amid the jeers and catcalls. The worst offenders were left hanging there, to rise and fall with the tides.

Before climbing the steps with the rope around his neck, Cusack said: 'Farewell earth. This is the last time I shall ever tread on thee.'

He mounted the steps, and the ladder was kicked away, ending the life and colourful career of the man they called The Great Pirate.

3

PIRATE PILGRIMAGE THE THIRD

Wexford Town

I am sitting in The Sky and The Ground and thinking about the sea.

The curiously named The Sky and The Ground is one of my favourite pubs in Wexford Town – and, indeed, in Ireland. But right now, I am not interested in the hypnotic ebb and flow and swell of conversation, nor tuning in to the primal rhythms of the traditional music. I am thinking instead about the pirates who founded this town and who dominated its history for centuries.

With the possible exception of Cork, there is no place in Ireland that is as rich in pirate lore as this southeastern corner that the Norse pioneers named *Waesfjord*, the mudflat inlet. In fact, some say that the sea-raiding traditions of the Vikings never really ceased in this part of the world, but simply continued uninterrupted, in various guises.

Pirate tales abound in County Wexford – from the remote cave at Cahore near Courtown, which a mysterious buccaneer named Gilligan adopted as his secret base; through the pirate nerve-centre of the salty Saltee Islands; all the way west to Duncannon, where an Elizabethan English landlord once went rogue and had a pitched battle with the sheriff in defence of his right to trade with outlaws of the sea.

Piracy here has often had a political motive, with freebooters acting as a *de facto* navy for whatever rising or rebellion was happening at the time. When Oliver Cromwell carried out his infamous massacre at Wexford in 1649, he wasn't punishing land-based insurgents – he intended it as 'God's righteous justice' against the local pirates.

I love Wexford, with its imposing, ghostly wharves no longer used by large shipping, its narrow mediaeval streets and its colourful pubs, which explode into frenetic life every summer. But today, Wexford is not living up to its reputation as capital of the 'sunny south-east'. Rainclouds gather ominously in the eastern sky like an avenging navy looming on the horizon, and the first plump drops of rain are already splattering like wet cannon-balls on the charcoal pavement, grey upon deeper grey.

I can't help thinking about another day in Wexford, just a few years ago, when the streets of the town exploded in fiesta colours and Latin-American rhythms, for a Mexican-style tribute to a Wex-Mex pirate. They were celebrating the extraordinary William Lamport, or, as locals like to call him, 'the real Zorro'.

William Lamport, the Wex–Mex 'Zorro'

It was a surrealistic spectacle, enough to make a man wonder whether he'd overdone it on the tequila slammers the previous night. Latin senoritas, their dark hair emblazoned with flowers, tossed and swirled their blue, red and golden dresses in a dazzling display of colour and dance as they performed in the street, flashing smiles at passers-by. Mariachi musicians in dark suits and sombreros strummed Mexican folk songs on outsized guitars. Wexford's ancient bull-ring had reinvented itself as a '*plaza del toros*', as the sober Irish seaport of Wexford came alive in a fantastic fiesta.

But no, this was not a hallucination induced by a bad burrito or a vengeful tequila worm. The colourful entertainers were celebrating the four-hundredth birthday of a Wexford native named William Lamport, a unique seventeenth-century rebel-philosopher who became a pirate captain (aged only thirteen!) after conspiring against the English King. His time as a buccaneer was a mere prelude to an astonishing career in which he served as a Spanish soldier and a secret agent, and was finally burned at the stake after a doomed attempt to free Mexico from Spain's iron domination.

His story doesn't even end there. Some historians maintain that Lamport was the inspiration for the fictional character Zorro, the masked swordsman who has been portrayed on screen by Douglas Fairbanks, Anthony Hopkins and Antonio Banderas. But before we launch into the story of William Lamport – pirate, spy and revolutionary – let's first set the scene with a general backgrounder on buccaneering in the pirates' paradise of Ireland's southeast.

With its odd mix of rugged promontories and suave golden beaches, the coastline of Wexford has always been a happy hunting ground for piratical predators. Here, the tradition of freebooting long predates modern history. The Vikings came here as sea raiders and settled in. Then came the Norman invaders – many of them actually descendants of other Vikings who'd settled in France. They morphed eventually into Old Establishment figures, distinctively Irish and proudly Catholic. Pirates were steadily elbowed out of the mainland by a burgeoning merchant class, but found a second home in the notorious French port of Dunkirk. They often used the Saltee Islands off Kilmore Quay as their springboard for raids and sea ambushes. In his history of Wexford, Philip Hore writes that the channel was then 'swarming with pirates', with the Saltees as their supply and service depot. The Privy Council in London complained that the King's ships sat idly by while mariners were 'open to spoil at sea'. But even as the English authorities seethed with impotent fury, some local landlords were helping themselves to a slice of the action.

The most notorious was Edward Itchingham, who occupied the crucially located promontory of Duncannon in the late 1500s. Edward, described as 'a dissolute character', provided a safe haven for the pirates who preyed on English and French shipping. In 1579, the Mayor of nearby Waterford complained that the area was 'much infested' by pirates who were 'succoured' by Itchingham.

Itchingham was told not to 'intermeddle' with pirates, and when he ignored the warning, the Wexford Sheriff marched on Duncannon with a small army. However, Itchingham was waiting for him with a similar force of pirates, and ambushed the Sheriff's men in the castle yard. Despite putting up a fierce resistance, Itchingham was eventually seized and ended his days in the Tower of London.

Sometimes the pirates took their captured ships right into the ports and auctioned off their loot on the quaysides. When freebooters captured a London ship named the *William* on its way to Duncannon, they brazenly escorted their prize into Wexford port and sold ship and cargo there for £370. Another victim, a French trader, complained that the Wexford pirates who stole wines from his ship were allowed to sell their haul in Waterford city.

There were many cases in which the pirates inflicted terrible hardship on merchants. In 1628, a Wexford man named Anthony Devereux was left destitute when his ship, the *Mary of Wexford*, was captured on its way home from London. Devereux 'lost everything', and was unable to support his wife and several children.

In 1566, a merchant ship called the *Sunday* was on its way home from La Rochelle when it was pursued by a pirate manned by 'Irish kerns' or mercenaries. After an arduous six-hour chase, the *Sunday* was eventually caught and stripped of her cargo and spares. Several crewmen were kept as hostages for more than two weeks before finally being set free in a small boat off the Channel Islands.

Wexford being Wexford – the heartland of every rising in the 1600s and the 1700s – it comes as no surprise that many local pirates were politically motivated. During the insurgency of 1641, London worried that Wexford was becoming 'a second Dunkirk' – quite a claim in view of the French port's extreme notoriety. Pirates later became a quasi-navy for the rebel Irish Confederacy. As Philip Hore put it: 'Besides the foreign pirates who preyed upon the merchant vessels of both countries, there were a score of fast-sailing frigates and sloops in Wexford Harbour, well manned and equipped, and their masters, who knew every rock and shoal around the south-east coast, were continually at war with the Parliament ships.'

When Oliver Cromwell came to quell the revolt in 1649, his men killed both soldiers and civilians in the infamous massacre of Wexford. He claimed later that the atrocity was divine revenge, not on the land-based rebels, but on the local privateers. 'God in his righteous justice brought a just judgement upon them ... who in their piracies had made preys of so many families,' he stated coldly.

Other Wexford pirates were forced into freebooting after backing the wrong side in a war. One intriguing example was John Gilligan, nick-named 'the pirate of Cahore', who set up his base in a remote cave at this north Wexford port. He had supported the Catholic King James II in the wars against William of Orange in the late 1600s, and had lost every-thing when James fled. Today, 'Gilligan's Cave' remains as a minor tourist attraction. Sadly, virtually everything else about his life has vanished in the mists of time.

But throughout the ages, in the annals of the rebel pirates of Wexford, one family name stands out above all others. That name is Lamport.

When William Lamport became a pirate at the age of thirteen, he had a lot of family freebooting history to live down to. His grandfather Patrick was one of the most feared sea raiders of the southeast. William was later to claim that Patrick was 'a Captain General who defended by sea and land all the province ... against the English heretics'. William's father Richard was said to have helped the 1601 Spanish Armada to invade Kinsale.

William was born in Wexford town sometime between 1610 and 1615. Both his father Richard – by then a legitimate merchant – and his his mother Aldonza Sutton came from old Norman families who were staunch defenders of the Catholic religion. William shared their grievances, and their militancy. His family's grief when his grandfather Patrick was captured and executed by Crown forces must have had a traumatic and embittering effect.

Later in life, William would often depict himself as a nobleman. The Lamports were, he argued, equal to kings and princes. His grandfather was 'Patrick The Great', and his brother was 'the Count of Ross'. The truth was less exotic, but one part of his inheritance was undeniable. Seafaring rebellion and privateering were built into his DNA.

While still a child, William was sent off to study, first in Dublin and then in London. His mother had died young, and his griefstricken father had disappeared into a monastery. William was a brilliant student, but was forced to flee from London when he published a seditious pamphlet attacking the English king.

According to his own account, he was fleeing to France on a Scots merchant ship when four English pirate ships swooped. Such attacks were common in the 1600s, and nearly always ended as bloodless victories for the attackers. The pirates travelled lightly in swift ships that could outrun and outgun most plodding merchant vessels. They could function in the wildest weather, 'by reason of the handiness of their ships and their skill as mariners', and in calm conditions could travel swiftly using oars. They would stalk a target for most of the day, dragging water casks or sea anchors behind them to give the false impression that they were heavily laden merchant ships, before swooping on their prey at sundown. The traditional pirate hail, 'We are of the sea!' would warn a merchant captain that it was pointless to put up a fight.

Once on board, the English pirates would have stripped Lamport's ship of its cargo, goods and tackle. As another victim of pirate attack described it: 'They went below ... and broke open all the trunks and chests, and plundered all our bedding, clothing, books, charts, quadrants, and every moveable article ... they then came on deck and stripped the clothes off our backs.' The trauma experienced by a young victim like William can only be imagined. In similar circumstances, another boy of fifteen recalled: 'The enemy seemed to me as monstrous, ravenous creatures, which made me cry out: "O, master! I am afraid they will kill us and eat us!"'

As the pirates celebrated their victory, they would scan the crew and passengers for likely looking recruits, and offer them the chance to join them in 'the trade'. With little to lose, Lamport threw in his lot with the outlaws of the sea.

The thirteen-year-old novice was soon blooded into the trade. His four ships ran straight into a Dutch naval patrol that was scouring the sea in search of pirates exactly like them. Battle was inevitable.

From accounts of similar Dutch actions, we know what a fever of activity preceded the clash. Soldiers would be armed and mustered on deck in fighting formation. Porthole covers flew open to reveal the gaping maws of cannon. Water casks and beer barrels were moved up on deck, where they could easily be thrown overboard, if need be, to lighten the ship and provide a turbo-charged burst of speed.

From the English pirates' viewpoint, the early stage of the clash was summed up in this breathless contemporary report of a pirate battle at sea:

'What, is all ready? Yea, yea. Every man to his charge. Dowse your topsail, salute him for the sea ... give him a chase piece, a broadside, and run ahead, make ready to tack about, give him your stern pieces ... we are shot through and through, and between wind and water, try the pump ... sling a man overboard to stop the leak. Done, done. Is all ready again? Yea, yea. Bear up close with him, with all your great and small shot charge him. Board him on his weather quarter, lash fast your grapplings and shear off, then run stemline the mid ships … the ship's on fire. Cut anything to get clear, and smother the fire with wet cloths. We are clear, and the fire is out, God be thanked … surgeon, look to the wounded. Wind up the slain, each with a weight or bullet at his head and feet, give three pieces for their funerals … gunners, sponge your ordnances. Soldiers, scour your pieces. Carpenters, about your leaks.'

The dense, choking smoke of battle eventually cleared to reveal the English pirate ships fleeing for their lives, their commander dead. They were lucky to escape at all. Once clear, their first task was to elect a new leader.

It is at this stage that Lamport's later testimony borders on the unbelievable. 'Appreciating [my] quality,' he told the Inquisition, 'they named [me] General of the four ships.'

It seems almost incredible that a band of case-hardened pirates should have elected a boy of thirteen to lead them. But piracy was a young man's business, with many freebooters no older than eighteen; so a mature-looking thirteen-year-old who'd acquitted himself well in the battle might have seemed like an impressive candidate. Besides, Lamport claimed to be of noble blood, and was thus assumed to have innate leadership qualities. So William may indeed have been telling the truth.

The new young commander soon proved his worth, with the four ships 'going on the hunt, robbing around most of the world'. Lamport's piratical spree lasted nearly three years. By that time he had built up such a reputation that – when he was still aged only sixteen – his raggle-taggle band was enlisted by the French King to help beat off an English fleet during a siege at La Rochelle. He rose to the challenge magnificently. His four ships sank nearly half-a-dozen English warships.

Lamport's fame spread so rapidly that, before long, he was able to hang up his pirate cap and unbuckle his swash to assume a more respectable land-bound role in Spain. Here, he was talent-hunted as a diplomat and secret agent by King Felipe IV's wily adviser, the Duke of Olivares.

Lamport was an agent more in the mould of James Bond than of George Smiley – he seduced a rich noblewoman and, when she became pregnant, disappeared to the other side of the world on the orders of his political 'M', the Duke of Olivares. After arriving in Mexico – then part of 'New Spain' – he ruthlessly enforced the Spanish court's interests before experiencing a political epiphany.

Touring the silver mines, he was appalled by the brutal treatment of local workers. Gripped by revolutionary fervour, he dreamed up a grand vision of a free Mexico. Admittedly, by that time he was taking the hallucinatory drug peyote, so he dreamed up a lot of things. He planned to lead an uprising of indiginous peoples and emancipated slaves, after which he would become the benign leader of a truly independent state in which everyone would be equal.

Pirate, spy, revolutionary – the remarkable William Lamport cheated the Inquisition of the pleasure of seeing him burn at the stake. But was this Wex-Mex freebooter really the inspiration for Zorro and Batman?

William was imprisoned by the Holy Inquisition, who couldn't touch him politically, but instead nailed him on charges of consorting with the Devil during peyote rituals. One indignant prosecutor denounced him as 'Don Demon'.

After suffering in jail for seventeen years, he was sentenced to a dreadful death by fire. But Lamport – ornery to the very end – cheated his tormentors of the pleasure of seeing him burn. From the high pyre, he flung himself violently forward, strangling himself on a metal collar. The year was 1649. He was in his mid-forties.

Within Mexico, Lamport is honoured as a founding father, the first man to issue a Declaration of Independence. Visitors can see his statue in the 'Angel', the memorial to independence in Mexico City: he is depicted as a long-haired, bearded, messianic figure in tunic and breeches, roped to a stake, gazing soulfully towards heaven.

Outside Mexico, Lamport is remembered for a totally different reason: as 'the real Zorro'. It is claimed that his real-life career of challenging the rich and powerful, romancing noble ladies and championing the poor may have inspired the masked avenger of fiction. Over the centuries, Lamport had featured in Mexican folk tales celebrating his exploits as a swordsman and romancer. In the 1870s, a Mexican writer, drawing on tales he'd heard as a child, wrote a novel about the Irishman he knew as 'Don Guillen Lombardo de Guzmán'. It wasn't until 1919 that the American thriller writer Johnston McCully created the character of Zorro. Some historians cite impressive evidence that McCully modelled his Zorro on Lamport. (Other researchers aren't so sure, and there are at least six other contenders.)

We could take it one stage further, since in 1939 a young graphic artist named Bob Kane watched a Zorro movie and, electrified by the idea of a masked avenger, dreamed up a character he initially named 'The Bat-Man'. So our Wex-Mex pirate William Lamport may have inspired not only the Hispanic swordsman Zorro, but also, indirectly, the Caped Crusader of Gotham City.

Among the experts, the debate goes on. But in the meantime, here in the town of Wexford, the legend of William Lamport will continue to fascinate, enthral and entertain.

4

PIRATE PILGRIMAGE THE FOURTH

Saltees, Dublin City, Rush

Ｆrom the seaside town of Kilmore Quay, County Wexford, the two Saltee Islands seem cheerfully jaunty, a couple of long, low-slung Morse dashes, like two whoops from a steam-train whistle, on the horizon. Few people pay much attention to these uninhabited islets: for most locals and visitors, they have happy associations of sunny sea trips, picnics or bird-watching expeditions.

The atmosphere in Kilmore Quay adds to that carefree vibe. As you drive south from Wexford, you find yourself in a picture-postcard landscape of country lanes and thatched and whitewashed cottages. Finally you come to the village itself, a busy fishing port that doubles as the sort of ice-cream-licking, fish-and-chips-savouring seaside town featured in jolly Pathé newsreels of the 1950s. And there in the background, always there to define the town, are the two Saltees.

But there is another view of the Saltees that is more sinister and for-bidding. You get it from the sea as you sail from the east, passing Ireland's southeast headland of Carnsore Point, on a route that has been followed by merchant ships for almost all of human history. From this angle, the two Saltees appear fused into one dark, low-lying, shape that resembles nothing more than a shark lying in wait. This is an apt simile, because for generations pirates lay in ambush at the Saltees, their ships waiting unseen in the gap between the islands – a gap that isn't visible to the passing victim until it is too late to escape.

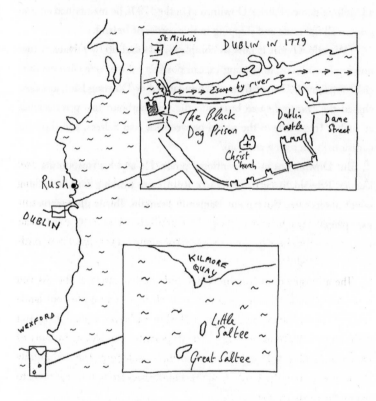

All through the mediaeval era and right up to the 1500s, 1600s and 1700s, the Saltees have been a pirate haven. Some pirates actually lived there for part of the year, using the islands as a base from which to plunder coastal towns and attack passing ships.

I made this sea trip on a cold, misty day, and it was not difficult to imagine the sense of foreboding and apprehension on board a merchant ship as the Saltees loomed closer. I thought of one particular ship, black as night and bristling with weaponry, lying in ambush like some predatory spider awaiting its next victim. It was called the *Black Prince*. Its commander was a Dubliner named Patrick Dowlin, and in the 1780s, he maintained an iron grip on all the trade and shipping in this corner of Ireland.

'[Waterford] port is now so completely blocked up by privateers that no vessel going out, or coming in, can possibly escape,' one customs official complained. 'One of them … commanded by Dowling [sic], just now chased the *Hunter Impress* boat into the very harbour; this privateer lies at anchor frequently in the sound between the two Saltees, and slips out occasionally on seeing any ship.'

But Dowlin was no conventional pirate. He and his freebooting colleagues, Edward Macatter and Luke Ryan, were working for Uncle Sam, under orders from the famous Benjamin Franklin. This is their extraordinary story.

The Three Privateers and the Rebel Yell from Rush

'Why do you fight your King?'
'Because he has done ill by me.'
  – Irish privateer Luke Ryan responds to criticism of his raids
  on English shipping

If France had its Three Musketeers, Ireland can lay claim to having three equally proud, prickly and free-spirited fighters. They could be dubbed the Three Privateers.

Like the Three Musketeers, the Three Privateers were fiercely independent men who waged war according to their own agenda. Like Athos, Porthos and Aramis, they caused major upsets at high levels in France and challenged powerful forces in England. The big difference is that Alexandre Dumas's famous trio were fictional, while Ireland's Edward Macatter, Patrick Dowlin and Luke Ryan were very much real.

Yet their story rivals any thriller dreamed up by a Dumas or a Walter Scott. They began as small-time coastal smugglers, based in the harbour village of Rush, to the north of Dublin. But one incredibly audacious raid on the Revenue men to reclaim a confiscated ship full of smuggled brandy changed their lives forever. It put them high on the wanted list and transformed them into men living in the shadow of the gallows.

With nothing to lose, they escaped to France and threw themselves into the David-and-Goliath conflict of America's Revolutionary War. Benjamin Franklin, America's representative in France, set them loose at the helms of three well-armed privateering ships, in which they terrorised King George III's shipping around the British and Irish coasts until many captains were afraid to put their noses out of port. The very names of the privateering ships *Black Prince, Black Princess* and *Fearnot* – sleek, swift and black as midnight – were enough to strike dread into the hearts of merchants and ship owners. The three men played a major part in an economic war that crippled British trade, drove insurance costs sky-high, and either captured or sank 114 ships.

Franklin, who was not given to hype, praised their contribution to his new nation. 'Between them they have taken and sent in, or ransomed or destroyed, an amazing number of vessels,' he said. And that was in an era when the word 'amazing' really meant something.

Their fascinating story began one wintry night in 1779, when Patrick Dowlin and Edward Macatter were captured by the Revenue men as they attempted to smuggle a cargo of brandy from the French port of Dunkirk into Dublin on a fast cutter named *Friendship*. The captive ship was forced to berth by the quays. The cargo was left on board, tightly guarded by customs officers, while the crew of smugglers were put in irons and escorted a mile down the quayside to a tall and ominous tower known as the Black Dog.

Located on the banks of the Liffey, near today's Brazen Head pub, the Black Dog prison was a notorious hellhole. Gentlefolk strolling along the south Dublin quays shivered as they looked up at the grim, forbidding turret and heard the moans of the inmates confined in its dank lower regions.

Innocent people were routinely seized and thrown into the Dog's filthy cells on the basis of blank warrants, pre-signed by city aldermen who collected a percentage of the bribes their victims had to pay to get out. The jailers demanded a backhander known as a 'penny pot' from new entrants. 'Prisoners refusing to comply with this demand were abused, violently beaten and stripped,' says one history. '… Prisoners unable to meet these demands were immediately dragged to a damp subterranean dungeon.' This twelve-foot-square cell held as many as twenty people, ranging from dissidents to street women, whose nightly presence gave the dungeon the black-humour nickname of The Nunnery.

Dowlin and Macatter were not destined to stay in the Black Dog for long. The third member of the trio, Luke Ryan, had escaped capture and galloped from Dublin to Rush to round up support. As night fell and the moon rose over the sleeping city, his rowboat glided stealthily along the darkened Liffey and moored beneath the grim silhouette of the Black Dog's tower.

No-one heard a sound as they stole into the prison. The warders, who were more accustomed to beating up defenceless middle-aged merchants, took one look at the menacing gang and surrendered. Within minutes, the captives were hauling oars down the River Liffey towards the sea and savouring the cool, salty air of freedom.

Further down the river, the *Friendship* lay moored to the wharf. The unsuspecting Revenue men were keeping minimal watch, convinced that their captives were still safely languishing in the Dog.

The Rush smugglers swarmed on to the ship, easily overcoming the men on watch. The lines and warps were slipped and the *Friendship* drifted away from the quay as silently as a spectre. At the river's mouth they set their sails, caught the wind, and melted into the night.

They released their Revenue captives on a deserted strand, well aware that this act of clemency would not save them from the gallows. As far as the British were concerned, they were now dead men sailing. The *Friendship* set its course for the only place in Europe where its crew could be guaranteed sanctuary – the pirate nest of Dunkirk.

Cometh the hour, cometh the ship. Just as the *Friendship* arrived in Dunkirk, a new opportunity opened up for the Rush smugglers. They were a solution to a problem they didn't even realise existed. US Commissioner Benjamin Franklin happened to be looking for a fast ship and a tough crew who could help the navy of his fledgling thirteen-state Union to harass their English oppressors in their own backyard. American navy vessels were already operating around England and Ireland, but their men were regularly captured and imprisoned. By early 1779, there were 500 American prisoners in England. London refused to regard these captives as prisoners of war: they were simply rebels, to be treated as traitorous scum. Franklin described their conditions as 'more than barbarous'. One American was left in a cell with guards who were ordered to deprive him of sleep until he died of fatigue.

Franklin, a Founding Father of the USA, a champion of the Enlightenment movement and a reluctant military strategist, could envisage only one way out of the dilemma: to accelerate the capture of English ships until he had taken as many prisoners of their nationality as they had taken of his. That could eventually lead to a large-scale exchange of prisoners, which was his main aim. He didn't want to become involved in the murky world of privateering, and he certainly didn't want to offend America's new ally, France. As he explained later: 'I have had no other interest [than taking] prisoners in exchange for my countrymen.'

When the footloose *Friendship* appeared in Dunkirk, two local entre-preneurs named Franz Coffyn and Jean Torris approached Franklin with a proposal. They would refit and re-arm the smuggling ship and put her to sea as an American-commissioned, anti-English privateer under the new name of the *Black Prince*. A US citizen would nominally command the vessel, but the real masters would be the Three Privateers from Rush. Franklin immediately saw the potential of a crew of 'old smugglers, who knew every creek on the coast of England'. He also realised that these were desperate men with little to lose. 'The *Black Prince* ... had been an old smuggler on the coasts of England and Ireland,' he explained later, 'and was taken as such and carried in to Dublin, where her crew found means to break prison, cut their vessel out of the harbour, and escaped with her to Dunkirk ... [They] were afraid to continue their smuggling business, lest if they should be again taken they might be punished as British subjects for their crime in Dublin, and were willing to go a-privateering against the English.' He believed that their Irish accents would enable them, at a stretch, to 'pass as Americans' if they were captured. He approved the plan, 'believing that such a swift vessel with a crew that knew so well all parts of the enemy's coasts might greatly molest their coasting trade'.

A typical privateering contract instructed the crews 'to give chase to, to capture, to hold in ransom and to destroy' enemy ships. But Franklin wanted this mission to be different: they must concentrate on captur-ing live prisoners for swaps. Coffyn, Torris and the Three Privateers had another viewpoint, because they depended on prize money. Right from the beginning, that difference in outlook posed a problem.

The *Black Prince* was painted jet-black and reborn as a light, high-speed cutter, with sixteen three- and four-pounder guns and another thirty-two swivels – small, manoeuvrable and blisteringly effective anti-personnel cannons. As she set sail for the first time in June 1779, she was nominally commanded by a Captain Stephen Marchant from

Ben Franklin, founding father of the United States, wanted a band of tough corsairs who could harass British shipping and help him in the battle for independence. He signed up the Three Privateers from County Dublin – 'old smugglers, who knew every creek on the coast' – and they didn't let him down.

Massachusetts. One of his lieutenants was a 'Richard Bennett of Boston', who was actually Edward Macatter. Around forty of the crew were Rush smugglers, and Ryan and Dowlin played prominent roles.

The initial mission lasted ten days, and did not help Franklin at all. First, there was a fierce firefight against two armed English cutters in the

Channel. The Irish crew won and killed several Englishmen, but they were no better off financially or in terms of prisoners. There followed several days of frustrating inactivity until, within a single explosive forty-eight-hour period, they captured eight merchant ships and more than three dozen prisoners – so many, in fact, that the *Black Prince* couldn't contain them all. However, the English pursued them and recaptured six of their eight prize vessels, together with their temporary Irish crews and sixteen of the prisoners. The *Black Prince* itself only narrowly evaded capture. Result: the privateers had lost as many of their own men as they had taken prisoners.

From now on, they decided, captured prisoners would be 'paroled' on an honour system after signing a pledge that, once they were home, an American prisoner would be released in their place. The plan was doomed: the British simply rejected the contracts as worthless.

Franklin may have been frustrated, but the shareholders were soon delighted with the *Black Prince*'s performance. 'She went around the coasts of British and Ireland,' recalled Captain Marchant, 'and in less than three months took 37 prizes: three were retaken, four burnt … [and] the rest either ransomed or arrived safe.' He added that 'the lowest men have made a little fortune'. The highest investors made a big one … at least on paper.

Luke Ryan soon dropped the 'American captain' pretence. In September 1779, he abruptly sacked Marchant and took command. However, after a month, he fell ill and nominated Dowlin as his replacement.

Emboldened by their triumphs, the Dunkirk financiers decided to expand the operation with a sister ship, the *Black Princess*. 'These successes,' Coffyn informed Franklin, 'have determined the proprietors to fit out another cutter, mounting sixteen three-pounders, 24 swivels and small arms, with 65 men, all Americans and Irish, under the command of Captain Edward Macatter of Boston [*sic*].'

For their part, the English were bewildered by this piratical pipsqueak of a ship that was wreaking so much havoc. They explained in obvious embarrassment that the privateer vessel was 'manned by several fellows who broke out of Dublin Jail' and were 'a desperate crew having the halter about their necks'.

The trio went on to command three separate ships – the *Black Prince*, *Black Princess* and *Fearnot* – and for a brief time, deterred Britannia from ruling the ocean waves. Franklin wrote to Congress: 'The *Black Prince* and *Black Princess* … have greatly harassed the English coasting trade, having in 18 months taken near 120 sail.'

Here are the individual stories of the the Three Privateers.

Edward Macatter

The man that Jean Torris described as 'the brave Macatter' was far and away the most successful of the three Irish privateers, bringing home prizes worth 1.8 million French livres (in comparison, a skilled tradesman earned around 100 livres a year). He also seems to have been the most politicised of the trio, declaring his allegiance to the new United States 'at the risk of my life and [my ship]'. Unlike Luke Ryan, he was totally focused on Franklin's central mission of freeing American seamen in England through prisoner exchanges. 'I shall fetch a great many more prisoners,' he promised to Franklin after landing one batch, '… to have a like number of my poor distressed countrymen exchanged, God may send it.' At one stage he reacted angrily to reports that the prisoners he captured were being exchanged for Frenchmen rather than Americans. Macatter warned Franklin: 'I would rather maintain them in jail at my own expense than to have them lost for the Congress.' If this continued, he warned, 'not one single man would go any more to sea with me'.

Macatter pretended he was an American, but he was actually born in the seaside village of Loughshinny, north of Rush. He used at least three aliases, one of them 'Edward Wilde', which may actually have been his real name. However, in official documents he signed his name as 'Edward

Wildallies Macatter', and his wife Mary continued to use 'Macatter' for herself and her husband after the wars were over.

The father of four children, Macatter was an experienced seaman, a brilliant naval strategist and – judging from his letters to Franklin – a man genuinely inspired by the ideals of American independence.

After serving his time as First Mate aboard the *Black Prince*, Macatter had taken command of the *Black Princess* in April 1780, with a crew of 'resolute fellows' and a 6.25 per cent interest in the mission. His first few days cruising jointly with Patrick Dowlin's *Black Prince* were spectacularly successful: seven ships taken, five ransomed, and sixty-eight prisoners captured. However, Macatter lost a dozen of his own men, and the *Black Princess* was damaged beyond repair.

Back in France, he was given a replacement *Black Princess*, bristling with eighteen six-pound guns, two stern-guns, and thirty swivel guns. Macatter also took on twenty-one veteran American seamen who had escaped from England. This unusual alliance of free-spirited Irish smugglers and disciplined US marines is the stuff that great movies are made of. Despite the inevitable culture clashes, it proved a winning combination.

It had its baptism of fire in May 1780, when three English warships caught up with Macatter and raked his decks and masts with gunfire. There was consternation aboard the *Black Princess* as shards of glass splattered into the timber. The English were illegally firing broken-glass shrapnel – outlawed by international agreement. As the other two pursuers closed in, defeat seemed inevitable. But this was the moment of sweet revenge the American escapees had been waiting for. They stayed cool and aimed their cannon at the leading attacker's mast. One shot hit true and the crew of the *Black Princess* cheered as the mainmast crashed down on deck, burying their cursing opponents under a spider's web of rigging and sail. Macatter raised canvas and streaked off without sustaining a single casualty.

The *Black Princess* went on to cause havoc off the Irish coast, attacking high-value ships bound for Youghal and Waterford. The ships were usually either ransomed or burned, although sometimes the ransom was imposed at gunpoint.

Other confrontations were slightly more civilized. A Captain George Cload, whose ship was seized off the Isle of Man with a valuable cargo of timber, was escorted into Macatter's cabin. It was 3am.

—You're very welcome aboard, Macatter said warmly. Would you like a glass of gin-and-bitters?

—No thanks, the victim replied. I've had bitters enough for one night.

—In that case, said Macatter, would you like to ransom your ship?

—Not unless you'd accept £300, said Cload.

Remaining pleasantly conversational, the privateer replied that, unless he doubled his offer, his ship would have to be torched. The captain refused. Macatter sighed and ordered an incendiary crew to sail across to the empty vessel. Then he invited Cload to take a ringside seat at the fireworks.

—Come up to the deck, he urged enthusiastically. We'll show you how it's done.

The sullen captain waited until the arson crew had almost boarded his ship before deciding that the Irishman was not bluffing. He met Macatter's demand.

Cload was exceptionally unlucky, for just six months later, he was in command of the same ship when it was wrecked in a storm.

Notes promising to pay a ransom were legally binding, and were highly valuable. But if the privateer vessel itself were taken, the captors could simply rip up the notes. For this reason, the privateers hid them in all sorts of ingenious places. One captured American privateer captain kept his profits safe from a thorough search by entrusting the ransom notes to his hunchbacked cook, who hid them under his hump.

Hostages were retained until the ransoms were actually paid, but niggardly ship owners often abandoned these prisoners. When Macatter took and ransomed a ship named the *Saville*, a seaman named Yates was ordered by his captain to go on board the privateer as a hostage, on full wages. However, the owners simply wrote off the *Saville*, and the unfortunate Yates was retained for nearly four years. On release, he was refused his back-pay. He sued and won his money.

Edward Macatter continued his run of successes throughout 1780, capturing a total of forty-three ships, with only one retaken by his enemies. In one single cruise, he captured twenty-nine ships. Cruising jointly with Dowlin, he captured twenty prisoners for direct exchange (Dowlin took forty-eight); alone, he captured thirty-six, for a grand total of fifty-six, with perhaps another three dozen released on parole.

Yet life as a privateer could be short and brutish. On one trip, Macatter had two men killed, five wounded and 'one burned'.

The last word on Macatter goes to Franklin: '[You] have much alarmed the enemy's coasts, and done great damage to their commerce, your bringing in so many prisoners is another considerable service,' he wrote warmly. '[I have] much esteem for your activity and bravery, Sir.'

Patrick Dowlin

In financial terms, Patrick Dowlin was the second most successful of the three privateers, taking an impressive 1.5 million French livres' worth of prizes. He could also be described as the most successful in the sense that he was never defeated, never captured and never brought to trial. After serving as First Lieutenant on board Ryan's *Black Prince*, he took over its command in October 1779. Ryan told Franklin that he was 'best calculated in every respect to replace me'.

Dowlin told Franklin, '[I] expect and determine to do as much hurt to the enemies of the United States as I possibly can.' He set sail in wintry December, cruising jointly with Macatter's *Black Princess*. 'I left Dunkirk the 21st of last month,' Dowlin wrote to Franklin in January, 'all hands well, hard weather ... [I] took three valuable prizes ... besides four ransoms [and] 43 prisoners.'

His next cruise, beginning in February 1780, elevated him into a legendary figure. One incident in the Irish Sea made him infamous. Cruising alongside Macatter, he set his sights on an almost impossible target: the ultra-fast mail ships that streaked between Dublin and Wales each day. No pirate had ever matched their speed.

Dark as a cormorant, the *Black Prince* emerged from the gloomy March twilight to chase down the *Hillsborough* mail ship. His men boarded her, looted the vessel and searched all the passengers, who later complained of their foul language and alleged the women passengers had been treated indelicately. Not content with one vessel, Dowlin hung around until midnight and took the second mail ship, the *Bessborough*. One enraged passenger said that Dowlin took all his money, but kindly left him a single farthing – the lowest coin in the realm.

After the two ships were ransomed, the authorities heard that Dowlin and Macatter intended to land in Rush for supplies. That night, more than 280 heavily armed militiamen marched from Dublin to catch them in the act. However, a storm scuppered the privateers' plans and they sailed directly to France, unaware of their narrow escape.

English merchants pleaded for naval protection. One Waterford customs official wrote that his port was completely blockaded. 'A lugger of 16 six-pounders commanded by Dowlin just now chased the *Hunter Impress* boat into the very harbour ... scarce a day passes that vessels are not taken in view of the people about Dunmore and Tramore.' He predicted that 'there [will] be an end to all trade here'.

However, the plucky *Black Prince* was living on borrowed time. Cruising in the Channel in April 1780, Dowlin was forced to flee from two fast warships flying English flags. The chase continued all night. By daybreak, they were skirting the French coast. Thousands lined the clifftops to cheer the *Black Prince* on. Finally a big gun roared out a warning shot from a French fortress. Two things happened in quick succession: the *Black Prince* smashed into a hidden rock, and the two pursuers swapped their English flags for genuine French colours. Incredibly, they had actually been 'friendly' French ships sailing under false flags – and they had attacked the *Black Prince*, thinking it was an English vessel.

Since no-one was hurt, Franklin was philosophical. 'The *Prince* was wrecked on this coast,' he wrote to Congress, '[but] the *Princess* still reigns.' Torris bemoaned that his ship 'deserved a better fate', but pledged: 'I would sooner sell my last shirt than not procure soon a large cutter for the intrepid and clever Captain Dowlin.'

Again, it is Franklin who best sums up Dowlin's legacy. 'I congratulate you on the success you have had against our enemies,' he wrote in 1780. '... The prisoners you have brought in will soon procure the liberty of as many of our countrymen ... It is therefore an essential piece of service to the United States.'

A sea duel between French and English ships. But when privateers used false flags, you could have an epic mishap in which two friendly ships, each unaware of the other's true identity, could become unintended foes. It was this sort of misunderstanding that led to the wrecking of Patrick Dowlin's ill-fated *Black Prince*.

Luke Ryan

Luke Ryan had a spectacular career. Like his two comrades, he terrorised English and Irish shipping, but he took things one step further by carrying out land raids. His exploits were famous in London and legendary in France, but he never achieved any recognition in America.

Ryan was born on St Valentine's Day 1750, in Kenmure, near Rush. His father Michael was a teacher, who apprenticed his only son to a carpenter. However, Luke found his true calling as a smuggler, and rose rapidly up through the tough ranks of the contrabanders thanks to his superior seamanship, sharp intelligence and sheer brass neck.

The 'astonishing' Luke Ryan from County Dublin, one of the Three Privateers who turned the tables on the British during America's War of Independence. Ben Franklin said he had 'done honour to the American flag'. Yet Ryan died penniless.

Later, a hostile English report would describe him in unflattering terms: 'He is of small stature, rather approaching effeminacy, his countenance is pale and sickly, but marked with the strongest sensibility, and his address is perfectly that of the gentleman.'

Ryan's dream was to secure a US naval commission, but it never happened. It wasn't for lack of courage. 'I have sailed with many brave men,' one American naval officer wrote, '… yet none of them equal to this Captain

Luke Ryan.' Benjamin Franklin himself was impressed with his 'activity and bravery', and sent Ryan a special night-vision telescope as a mark of his appreciation.

During his first successful cruises, the *Black Prince* 'took, ransomed, burnt and destroyed above 30 of their vessels within these three months,' Franklin reported. After a short illness, Ryan set sail again in March 1780 in a new ship, the *Fearnot*, with fourteen six-pound guns, a dozen swivels, and nearly 100 men. He promised Franklin that the vessel would 'do as much harm to the enemy as one double her force'. Franklin replied: 'I make no doubt you will do honour by your bravery and good conduct.'

Strange things could happen on a Ryan expedition. Off Tory Island in Donegal, the *Fearnot* exchanged gunfire with a British privateer and captured its skipper, Captain Sinclair. Shortly afterwards, he took a second ship, whose master refused to pay a ransom.

—Very well, said Ryan, then your ship goes up for auction. What am I bid?

—Five thousand guineas, shouted his first victim, Captain Sinclair.

—Sold, Ryan declared.

And so the first captive bought the second captive's vessel.

Some disenchanted seamen actually *wanted* to be caught. When Ryan boarded one ship, he found the crew eagerly packing up and raring to go. The captain congratulated Ryan on his capture and shouted happily: 'Fortune of war, I am caught!'

Off the north Scottish coast, there was a surreal episode when Ryan boarded a small sloop to find a wealthy landowner escorting a party of rich gentlemen from Derry, who had 'come a-pleasuring' to shoot game on his estate. The landowner, clad in full tartan, 'remonstrated' with Ryan. 'I having my Highland clothes on,' he later recalled, 'the captain [acted] in the most agreeable and genteel manner.'

Ryan was courtesy itself. Posing as an American, he apologised for the inconvenience and chatted with them for a while about hunting. When he finally said, with sadness, that he'd have to levy a small ransom, the gentlemen were so enchanted with his fine manners that they paid up willingly. They even invited Ryan to come hunting with them, but the buccaneer regretfully declined.

Ryan was famously unpredictable. In the Hebrides, he threatened to burn the town of Stornoway and held back only when its leading inhabitants surrendered themselves as hostages. Yet when he targeted Portree, his only demand was for some provisions, which he paid for in full. Another time, he sailed up a channel, more than ten miles inland, at great risk ... for no other reason than to visit a pub.

Panic spread along the coastline, with one man complaining that Ryan attacked them almost daily, 'carrying away the cattle, or plundering the houses of the wretched inhabitants'. A London newspaper wrote: 'Luke Ryan reigns uncontrolled.'

Ryan's *Fearnot* sailed on two missions, but returned to France without a single live prisoner. Overall, his record as a privateer for Uncle Sam was not particularly impressive. Macatter and Dowlin had brought back more than 100 prisoners, compared to Ryan's zero, and in financial terms, Ryan's prize total of 675,521 French livres was far less than the others'.

However, Franklin summed up Ryan's seafaring legacy in 1779, when he wrote: '[I am] much pleased with your activity and bravery, in distressing the enemy's trade and beating their vessels of superior force, by which you have done honour to the American flag.'

The Irishmen's privateering party could not last forever, and it all turned sour when Macatter and Dowlin, separately, made stupid mistakes. Macatter took on some French Navy deserters, and nearly ended up in jail. Dowlin seized a ship from neutral Holland, sparking an international incident.

The furious French authorities ordered Franklin to call a halt, and Torris was told: '[You] can no longer sail your vessels under any other flag but that of France'.

The three privateers adjusted to the new reality. Dowlin joined the French Navy, and Macatter and Ryan continued to sail as privateers for France.

Luke Ryan finally met his equal, in the form of a Scottish skipper who matched him in devious trickery. The Irishman was cruising near Scotland's Firth of Forth in a thirty-two-gun French privateer, *La Calonne*, when he captured the brig *Nancy* from Aberdeen. The skipper, John Ramsay, agreed to ransom back his boat for 300 guineas, but mentioned casually that there were several large fishing boats close by. There were indeed ships nearby, but – as the devious Scotsman well knew – they were disguised navy vessels. Ryan took the bait and set off in pursuit. On 16 April 1781, he confronted what he thought was a defenceless fishing craft. It was actually the massive seventy-four-gun navy ship *Berwick*.

A line of concealed portholes flew open and Ryan found himself staring down the mouths of three dozen Navy cannon. Realising that he'd been played for a fool, the Irishman fled. He might have outpaced the lumbering *Berwick*, but he was cut off by its companion ship, the thirty-two-gun *Belle Poule*. The *Calonne* and the *Belle Poule* fought it out on equal terms, but when the *Berwick* caught up and joined the fray, it was all over.

Ryan was taken under heavy escort to London, where he was remanded to Clerkenwell Prison. 'Both Ryan and his mate seemed much affected with their commitment, wrung their hands and wept, and seemed in very great agitation,' reported *The Universal Magazine*. However, another press account said: 'Luke Ryan appears perfectly at ease in his confinement' and seemed totally unconcerned by his predicament.

In October that year, Macatter was captured off the Scilly Islands. Although he claimed indignantly to be a Boston man, he was declared a British subject and duly charged with piracy and felony.

At nine o'clock on Saturday, 30 March 1782, Ryan came to trial. The Scots skipper John Ramsay took the stand and identified the defendant's handwriting on the ransom note. The evidence was damning, but observers were struck by the prisoner's apparent coolness. 'Ryan was elegantly dressed,' one wrote, 'and seemed little affected with his fate.'

In his defence, Ryan claimed he was not the Irishman Luke Ryan, but a French-born soldier named Joseph Ryan. Since he was a licensed French privateer, he could not be convicted of piracy. There were, no doubt, gasps of astonishment around the court when he produced a witness bearing his French birth certificate and documents 'proving' his military career there. However, two officers from the *Belle Poule* claimed that Ryan had admitted he was an Irishman, born in 'a place near Dublin'. Another officer, fluent in French, had talked to him in that language, but found Ryan struggling to keep up. 'You do not speak like a Frenchman,' he had accused Ryan at the time.

Another officer on the *Belle Poule* claimed Ryan had disclosed the motive behind his attacks on English shipping.

'Why do you fight against your King?' he had asked him.

'Because I have been ill used by him,' Ryan had replied.

Ryan's defence was finally demolished when a line-up of Irish people from Rush testified to his real identity. They were later to pay a heavy penalty. Patrick Dowlin, who was still at liberty, launched a reprisal raid on Rush and burned their homes.

The jury deliberated for only an hour before returning their verdict: guilty.

Macatter came before the same court and was also pronounced guilty. It was ruled that both privateers had been 'under colour of commission from the French king, although natural-born subjects of this Kingdom'.

Judge James Marriott imposed the worst possible sentences. Ryan and Macatter would be taken to Wapping, hanged, and left to rot in the rising tide of the Thames.

Thomas Digges, a pro-American advocate in Britain, worked hard on their case, but privately conceded to Franklin that they were 'both condemned and likely to suffer'.

What happened next was enough to turn the most courageous man insane. Four times Ryan and Macatter were fetched from their cells to meet this dreadful death, and four times the hangings were postponed.

Back in France, Torris was pushing for his Government to intervene 'in saving the life of this brave sailor'. Fortunately for the duo, some delicate peace negotiations were taking place between England and France, and when Queen Marie Antoinette personally begged for their pardon, 'his Britannic Majesty was pleased to grant' it.

On their release, Ryan and Macatter found themselves rich beyond any wild dreams they'd ever had as scruffy small-time smugglers in Rush. From his French bank account alone, Ryan stood to collect a fortune equivalent to €8 million today. However, he never saw a penny.

'[He] expected to enjoy the spoils of his adventurous life, a fortune of £70,000, which he had lodged in a mercantile bank in Brittany,' said one early historian, 'but his wary bankers, taking advantage of his legal incapacity to sue, withheld the sum for their own use.'

The bankers claimed that a mystery lady claiming to be Ryan's wife had turned up unexpectedly at the bank, and had withdrawn the lot. There was nothing they could do, the bankers said, no doubt with an apologetic Gallic shrug.

Separately, Ryan was owed 160,000 livres in back-payments from Jean Torris. But 'when he returned from imprisonment', says one early French history, 'he found Torris in bankruptcy and he thus lost the larger part of all he had gained during the war'. Even King Louis intervened on Ryan's behalf, but the Irishman never saw any money.

Nominally rich but penniless, Ryan ended up in a debtor's jail over a £200 debt. He died there in 1789, and his passing rated only a small paragraph in the Deaths column: 'Yesterday morning, in the King's Bench Prison: the notorious Luke Ryan, who commanded the *Black Prince* privateer and captured more British vessels than any other single ship had done in the same space of time.' The *Gentleman's Magazine* added: 'The various scenes he went through are astonishing.'

Macatter was equally down on his luck. In 1782, we find his wife Mary begging for help from Franklin. 'This Torris says he owes Macatter very little money, and cannot pay it, as he says he did not receive the price of the prizes they took, which were vast, many and very valuable,' she wrote. 'But this is only a false and villainous excuse.' She claimed Torris had used the privateers' money to buy lavish properties, and yet 'says he cannot pay a poor starving family'. But when the war ended in 1783, Franklin had other priorities. Macatter also died poor.

Although undefeated, Patrick Dowlin was finally laid low by a different sort of enemy: alcohol. His heavy drinking interfered with his naval duties, and when his fellow officers boycotted him in 1788, he was discharged for bad conduct. According to contemporary sources quoted by historian William Bell Clark, he was living 'a life of the greatest debauch by passing days and nights in drinking in dens with the worst riff-raff of English sailors'. And with that suitably piratical image, one of the greatest Irish privateers in history disappears from the record.

Two of the Three Privateers have had a raw deal from history. Our human need for one strong central character in our historical narratives has elevated Luke Ryan to the status of superstar, with Macatter and Dowlin reduced to minor supporting roles. Ryan was indeed a remarkable man, but some eighteenth-century letters and reports gild the lily. For instance, King Louis XVI wrote in 1786 that Ryan had personally 'captured 80 English vessels without counting those that he had sunk, captured 60 cannon, made more than 500 prisoners, and had fought through 13 combats, receiving many wounds'. Today, Ryan is often given credit for *all* the successes of the *Black Prince*, although for the most part that ship was commanded independently by Dowlin. Ryan is also sometimes credited with capturing 161 exchange prisoners for Franklin, but that is actually the overall total of the three men combined. Figures painstakingly compiled by William Bell Clark show that the trio, sailing together in the *Black Prince* under Ryan/Marchant, took thirty-five prizes and brought in fifty-seven prisoners; Dowlin and Macatter sailing jointly in the *Black Prince* and *Black Princess* took twenty prizes and sixty-eight prisoners; Macatter alone in the *Black Princess* took forty-three prizes, thirty-six prisoners; and Ryan alone in the *Fearnot*, sixteen prizes and no prisoners. (Many more captives were paroled, unproductively.) Altogether, 114 ships were taken by the trio during their two-year rampage. The three men had contributed considerably to the £8 million in damages that privateers had cost Britain during the war. The words 'amazing' and 'astonishing' used by Franklin and the *Gentleman's Magazine* about the trio were fully justified – although most American schoolchildren will never learn that they owe their freedom as a nation, at least in some small degree, to three bold smugglers from Rush.

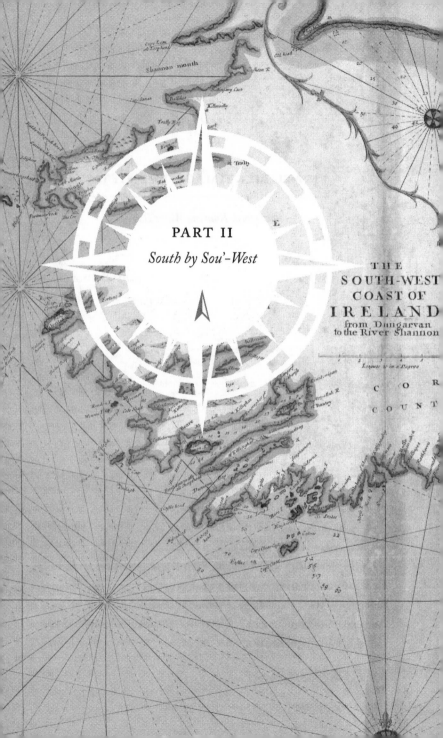

PART II

South by Sou'-West

5

PIRATE PILGRIMAGE THE FIFTH

Waterford, Roaring Water Bay

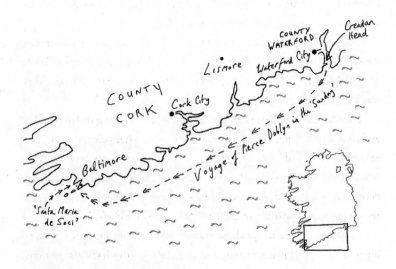

A pitiless North Atlantic wind scythes sharply across Waterford's Creadan Head, flattening the grass into sea-like ripples and making the trees shiver with apprehension. Even the seagulls have taken to dry land, gathering in morose, muttering bands as they sulkily await an imminent squall. Racing clouds send phantom shadows scudding across the fields, seeming to mimic and mock the few remaining boats in the estuary, hurrying towards the safety of port.

I've travelled here from the Hook Head peninsula in County Wexford, taking the ferry to the western side of Waterford Harbour estuary, and driving south through Crook, a village made famous by Oliver Cromwell's supposed warning that he would capture Waterford 'by Hook or by Crook'. (The phrase had been around for centuries in a farming context, but Cromwell may have been making a wordplay on the placenames.)

The remote promontory of Creadan Head is not easy to access by land. From Liccaun village, a narrow boreen takes you – eventually – to a tiny cove under the headland. No wonder this spot once proved so attractive to buccaneers and smugglers.

The tide is quite far out, so on the beach I wander out along the northern flank of the headland, checking out the Swiss-cheese maze of sea-hollows and cavelets that lie under its fringe of May-flowering hawthorn trees. (This was a stupid idea, as I'll explain in a moment, so don't try it.)

Each of these cavelets would have been ideal for hiding stolen plunder and contraband. Some are dark and gloomy, others strangely mystical. One sea-grotto surrounds a central, thigh-high rock that shines brightly with white lichen, green moss and mauve thrift flowers, for all the world like a decorated church altar. At times I feel as though I am wandering through the supernatural backdrop of Leonardo's *Virgin of the Rocks*.

I look up and see to my alarm that the tide has raced in at a frighteningly fast rate, and is threatening to cut me off. I hurry back just in time, and realise that this natural phenomenon is just one booby-trap that the pirates used to their advantage.

From the beach I climb up a laneway to the headland itself. (On that day I had no trouble getting in, and did so innocently, but I'm informed that the entire promontory is actually private property and is now sealed off by a locked gate and 'No Entry' signs.)

After a short uphill trudge, I find myself on a beautifully bleak headland, vibrant green with long, lush grass, and dotted yellow and white with buttercups and daisies. From here, I can get a clear view out into the busy channel that once ushered thousands of merchant ships into Waterford port. However, not every cargo made it safely into harbour to be tallied and taxed. Some stolen ships made unauthorised stops in the dead of night, on the southern flank of Creadan Head. Smuggled and pirated goods were hauled up from a tiny strand near the base of the headland, and spirited away through country roads by moonlight.

At that lonely strand, usually accessible only by sea, there is a pirate relic set in stone. Such a thing is extremely rare. Pirates inhabited a universe of wood, rope and canvas – materials that soon rot and disintegrate. Few things survive the centuries. So, as a rule, pirates tend to leave no monuments.

The 'Forty Steps of Creadan' are an exception. This stone stairway, rough-hewn into the rocks, is well worn by the feet of generations of pirates who grunted and shunted their way up the ascent, carrying casks of stolen rum, bolts of silk, and rare spices. But if one local tradition is true, there were much more tragic cargos. The road leading inland and westward is known locally as 'The Road of the Black Women', which some believe refers to female slaves from Africa who were landed here illegally for transfer by foot to Cork and then by ship to the New World. Truth or legend? I don't know, but as I zip up my windcheater against a biting sea-breeze, I seem to hear, amid the eerie howl of the wind, the pitiful keening of those captives.

These Forty Steps in Waterford, and the contrabander's road that links them with Cork, make Creadan Head as good a place as any to begin my next true-life pirate tale: the remarkable story of the merchants of Waterford City and their long, bitter war against the pirates of Baltimore.

'He Led Them in a Carol, Then Clapped Them in Irons'

Waterford versus the Baltimore Buccaneers

Baltimore, West Cork. April 1537.

William Grant was, for all practical purposes, a dead man. Standing on the ramparts of Dún na Séad Castle in Baltimore, he watched the crackling flames leap up the stairway beneath him. His lungs filled with the stench of scorching wood as the Great Hall of the O'Driscoll Clan was devoured by fire. Grant glanced around him and confirmed that his situation was hopeless. There was no way down through the raging blaze, and a leap to earth would mean certain death.

Grant was a fighting marine from Waterford. He'd been taking part in a punitive raid on the then-notorious pirates' nest of Baltimore, aimed at avenging a series of attacks against Waterford by the sea-rovers of the O'Driscoll clan. He and his comrades had stormed the seaport at night, completely surprising the pirates and decisively defeating them. The much-feared O'Driscoll galleys had been torched into ashes.

Acting alone, William Grant had stormed into the tower-house of the O'Driscolls before it had been set aflame. He was searching through the upper floors when, to his horror, he heard the crackle of fire from below. His comrades – who hadn't realised he was there – had tossed in their torches to destroy this infamous and iconic castle where their enemies had plotted their assaults on Waterford city, where they had orchestrated their attacks on its shipping, and where, after a victory, they had often retreated to toast their successes in stolen Spanish wines. There were cheers as the fire took hold. The layers of dried rushes which the O'Driscolls had used as carpets, and the heaped-up straw they'd used for bedding, could not have been more efficient at fuelling the blaze. The flames roared hungrily through the woodwork and licked the tapestries on the walls.

Down below, the arsonists were retreating from the intense heat when they heard the desperate shouts for help. Looking up in horror, they saw their comrade trapped on the roof.

Just when it seemed that William Grant was doomed to die, a quick-thinking bowman leaped into action. He found a long piece of thin cord, little more than thread, and attached it to the end of an arrow. Aiming carefully, he sent the arrow in an arc just above Grant's head. The trapped man grabbed the cord as it fell across the rampart. Down below, eager hands tied a strong rope to its other end. Grant hauled it up, tied the rope around the stonework, and abseiled safely to earth just moments before the pursuing flames, cheated of their victim, raged furiously through the topmost part of the tower.

That story may sound like a scene from an Errol Flynn movie, but it is true, and it formed the climactic moment of the epic war between the long-suffering merchants of Waterford and the O'Driscoll pirates who had tormented them for 500 years.

The O'Driscoll Clan was one of the three main pirate families in Ireland. In their heyday, the O'Driscolls ruled over the entire southwest coastline from Kinsale to Kenmare – a near-perfect turf, overlooking a major shipping route from Europe. They had a formidable private navy of up to eighty pinnaces (light sailing vessels), led by a flagship war galley powered by thirty oars. The family levied 'taxes' on passing merchant vessels, and ransacked those ships whose captains wouldn't play along. It was in effect a protection racket, and it enabled the O'Driscolls to enjoy a fine lifestyle. They grew rich on the sale of exotic metals, fabrics and spices. The fish and beef they levied from their local vassals were always washed down with the best clarets and Burgundies.

Their main victims were the merchants of Waterford, a burgeoning city economy some 140 miles to the east. They watched their ships arrive empty, or with seriously depleted cargos, or not at all, and swore that one day they would wipe out the pirate menace forever. Sensing this determination, the Baltimore pirates raided Waterford itself, and fomented revolts in the area.

The towns' bitter rivalry began way back in the eleventh century, when an O'Driscoll pirate leader launched a seaborne raid on Waterford, but died in the process. It gained momentum in 1368, when the O'Driscoll galleys joined a belligerent Norman family – the Powers from Tramore – in a joint attack on Waterford town. Although nearly 100 died in the battle, including many O'Driscolls, the result was a resounding defeat for Waterford. Many of the top city officials were killed.

This set the pattern for centuries of bitterness between the two maritime towns. It took the men of Waterford nearly half a century to wreak their revenge, but they did so in style.

In December 1413, Waterford Mayor Simon Wickens set sail for Baltimore Castle 'with a strong band of men in armour'. He timed his arrival for Christmas Day, when the entire O'Driscoll family would be drinking and feasting. In an astonishing show of bravado, Wickens walked right up to the fortified castle and sent a conciliatory message to the O'Driscoll lord. He had arrived with a ship full of wine, and 'would gladly come in and see him'. When the O'Driscolls opened the door, Wickens and his squad marched in. An extraordinary scene ensued:

'They walked into the Great Hall, where O'Driscoll and his kinsmen and friends were seated at the boards ready to sup. The Mayor commanded O'Driscoll and his company not to move, or fear, for he meant to draw no man's blood in the same house, more than to dance and drink and then depart.'

As his armoured soldiers stood guard, Wickens demonstrated his Christmas spirit by downing a glass of wine and striking up a dance. The astonished O'Driscolls looked on open-mouthed as he led the company in a cheery Christmas carol ... before clapping his hosts in irons, and ferrying them back as prisoners. The entire party arrived back in Waterford within twenty-four hours, in time for the gloomy O'Driscolls to celebrate New Year in jail.

After that deadly insult to Baltimore, things could only get worse – and they did. The O'Driscolls were officially outlawed in a 1450 proclamation: 'As [many] of the King's subjects have been taken and slain by Fineen O'Driscoll [a prominent pirate of the era] ... any town that receives O'Driscoll or any of his men shall pay £40 to the King.'

Eleven years later, in 1461, there was a replay of the Baltimore vs. Waterford match of 1368, with a completely different result. It began conventionally, with the O'Driscolls joining the warlike Powers in an attack on Waterford. However, this time the Waterford men had been tipped off well in advance. The resultant battle ended in complete victory for the home team, with 160 of their enemy dead and an O'Driscoll chieftain in chains.

Ships bound for Waterford would usually give Baltimore a wide berth, but during winter storms they could be driven wildly off course. On 20 February 1537, four Portuguese merchant vessels were carrying a substantial consignment of Spanish wine towards Waterford when a raging Atlantic gale forced them off course. *La Santa Maria de Soci*, carrying 100 tuns (over 25,000 gallons) of wine, was blown into the very entrance of Baltimore harbour, where she beat back and forth in a desperate bid to save herself from foundering on the treacherous rocks.

The reigning chieftain of Baltimore – another Fineen O'Driscoll – climbed up to what is now the Beacon and watched the *Santa Maria*'s ineffectual efforts, while discussing tactics with his sons Conogher and Giolla Dubh. They sent word to the captain that they'd help his stricken ship ... for a price. In return for a fee of three pipes (around 324 gallons) of wine, Fineen's men would guide him into the harbour. Once the storm passed, he could continue his voyage safely.

A pilot took the ship into port, and the wine changed hands as promised. The captain had sacrificed a mere 1.3 per cent of his 25,000-gallon cargo. When he was invited to dine at Dún na Séad castle, he probably wondered whether all the stories he'd heard about the savage O'Driscolls had been exaggerated.

He was walking into a trap. Fineen and his sons had wasted no time in sampling the Spanish vino, and liked it so much they had decided to liberate the entire cargo for themselves. When the captain and his officers walked into the Great Hall for dinner, they were immediately clapped in irons. Fineen could take satisfaction from the fact that the infamous 'Christmas Carol' raid in that same Great Hall had finally been avenged.

The O'Driscolls were prepared for the inevitable reprisal. What they didn't anticipate was its speed or its ferocity. Within eleven days, news of this latest indignity had reached Waterford. Instead of waiting to mount a full-scale retaliatory expedition – a process that could take several days – Waterford immediately sent out a commando-style raiding party on one of the most daring and courageous missions of the era. Using a light, fast ship named the *Sunday*, Captain Pierce Doblyn set sail with twenty-four of his best marines, arriving in Baltimore the following day.

The O'Driscolls were taken completely by surprise. The *Sunday* sneaked alongside the *Santa Maria* while Fineen's unsuspecting son Giolla Dubh stood on guard with twenty-four men, who were still busily unloading the wine. There wasn't even a skirmish. As Doblyn's men boarded the ship on one side, Giolla Dubh scarpered off the other.

Pierce Doblyn freed the prisoners and took command of the *Santa Maria* and what was left of the wine. He even fired a few contemptuous shots at the O'Driscoll's Great Hall, which had become something of a symbol for both sides, before returning to Waterford.

The business was far from over. While Doblyn was away, Waterford's elders had decided to wipe out the O'Driscoll threat for good. This time, there would be no half measures. Two large craft, one of them the Great Galley or chief warship of the city, were being equipped for all-out war. The *Sunday* joined them, and on All Fools' Day, with 400 fighting marines on board, the three ships set sail.

The expedition arrived in Baltimore under cover of darkness. The three warships anchored within range of Dún na Long castle on Sherkin Island and lined up their artillery. All through that night, they blasted their big guns at the fortress. The O'Driscolls, hopelessly outclassed and outgunned, abandoned the castle to their ancient foes. As the sun rose, the flag that fluttered over the blasted fortress was the Waterford men's Standard of St George.

The conquerors' revenge was total. They began on the islands, tearing down the castle of Dún na Long and hurling its giant stones into the sea. They laid waste the beautiful old Franciscan abbey. O'Driscoll's fine orchards and gardens were razed into the earth.

After that, they turned their attention to the mainland. 'Then, landing … they burned and destroyed Baltimore, and broke down O'Driscoll's goodly castle and bawn.' It was at this stage that the trapped William Grant had his dramatic escape.

Before they set sail for home, the Waterford men destroyed the O'Driscoll fleet, burning fifty of the eighty pinnaces and seizing the rest as prizes. The war was over – and nobody was in any doubt about which side had won.

The O'Driscoll pirates revived and regrouped, but their glory days were over: they'd been beaten by the fearsome artillery power of modern warfare. Yet their memory is still celebrated in a ballad that toasts the buccaneering Fineen with an Irish 'sláinte'. The song features in some folksingers' repertoires to this day:

> *Then sláinte to Fineen the Rover*
> *Fineen O'Driscoll the free*
> *Tall as the masts of his galleys*
> *And wild as the might of the sea.*

I leave Creadan Head behind and drive northwest to Waterford City – the oldest city in Ireland, established in 914 AD by those most efficient of sea-raiders, the Vikings, who gave it its name. The sun has re-emerged, and it is a sheer joy to wander around the 'Viking Triangle', savouring the old Friary, the Mediaeval Museum and Christchurch Cathedral, before treating myself to a coffee near the giant mediaeval chess set in Cathedral Square. Nearby, the thirteenth-century fortress of Reginald's Tower stands on the site of an earlier Viking turret. If you are at all interested in the Vikings – and we'll hear a lot more about them in Chapter Eighteen – then you'll really enjoy this city.

However, there is a different atmosphere down by the waterfront, where a rough-looking hustler tries to shake me down for cash as I retrieve my car. It's nice to see that some of the freebooting spirit has remained.

And at least I can draw comfort from the fact that, in an earlier century, I might have been knocked unconscious with a marlin-spike and woken up as an unwilling deck-hand somewhere around the Spice Islands.

I'd love to spend more time in Waterford – maybe next trip – but right now I have to drive further west, to Lismore Castle, once the home of two fascinating figures in Irish privateering lore.

The first was Sir Walter Raleigh, who bought and restored the former Norman castle in 1589, in the hope of creating an English colony. It was supposedly here – although the location is disputed – that a servant spotted Raleigh smoking tobacco and threw water over him, thinking he was on fire.

Raleigh was one of the most successful privateers of this or any era. In 1592, he organised the capture of what many historians believe was the richest single pirate prize in history – the *Madre de Dios*, a Portuguese carrack or transport ship carrying 1,600 tons of luxury goods, including rubies, pearls, exotic woods and spices, from India to Lisbon. It was a cargo valued, even then, at half a million pounds. Raleigh had masterminded the mission and set off on it, but was recalled to London and locked in the Tower by a furious Queen Elizabeth, who'd just found out he'd impregnated one of her ladies-in-waiting. When the *Madre de Dios* arrived safely in Dartmouth that September, on the Queen's birthday, cheering crowds lined the quays.

Unfortunately, the seething Raleigh had to cool his heels in the Tower as his prize was rifled by pilferers. 'My Lord,' wrote the statesman Robert Cecil, 'there never was such spoil.' Half the cargo went missing. Cecil reported that for seven miles outside Dartmouth, everybody he met smelled of amber or musk, and seed-pearls were hidden in many bags. Like so many freebooters, Raleigh had found that there were 'pirates' on land who were happy to do to him what he'd done to the Spanish at sea.

Back in Waterford, political upheavals had strangled Raleigh's Irish colony at birth. He was forced to sell Lismore for a knockdown price of £1,500 to a shrewd English carpetbagger named Richard Boyle. Boyle was exceptionally lucky. He rode a post-war boom to become fabulously wealthy, and turned Lismore into an opulent mansion. He is of interest to us because he was the first person to launch an efficient counter-intelligence network to penetrate the pirate gangs.

Boyle was a key target for pirates, and for this reason, he ran a string of double agents. These agents would often turn rogue again – 'Redmond Fitzjohn has turned pirate for the third time, God damn him!' Boyle wrote in frustration at one point – but they usually gave him reliable warnings of impending attacks. He could use these not only for his own security, but as currency to advance his career. For instance, in 1613, he dispatched a mariner by sea to Cornwall to warn the son of the Irish viceroy, Lord Chichester, that pirates were lying in wait for his ship.

Later, in July 1630, three earls were about to set sail from Holyhead to Ireland when a breathless mariner arrived at the quay. He had sailed alone from Howth near Dublin in a light craft, at top speed, hoping that he'd arrive in time to warn them to cancel their journey. Richard Boyle – by then Lord Justice of Ireland – had sent the messenger after receiving a last-minute warning from his pirate contacts that all three earls were to be kidnapped on the voyage. But, as the historian Dorothea Townshend perceptively observed, 'It was somewhat humiliating that the Lord Justice of Ireland could do no more to secure his friends' safety than pay a messenger to warn them of the danger.'

However, Boyle's own intelligence let him down when he set off from Lismore in May 1628 to travel to Wales with most of his family. He encountered a fleet of Dunkirk pirates who were determined to seize this most promising of targets. As dawn broke, the pirates swooped. They quickly captured an auxiliary boat that carried the Boyles' three servants and their horses, but as they zeroed in on the main ship they found Boyle armed and prepared. 'Having [the pirate ship] in our sight and hearing, [we] shot twenty pieces of ordnance at it,' Boyle wrote.

The pirates retreated, but before returning to France they made an unscheduled landing. As a contemporary journal reported wryly: '[They] were so courteous as to restore my Lord's horses and land them in Wales.'

6

PIRATE PILGRIMAGE THE SIXTH

Kinsale, Carolina, Caribbean

After a long and frustrating drive through heavy traffic, the lush, verdant boreens of the Old Head of Kinsale were as refreshing as a summer shower in the muggy late-spring heatwave.

The south-pointing peninsula that leads to the mariner's landmark of the Old Head is a rambler's paradise. You can leave a standard blacktop road and, within minutes, end up happily lost in a labyrinth of enchanting little country lanes where the grass grows calf-high in the middle of the asphalt surface. An unsigned track can lead to unexpected rewards. You can descend a stone stairway that is as remote as a contrabander's gangway, and emerge into an impossibly photogenic scene: an abandoned granite church with its famine-era graveyard, standing sentinel over the breathtaking sweep of Kinsale Bay: all the way from dark and lonely Sovereign Island at the seaward approach, across the wide harbour mouth towards Kinsale port, and, to your left, a dramatic, deserted and almost inaccessible smuggler's cove of jagged rock and shingly sand.

Retracing your steps, you can take a minor country road where the already-narrow throughway is further choked by foxgloves and scarlet-flowering fuchsias that thrive, wild and rampant, on the verges. It is tempting to see these flora as soft, tender and delicate, yet they are tough

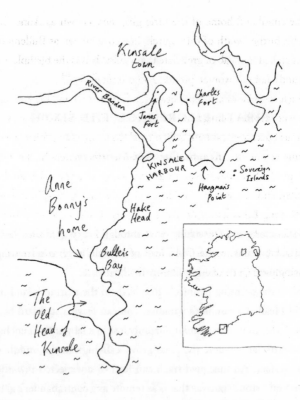

and aggressive in their determination to break free of their designated area on the margins. You could not hope for a better metaphor for a female pirate, and by happy coincidence, this small peninsula was home to the second most famous she-pirate in history: Anne Bonny, the Irishwoman who spurned conventional ideas of womanhood in the 1700s to carve out a lucrative career for herself in the overwhelmingly male domain of buc-caneering. This bewitching region was her childhood stomping ground, from the rugged Old Head in the extreme south to the bays at Sandy Cove, close to Kinsale town. That ancient granite church was probably her parents' place of worship.

The childhood home of the little girl, then known as Anne Cormac, was a bit further south of this church, in a cove known as Bullen's Bay. Its fame is etched in a slab of grey slate that reads: 'This is the birthplace of one of Ireland's famous women pirates: Anne Bonney, 1697'.

The love-child of an affair between a Cork lawyer and his kitchenmaid, Anne was forced to emigrate to the Americas. There she fell in with the notorious buccaneer captain 'Calico Jack' Rackham, and achieved everlasting fame as one of only a handful of female freebooters in the annals of world piracy. She may never be as well-known as the celebrated Grace O'Malley, and she was not as rich and powerful as the Chinese woman pirate Cheng I Sao. Her career was not particularly lengthy or successful. But because a biographer made her a household name just four years after her trial, her influence has been immeasurable. This is the amazing, and surprisingly true, tale of Anne Bonny from Kinsale.

Anne Bonny, Scourge of the Caribbean

Anne Bonny, late of the Island of Providence, Spinster: that on the first day of October, in a pirate sloop, about three leagues from Hispaniola, you did, piratically and feloniously, set upon, shoot at, and take two sloops, and put the mariners in corporal fear of their lives; and that you did steal the two sloops, to the value of £1000 of current money in Jamaica.

– Charge sheet, Jamaica, 1720

The fearsome figure who stood cursing and swearing on the deck of the pirate ship looked like everyone's idea of the ultimate badass buccaneer.

Dressed in rough canvas jacket and trousers, with a coloured handkerchief tied around his head to fend off the burning Caribbean sun, he barked orders at the crew as they closed in on their target vessel. In one hand he carried a pistol, and in the other a long-bladed hacking machete.

As the two vessels bobbed side by side off the coast of Jamaica, the victim of the attack – an Englishwoman named Dorothy Thomas – was able to get a close look at the alpha-male buccaneer who obviously held sway over most of the other pirate crewmen.

But something wasn't right, and it didn't take the observant Dorothy Thomas long to work out what it was. The pirate could dress like a man and curse like a man, but she couldn't hide the generous curves that distorted the front of her jacket. As Miss Thomas was later to testify in court, she identified her attacker as female 'because of the largeness of her breasts'.

One badass mother – Kinsale's Anne Bonny, the scourge of the Caribbean. She disguised herself as a man, but one victim who narrowly escaped death at her hands identified her as female 'because of the largeness of her breasts'.

Dorothy Thomas didn't know it at the time, but she had come face to face with the legendary Anne Bonny – the Kinsale-born Irishwoman who had achieved notoriety all along the Caribbean coast as the piratical scourge of shipping, and the favourite moll of the infamous buccaneer captain 'Calico Jack' Rackham.

When the pirate crew had completely emptied Thomas's vessel, a small tender known as a *canoa*, they cast off and prepared to set sail. But Anne Bonny was not happy to leave her victim alive. She cursed and pointed at Thomas.

—Kill her, she snarled at her seamen. We don't want her alive and coming after us in court.

For a few dreadful seconds, Dorothy Thomas's life hung from a thread. The pirates hesitated: they may have been thieves, but they hadn't yet resorted to murder. The exasperated Bonny looked capable of dealing the death blow herself, but at the last minute she appeared to change her mind. Kicking the two boats apart, she ordered the men to set the sails and before long, the pirate ship had dwindled to a mere dot on the horizon.

Bonny's worries about Dorothy Thomas were to prove entirely justified. Not so long afterwards, the two women were to face each other again, in a sweltering Jamaican courtroom. The victim's courageous evidence helped to identify Bonny as a ringleader in a series of pirate attacks, and secured a sentence of death against her.

However, the execution was postponed for humanitarian reasons. Dorothy Thomas may have noticed the curve in Bonny's chest, but she did not notice a similar giveaway curve below her waist. Incredible as it seemed, the swearing, snarling sea-warrior who had been at the forefront of the action was not only female ... but also an expectant mother.

The remarkable Anne Bonny was born sometime around 1698 in 'a town near Cork', which historians have identified as Kinsale. Her precise birthplace is unknown, but one historian has pinpointed her childhood home as Bullen's Bay, a windswept cove on The Old Head. She was born into a well-off middle-class household – although the circumstances of her birth were to shatter that comfortable existence for everyone involved. Right from the moment of her first breath, Anne Bonny was Trouble.

Bonny was actually her married surname. Her childhood surname is uncertain. Although I have trawled extensively through the archives, I have yet to find any contemporary historical documentation that names her parents as William Cormac and Peg/Mary Brennan, as is generally supposed. It's just about possible that her childhood surname was 'Fulford' since she was later described in a Wanted poster as 'Anne Fulford, alias Bonny'.

Almost everything we know about her Anne's early life comes from the eighteenth-century biographer Captain Charles Johnson, who despite his chatty style has been proven generally reliable on facts. (Some say he was the true author of *Robinson Crusoe*, but others dispute that. The debate rages on.) Frustratingly for historians, Johnson does not name her parents, although he goes into endless salacious detail about her family history.

Anne's father was a prominent Cork lawyer and her mother his household maid, 'a handsome young woman'. Their affair began when the lawyer's wife was away from home due to illness. On her return, the wife became suspicious, and entrapped her husband by secretly sleeping in the maid's bed. She said nothing when her husband joined her and began smooching in the darkness with the woman he supposed was his maid and lover. As a result, the wife became pregnant with twins. Meanwhile, the maidservant announced that she, too, was expectant.

After this almighty marital omnishambles, the couple's separation was inevitable. The attorney's clients abandoned him, so he sold up and sailed off to the New World along with his mistress and their child, little Anne.

It was a wise move. The thriving colony of Carolina suited him perfectly. He diverted into trade, made a bit of money, and bought a plantation near Charleston. Anne's mother died a few years later, and Anne grew up to become a formidable force in her own right.

'She was of a fierce and courageous temper,' writes Johnson, although he denies the story that Anne stabbed an English servant in a fit of fury. However, another story was true: when attacked by a would-be rapist, Anne beat the man so badly that 'he lay ill of it for a considerable time'.

Her father had high hopes that his daughter would marry into money, but Anne had no intention of being a trophy wife. Instead, she married a penniless seaman named Bonny, whose real aim was to get his hands on the family plantation. This was his first mistake, because Anne's father rapidly disowned his wayward daughter and cut her off. Bonny's second big mistake was to take his new wife off to the Caribbean island of New Providence, in the Bahamas. Because it was here, in this sunblasted snakepit of thieves and pirates, that she met the real love of her life – the colourful pirate Calico Jack Rackham.

On the sweltering, stinking, deafening, rollicking wharves of Nassau town, Calico Jack Rackham must have stood out like a peacock amid a congress of crows. With his arrogant attitude, his propensity for violence, and his taste for the distinctive trousers in Calcutta cotton that gave him his nickname, he was a striking figure in every sense of the word. Yet even he must have done a double take at the sight of Anne Bonny, as she negotiated through the heaving crowd of pickpockets, prostitutes and pirates that thronged the waterfront in the Caribbean's most lawless town. Thanks to her upbringing as the daughter of a wealthy plantation owner, Anne exuded an air of entitlement that set her aside from the usual weary maidservants and sunburned farmers' wives who pushed their way along that muddy, litter-strewn quayside. If a drawing in Johnson's book is in any way accurate, she had shoulder-length, curling dark hair, an oval face with fierce, blazing eyes, a jutting, determined chin, and a mouth twisted in a snarl. (Admittedly, she is depicted in the middle of a fight.) However, another contemporary drawing depicts her with curiously catlike features: narrowed eyes, an upturned nose and small, rosebud lips. Either way, the overall impression was of a strong and determined woman who was used to having her own way. Rackham probably took one glance at her and recognised a kindred spirit.

English-born Rackham had already chalked up an impressive CV as a pirate. He had served as quartermaster under the privateer Charles Vane, but the two men had fallen out and the crew had chosen Rackham over the captain. On 24 November 1718, Calico Jack assumed his first command. Spurning an offer of pardon, he sailed his brigantine to the Caribbean and made his base in New Providence.

New Providence was at that stage at the very epicentre of the buccaneering boom that would later be labelled

Anne Bonny's lover, the infamous Jack Rackham. 'If you had fought like a man,' Bonny admonished him as he awaited execution, 'you would not have been hanged like a dog.'

the Golden Age of Piracy. A peace deal ending a long-running war had left thousands of seamen out of work, just at the same time as a post-war economic surge was creating an increase in shipping traffic in the Caribbean. Meanwhile, New Providence's main city of Nassau (named, incidentally, after William of Orange-Nassau, of Battle of the Boyne fame) had become a lawless ghost town as a result of the war. For a pirate, conditions could hardly have been more suitable.

A 1700s chart of the Caribbean. After eloping with Jack Rackham in the Bahamas (top right), Anne Bonny gave birth to his child in Cuba. Leaving the baby with foster parents, they went on to terrorise the waters around Jamaica (centre), where her second pregnancy saved her from the hangman.

By the time he met Anne, Calico Jack had already established his piratical reputation when 'he took and plundered several vessels'. According to some sources, he had also designed his own personal pirate flag: a grinning skull with crossed cutlasses.

The Rackham gang had hit the jackpot near Jamaica when they'd captured a ship full of fine food and excellent Madeira wine. They 'spent their Christmas ashore, drinking and carousing as long as they had any liquor left, and then went to sea again for more'. They weren't so lucky this time: off Bermuda, they captured an English vessel, but were disgusted to find that its cargo consisted of miserable thieves from London's Newgate Prison, bound for the Plantations. They freed the prisoners, but the Royal Navy captured them again.

We aren't told exactly how Anne and Jack met. Anne's marriage to Bonny was rocky, to say the least, and it didn't help when her husband 'surprised her lying in a hammock with another man'. (Not Rackham.) According to Johnson, she had become a 'libertine'. She also moved in with an older woman whom she described as her mother, and who actively encouraged her romantic liaisons.

That last part sounds a bit shady, but there's no evidence that she worked as a professional prostitute, as has been suggested. She may simply have enjoyed the company of those raffish, rumbustious sea rovers with their live-fast-die-young attitudes. There were the privateers, who were licensed to attack enemy nations. There were the buccaneers, who lived wild on remote islands and ate salted meat called boucan. And there were the outright pirates, who attacked anyone and everyone. All these people came to Nassau to sell their stolen goods and buy supplies. It was noisy and colourful and a bit crazy, and Anne obviously loved it.

For his part, Rackham was hopelessly besotted by Anne. He'd just sold a stolen cargo and wanted to spend all the money on her. 'He had nothing but Anne Bonny in his head,' writes Johnson.

James Bonny offered to divorce Anne in a semi-legal transaction known as a 'wife sale'. Rackham agreed to pay the money. They hired an official named Richard Turnley to do the paperwork. However, Turnley tipped off the Governor, Woodes Rogers, who was so outraged at Anne's behaviour that he condemned her to a public flogging and ordered her lover Rackham to wield the whip.

The couple escaped and 'resolved to run away together, in spite of the world'. They had no ship, but that didn't deter Jack. He already had his eye on an ultra-fast privateer sloop called the William, which lay at the quayside, supposedly under heavy guard. It had six guns and was so swift that its owner was nicknamed 'Catch him if you can'.

Anne volunteered to do the reconnaissance. She sashayed aboard the ship in her haughtiest plantation-daughter manner, telling the guards she had important business with the owner. Meanwhile, she was checking out the security. She reported back that there were only two guards, both sheltering inside the cabin.

At midnight on a moonless, rain-blasted night, eight of Rackham's pirates boarded the ship. Anne, who knew the layout, led the way. 'As soon as they got on board,' writes Johnson, 'Anne Bonny, having a drawn sword in one hand, and a pistol in the other, went straight to the cabin where the two fellows lay … [She] swore that if they pretended to resist, or make a noise, she would blow their brains out. That was the term she used.'

They bluffed their way past soldiers at the harbour mouth and sailed off to freedom. Jack's first mission was to settle accounts with Richard Turnley, their betrayer. The pirates tracked him down to an isolated island where he'd gone hunting. Rackham waded chest-deep through the pounding surf and searched the island for his target, shouting at Turnley to come out and fight. Wisely, the hunter lay low, and Calico Jack was cheated of his prey. However, he got his revenge by sinking Turnley's boat and leaving him stranded.

Once at sea, Anne abandoned her petticoats and put on the standard sailor's gear of wide trousers, shirt and tunic. She tied her hair under a hat or piratical scarf. In order to disguise her identity, she dropped the final letter 'y' from her surname. For the former Anne Bonny, it was now a case of: 'The name's Bonn. Anne Bonn.'

Anne knew that to survive, she would not only have to be the equal of the fighting mariners, but to outmatch them. During assaults, she would pretend to be a man. In attack, she was always first; in defence, she was always last to yield. 'Nobody was more forward or courageous than she,' says Johnson.

Just when Anne had established her status as a macho mariner, Mother Nature intervened and Anne discovered she was pregnant with Jack's child. Rackham took her to Cuba, where he had 'a little kind of a family' who could look after Anne. No-one is sure what happened to the child, but before long, Anne rejoined the pirates, as free as ever.

On their next voyage, they were accompanied by an English sailor. According to Johnson, Anne made a move on him, only to discover that the new recruit was actually a woman posing as a man. Madly jealous, Jack Rackham threatened to kill the new 'seaman' before he, too, was let into the secret.

The Englishwoman's name was Mary Read, and she had spent years serving in disguise as a male soldier in Europe. A picture in Johnson's book depicts her as a fearsome figure, slashing the air with a cutlass. She carries a hatchet in her belt, and a pistol and machete in her sash. Long, curly dark hair cascades from under her sailor's cap. Her dark eyes are burning and resolute. In reality, she was as formidable as her pose suggests. She fell for one of the crewmen, and when her lover foolishly challenged someone to a duel she thought he would lose, she seized the initiative by deliberately insulting the same man so that she could fight him first and win.

In September 1720, a proclamation declared the Rackham gang to be 'pirates and enemies of the Crown' and newspapers as far away as Boston were cautioning sea captains to beware of the now-enlarged band of 'twelve men and two women' who were terrorising New Providence. 'The pirates swear destruction to all those who belong on the island,' they warned.

Rackham's gang retreated to Cuba. One night, they were warned that a hostile Spanish navy ship had arrived secretly in the next bay. The Spaniards had already captured an English ship and planned to capture Rackham's vessel next morning.

In the dead of night, the pirates abandoned their own ship, sneaked into the bay on rowboats and silently boarded the captured English ship. At dawn, the unsuspecting Spanish sailed their warship in as planned and blasted at the empty pirate vessel. Meanwhile, amid the mayhem, the Rackham gang escaped in their new ship.

Jack returned to Jamaican waters and snatched several fishing boats, a schooner and another vessel. Infuriated, Governor Rogers put Rackham at the top of his wanted list, and despatched a well-armed sloop under a Captain Barnet to put an end to his piracy.

Throughout all of this action, Anne Bonny and Mary Read had been Rackham's main lieutenants. Witnesses were later to testify that 'no person among them was more resolute, or more ready to board or undertake anything that was hazardous' than the two women.

In one incident off Jamaica, Rackham seized a schooner and forced two of its French crewmen – John Besneck and Peter Cornelian – to join his pirate band. They later testified that Anne Bonny was particularly gung-ho during attacks. She was 'very active on board and willing to do anything'. She and Read carried weapons and weren't afraid to use them in a fight. 'Ann Bonny handed gunpowder to the men,' they added. The two seamen were absolutely convinced of one thing: 'They did not seem to be kept or detained by force, but of their own free-will and consent.'

By this stage, Bonny and Read had abandoned the gender-bending pretence, and posed as men only when an attack was imminent: 'When they saw any vessel, gave chase or attacked, they wore men's clothes,' said the French witnesses, 'and at other times they wore women's clothes.'

In another Jamaica incident, Rackham sailed into the quiet inlet of Dry-Harbour, where the sloop *Mary and Sarah* was peacefully bobbing at anchor. He blasted a warning shot and the merchantman's Irish captain, Thomas Dillon, fled to the shore to get weapons. 'Several shots were fired at [us],' Dillon testified.

By the time the gunfire died down, the attackers had taken the ship. 'We are English pirates,' they shouted at Dillon. 'Do not be afraid. Come on board.'

Cautiously, Dillon rowed out to his captured ship. One threatening figure, in particular, came to his notice. 'Anne Bonny had a gun in her hand,' he recalled later. She was 'very profligate, cursing and swearing much, and very ready and willing to do anything on board.'

Rackham's reign of terror could not continue forever. In November 1720, the dogged Captain Barnet intercepted the pirates near Point Negril. As the navy man's sail appeared on the horizon, Rackham weighed anchor and fled. The navy ship gave chase. Luck was on the side of the lawmen, who found a fortuitous offshore breeze and soon caught up. As Captain Barnet closed in on the buccaneers, he saw that 'some were drinking, and others walking the deck'. The pirates opened fire with cannon and small arms. Barnet shot back. When the two ships drew alongside, the navy men were confronted by an almost incredible scene.

Almost all the men – drunk and sober – had scuttled down into the hold like frightened mice. The only defenders on deck were Anne Bonny, Mary Read and one sole male crewman. They shouted down the hatch for help. When there was no response from their cowering comrades, Mary Read lost patience.

—Come up and fight like men! she yelled.

The men stayed put, cowering in the cargo hold. Furious, Mary Read stuck her gun down the hatch and fired it blindly, killing one of her comrades and wounding several others.

The battle was as good as over. 'After a very small dispute,' writes Johnson, '[the sloop] took her and brought her into Port Royal, Jamaica.' Calico Jack was hauled ashore in chains.

The authorities wasted no time. On 16 November, Rackham and his male crewmates were arraigned at an Admiralty Court at St Jago de la Vega, Jamaica. Within two days, they were convicted, and on 18 November, Rackham and four others were hanged at Gallows Point in Port Royal. Rackham's body was removed to a promontory known as Plumb Point, where it was hung 'on gibbets, on chains, for a public example, and to terrify others from suchlike evil practices'.

Ten days later, with the dreadful knowledge that her lover's corpse was festering in chains on Plumb Point, Anne Bonny was hauled into court. She was arraigned both under her real name and her alias of 'Anne Bonn'. She and Mary Read faced four charges of 'piracies, felonies and robberies on the High Sea'.

In the stifling heat of the courtroom, the judge Sir Nicholas Lawes listened impassively as witness after witness pointed the finger at the Irishwoman. Dorothy Thomas's testimony that Anne and Mary had ordered her murder was especially damning. Throughout the trial, Anne Bonny remained stolidly silent.

'Have you any defence to make, or any witnesses to call?' the judge asked.

'I have no witnesses and no questions,' Bonny replied.

After a short recess, the judge and commissioners reached a unanimous verdict: guilty on all charges.

Lawes asked gravely: 'Have you anything to say, or offer, why sentence of death should not be passed against you?'

The two women silently shook their heads.

The courtroom fell silent as Sir Nicholas read out the sentence: 'You, Mary Read and Anne Bonny, are to go from hence ... to the place of execution, where you shall be hanged by the neck till you are dead. And God, of his infinite mercy, be merciful to both your souls.'

It was only then, at the last minute, that the two silent women played their hidden aces. They 'informed the court that they were both quick with child'. The judge was sceptical, but stayed the execution pending a medical examination.

Poor Mary Read did not last long in the filthy, rodent-infested Jamaican dungeon. She caught an infection, developed a high fever, and died along with her unborn child.

Bonny had one advantage over her shipmates: she had connections in high places. Many of the 'gentlemen planters of Jamaica' had known her wealthy father. Some had actually visited the family home in Carolina and remembered his feisty daughter. One word in the right ear would have gone a long way. However, it was Anne's free-loving, rather than her freebooting, that put them off. 'They were inclined to show her favour,' says Johnson, 'but the action of leaving her husband was an ugly circumstance against her.'

No-one knew quite what to do with her, and in the end the authorities did a classic fudge. She was paroled to have her child, and 'reprieved from time to time' until it was made very obvious that nobody in Jamaica would lose any sleep if she quietly left the island.

Johnson, writing only a few years after the trial, admits that 'what is become of her since, we cannot tell'. However, the *Oxford Dictionary of National Biography* fills the gap with information from her descendants in America: her father organised her passage home to Charleston, and she gave birth without mishap. She went on to live a long and peaceable life, marrying a Carolina man named Joseph Burleigh and having another eight children. She died in April 1782, at the fine age of eighty-four, thousands of miles away from her childhood home in Kinsale.

We can't say farewell to the remarkable Anne Bonny without recording her most famous quote. According to Charles Johnson, she had been allowed to visit Calico Jack Rackham in his cell as he prepared to face the hangman. Far from expressing sympathy, Anne was characteristically blunt. 'I am sorry to see you here, Jack,' she told him, 'but if you had fought like a man, you would not have been hanged like a dog.'

7

PIRATE PILGRIMAGE THE SEVENTH

Cork City, Brazil, Boston

'Sharks off the port bow!'

These were words I never thought I'd hear myself saying, especially in the cold grey waters just outside Cork Harbour.

Was I seeing things? No, the nest of sinister black triangles breaking through the surface was unmistakeable, especially to anyone who'd lived through the *Jaws* hysteria of the mid-seventies. There must have been a dozen of them, each large enough to smash a hole in the side of our vessel with a flick of her tail. However, we were in no danger. These sleek black torpedoes scything through the sea were Atlantic basking sharks, beautiful and wild, but as gentle and harmless as a grazing herd of cows.

We cut the engine of the yacht and waited, careful not to disturb the ten-foot-long sharks as they drifted around and under our boat, ingesting plankton through their open mouths. It was a rare and precious moment, one that few people get to experience. Yet – damn you, Peter Benchley – deep inside, part of me still shuddered at the sight of the circling black triangles. For my generation, such a sight will always be accompanied by a mental soundtrack of a percussive cello. *Dum–dum dum–dum dum–dum …*

I wonder if the Lord President of Munster, one Henry Danvers, had the same experience when he first sailed into Cork Harbour in the early 1600s? It's entirely possible, because when the harbour was totally sealed off by a blockade of pirate ships in 1609, he looked out at the sinister flotilla of corsair vessels, with their triangular jib-sails showing dark against the horizon, and spat out two words of pure hatred: 'Sea sharks.'

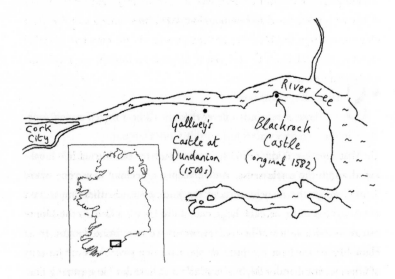

Danvers had been sent to the troubled city of Cork to maintain law and order, but had instead been humiliated by the great pirate armadas that dominated the entire coastline in the early 1600s.

That winter, a flotilla of four pirate ships carrying hundreds of heavily armed buccaneers had positioned itself at the harbour entrance, refusing to let any shipping in or out. They were 'strong enough to land 300 men' at any time they wanted. Another fleet of eleven ships, carrying 1,000 pirates, was soon to join them. It was a formidable show of strength, and Danvers had nothing to challenge it. He candidly admitted that he was too afraid to set out to sea, 'subjecting himself to the mercy of these pirates', who were prepared to use force 'to those that resist them'. Instead, this representative of the mighty English colonial power was stuck in Cork city for 'so long', unable to do much more than dream up a range of colourful insults to describe his piratical tormentors: 'Sea sharks', 'caterpillars' and 'weeds' were the best he came up with.

For pirate-power in Ireland, it was an all-time high, and for the forces of law and order, a nadir of humiliation. We'll hear more about the great pirate armadas of the 1600s in the next chapter, but for now, I was headed into the heart of Cork to seek out a tangible symbol of this city's rip-roaring pirate past.

The first time I visited Cork City – surprisingly late in life – I had a profound and inexplicable sense of déjà vu. I knew I had never been here before, and yet I had been here before. Perhaps the bewildering warren of vertiginous streets climbing its steep hillsides reminded me of Montmartre in Paris; perhaps the sweeping wharfs seemed like Copenhagen or Hamburg; or maybe it was just that the artsy, boho buzz was reminiscent of Greenwich Village or Berlin. I couldn't explain it, but I knew that I liked what I'd found, and that this was not a copy of any other city. Cork was purely Cork, and it was exuberantly proud of it.

Now, on my current pilgrimage, I found the pirate touchstone I was looking for in the breezy suburb of Blackrock, a few miles south of the city. With some difficulty, I located the ruins of Gallwey's Castle at Dundanion (the name means 'strong fortress') near the Marina walk. This fine limestone tower house once sat proudly on the shoreline, but is now stranded a few hundred yards inland thanks to land reclamation. Today it lies neglected, choked by rampant trees, shrubs and undergrowth. In the 1680s, William

Penn, who gave us Pennsylvania, is supposed to have sailed from Dundanion to found his new colony. But I'm more interested in the early 1500s, during the reign of Henry VIII, when the fortress featured in one of Cork's first pirate tales.

Cork, ideally placed on main shipping routes and blessed with the world's second-largest natural harbour, has always attracted pirates, like ice cream attracts wasps. But while many of its merchant princes battled to suppress piracy, there were others who actively encouraged it.

Step forward Mayor Richard Gallwey, owner of this castle at Dundanion. As a mainstay of one of the ruling families of Cork, Gallwey was supposed to stamp out the pirates. But, like many of his contemporaries, he couldn't resist the temptation to stick his hand into the honey-pot. In 1533, a richly laden Portuguese merchant ship named the *Santa Maria Desaie* was boarded by thirty-five pirates. The buccaneers sailed their stolen ship to Cork, knowing they would get a warm welcome at Dundanion Castle. Gallwey not only forgave their crime, but helped them secure a good price for the captured ship at auction: it fetched an impressive 1,524 crowns. The *Santa Maria*'s indignant captain demanded justice from the authorities in London. They ordered Gallwey to return the ship or refund the owners. Gallwey mumbled some lame excuse about thinking the vessel was Scottish. He flat-out refused to return the ship or pay compensation … and he got away with it. No doubt part of the money went towards the rebuilding of his castle.

So it is hard to feel much sympathy for the merchant princes of Cork who, fifteen years later, complained that pirates were starting to lean on them. 'Since we do not victual the pirates, they boast they will do us as much hurt as they can,' the then Mayor wrote to London in November 1548. 'We write to know whether we shall apprehend them and, of need, kill them, or not.' Every other port on the south coast of Ireland was growing rich on such proceeds, he protested. 'We have the name [i.e., the reputation] but they have the profits.'

By 1563, pirate attacks were becoming relentless and invasive. The buccaneers not only captured Cork-bound ships on the open sea, but even sailed right into the harbour to snatch them.

In April 1563, the Mayor protested to Queen Elizabeth: 'Our haven and river being large and long, we are by pirates and other malefactors grievously hurt … [We need] sufficient munition and artillery to resist them.'

Something had to be done. In order to discover their solution, I had to drive a little further along the south bank of the River Lee, to Blackrock Castle. Locals know this castle today as a romantic eighteenth- and nineteenth-century edifice, resembling a clutch of giant pepperpots or chess-pieces, and topped with a modern observatory. But it is built over the foundation of a circular limestone tower, which remains intact in the cellars. I descended the spiral stairs to inspect the single-room fortress. A large cannon mounted at an aperture gave me some idea of what this stronghold would have looked like in 1582, when it was constructed by the traders of Cork specifically to defend the city from pirate invaders. The walls are up to seven feet thick, designed to withstand the most powerful gunfire. This wasn't just a fortress, it was a message in stone. It said that Cork meant business when it came to deterring pirates, and that the city would at last live up to its motto of 'a safe harbour for ships'.

Well … not quite. As we've seen, Cork continued to be plagued by the pirate menace through the early 1600s. But, in fairness, the region was pretty good at producing pirates of its own. Anne Bonny from Kinsale was by no means unique.

In choosing a good pirate story to represent Cork city, I faced a dilemma. So many pirates, so little space. For instance, the successful privateer William Dampier, who circled the world twice, prepared his vessels at Cork and set sail from Kinsale in 1703. One of the men on board was Alexander Selkirk, the model for the fictional Robinson Crusoe, who was abandoned on uninhabited Juan Fernandez Island and managed to survive until he was rescued in 1709 by the privateer Woodes Rogers – who also set sail from here. (Before he left, Rogers amazed the citizens of Cork by blowing a fortune in a lavish and unprecedented spending spree.)

Instead, for my main story from this city, I want to tell the extraordinary tale of Peter Roach – a Corkman whose remarkable American odyssey of piracy led him from his home by the River Lee all the way to the steaming Rio de Plata estuary in South America, where he stole a fortune in gold dust before being hanged as a pirate at low tide on the banks of the Charles River in Boston.

Boston Harbour in the 1700s: Corkman Peter Roach set sail from here as a seaman, but returned as a pirate accused of 'horrible crimes, that all the world must detest and abhor'.

The Strange American Odyssey of Peter Roach

June 1704

Peter Roach was on the run, and could run no more. The Cork pirate was trapped on Cape Ann, a headland of Massachussetts Bay, with an angry posse of hundreds of local militiamen and volunteers in hot pursuit. Cape Ann was a rugged region of salt marshes and dense woodland bounded by granite sea-boulders: beyond them, to the east, the vast Atlantic separated him from his homeland by thousands of miles. He was exhausted, footsore, insect-bitten and soaked to the skin by the unseasonal June downpours. Roach had been either accidentally left behind, or deliberately abandoned, when his fellow pirates made their getaway by ship from the cape the previous night. Now he searched the shoreline in vain for a small fishing craft, or even a tiny rowboat, that could spirit him away from the avenging citizens' army whose hounds he could hear howling ominously in the near distance. His capture was inevitable – just as inevitable as the gruesome death he would meet at the end of a rope at low tide on the Charles River in Boston.

Roach had nowhere left to hide. He was – as one report put it – 'a stranger, destitute of all succours'. He sat down wearily and prepared to give himself up.

As they marched Peter Roach back in irons, he would have passed Cape Ann's distinctive nests of drumlins, the swollen egg-shaped hills that were so reminiscent of the landscape of his early life in Ireland. He had left that country as an innocent mariner. Now, he was an internationally wanted pirate, with the blood of two innocent sea-captains on his hands. He had been marooned in Massachussetts Bay carrying a large purse of gold dust and a pile of pieces of eight that he had stolen during an epic buccaneering voyage around the coast of Brazil.

Where had he stashed his treasure? Where had the other pirates hidden theirs? That's what the authorities in Boston would dearly love to know.

Details of Roach's early life in Ireland are obscure. All we know is that he was born in Cork around the year 1673. At that time, Cork was not the happiest place to grow up: it was one of the flashpoints in the war between kings William and James, and had endured a savage siege. Roach opted to go to sea. Mariners were badly paid, badly abused and often unemployed for long periods, and in 1702, when England went to war with Spain and France, many Irish and English mariners grabbed the opportunity to travel to the Americas to become privateers.

So, on July 1703, Peter Roach arrived in America and joined a queue of seamen standing in line to sign up for the eighty-ton brigantine *Charles*. Its captain, Daniel Plowman, was heading northwards from Boston to Canada, with a licence to 'war, fight, take, kill, suppress and destroy any pirates, privateers, or other subjects and vassals of France or Spain'.

As Roach waited his turn, he heard some familiar, yet differing, accents among his future shipmates. The gruff Dublin accent belonged to a young man named John Clifford who, at only twenty-three, was signing up for his first stint as a mariner. He was a professional 'malster', a brewery craftsman who had learned his trade in Dublin's breweries. Why was he here? Roach knew better than to ask. The soft Sligo accent belonged to John Carter, a mariner who, at forty, was the eldest of the Irishmen. The more nasal Derry brogue was that of thirty-two-year-old Dennis Carter.

One clause in the *Charles*'s contract stressed that the men who sailed her were 'in no wise to hurt or injure any of Her Majesty's subjects, friends or allies'. It was an innocuous clause – but one that would later become Peter Roach's death warrant.

The mission was in trouble from the beginning. Captain Plowman returned from its first trip not only physically ill, but deeply worried about the reliability of his crew. 'I find every day I grow worse and worse,' he wrote to the owners from his sick bed aboard ship on 1 August 1703. The investors should 'save what we can' before it was stolen. It was vital to disband the current crew, he warned darkly, 'for it will not do with these people'.

His enemies on board must have got wind of his plan, because within two days the *Charles* went missing. In mid-August, the authorities announced that the vessel had been stolen, and that its seventy-strong crew were wanted men. As far as they knew, the *Charles* had headed south, to 'parts of the West Indies' or the Caribbean. 'The commander, we fear, is dead,' they warned. 'The men are in rebellion.'

Some of them were, some of them weren't. But just three ringleaders had masterminded the takeover of the ship: and one of them was Peter Roach.

John Clifford later gave evidence as to how the mutiny had started. As Captain Plowman lay desperately ill in his cabin, a group of six mutineers took over the vessel. The main movers were Peter Roach, the Derry seaman Dennis Carter, and an Englishman named Anthony Holding. (A man called John Quelch, who was later to command the pirates, was not on board at the time.) Their first act was to blockade the captain's cabin, using a metal spike. Clifford, who remained loyal, was worried about the captain's wellbeing, and asked the mutineers if he could tend to Plowman in the locked cabin. But 'Peter Roach guarded the door, with sword in hand, and would not let [me] go in,' he said.

Clifford's fears were justified. Plowman's condition worsened without help, and two days later he died at sea. Whether he was actively murdered by the pirates, as some sources say, or simply left there to die, the intention was much the same. 'For some time, [they] bolted the cabin door upon him,' their trial would later hear. Their treatment of a sick man was 'inhuman and murderous'. At the time, the mutineers could not have cared less: they callously heaved the captain's body into the ocean.

John Quelch, a thirty-eight-year-old Londoner from Boston, joined them at sea, and 'did not object' to the new regime. With more experience than the others, he was elected as captain. He set course for Brazil, where the men 'intended murders, piracy and robberies'. They were to achieve all three aims – the latter two on a scale they could not have begun to imagine.

Brazil coast, December 1703
Sweating in the antipodean summer sun, Roach and his piratical shipmates stalked the distant Portuguese brigantine like feral cats stalking a mouse.

The ship was about thirty-five tons, they reckoned, and probably headed for Rio. It flew the Portuguese flag, which should have made it immune to attack. Earlier that year, England and Portugal had signed a treaty of alliance.

But that had not deterred the *Charles* pirates. Since arriving in these waters, they had taken seven other Portuguese ships, ranging from a tiny fishing boat on 15 November to a forty-ton brig on 24 November. The results had been underwhelming: fish, salt, sugar and around £50 in cash.

However, their luck was about to change. When they boarded the eighth vessel, this brigantine bound for Rio, they found sixteen wealthy passengers – fourteen men and two 'women of good fashion' – who were carrying a breathtakingly large hoard of gold and silver. We can imagine the passengers' reaction as Peter Roach and the other pirates, dirty and dishevelled, stood on the deck roaring their demands for money and valuables. If they behaved like their chief, Captain Quelch, they each carried 'a cutlass and two pistols'. A thorough search confirmed that they had hit paydirt at last: 900 gold pieces worth £500, and a staggering hundredweight (112 pounds' weight, or fifty kilograms) of gold dust, then valued at £6,000. Whooping joyously, the pirates ferried their haul back to the *Charles*, where they carefully weighed it and shared it out.

The emboldened pirates upped their game. Their next target was a 200-ton Portuguese merchantman armed with a dozen big guns. When the pirates swooped, the merchant captain responded with a volley of gunfire. The *Charles* blasted back with its superior weaponry. Eventually the victim yielded and the pirates swarmed on board, none too happy about having been on the receiving end of violence.

Bristolman Christopher Scudamore, the pirate ship's cooper, was among the first on board. He was incandescent with murderous fury. 'Kill him!' he yelled, pointing at the Portuguese captain. When no-one obeyed, he pulled out a pistol and shot the man in cold blood. 'He died immediately,' one witness said. 'His body was thrown overboard.'

The pirates commandeered the big guns and ammunition for their own ship. They also stole a slave, who was auctioned to one of the gang for £40.

This ship, the *Charles*'s ninth victim, also yielded two hundred pieces of eight. All told, the mission had stolen a fortune in gold and silver – around £7,500, equivalent to €1.2 million-plus in today's money, but actually worth substantially more in an economy of low-priced labour.

By this stage, however, the pirates had been away for six months and were growing restless. They were tired of Brazil, and they longed to spend their money. Anyway, the *Charles* was no jolly pirates' club. Quelch enforced discipline with vigour and some relish. One crewman who carelessly told a victim the ship's port of origin was viciously whipped at the mainmast.

Under pressure from the fractious crew, the pirate ringleaders huddled and came up with a proposal. It was quite a brilliant plan – and, if it succeeded, it would allow the *Charles*' crew to return home to a hero's welcome.

In May 1704 – after having vanished for a full nine months – the *Charles* brazenly sailed right in to Marblehead Harbour, near Boston. The pirates reacted to the shock and outrage of the citizens with open-eyed innocence. They claimed they had no idea that they'd been the focus of an international manhunt.

—Poor Captain Plowman passed away early in the voyage, Quelch explained solemnly. We buried him at sea with full honours. It was my sad duty to take his place.

While the authorities struggled to come to terms with this alternative reality, Quelch deftly diverted their attention to the ship's hoard of treasure. There was enough here to keep everyone happy and to suspend disbelief.

—We encountered a tribe of Indians who led us to a sunken Spanish galleon, Quelch lied. We salvaged the wreck and found this hoard.

The investors, who hadn't even expected to get their empty ship back, were overjoyed. On 15 May, a local newspaper enthused: 'Captain Quelch is said to have arrived from New Spain and made a good voyage.'

Roach, Carter and the other crewmen, who had concealed a good part of their share, hit the taverns to celebrate. It seemed as though their audacious plan had worked. But they hadn't reckoned on the greed of the Massachusetts authorities, who could have given them all a few lessons in the art of thieving with impunity. They wanted their hands on that gold … and they were men who knew how to use the law to get exactly what they wanted.

When the customs men carried out a full search of the *Charles*, they found some unsettling evidence. There was a captured ship's flag from friendly Portugal. Recently minted coins from Lisbon appeared, incongruously, among the money supposedly found on an ancient Spanish galleon. Questioned, a local goldsmith confirmed that the pirates had exchanged more Portuguese coins, and that Quelch had used his workshop to melt some into pure gold.

The game was up.

Quelch was arrested, but Roach and many others managed to escape. On 25 May, the authorities proclaimed that the crew had obtained their gold through 'piracy and felony', and demanded their capture.

Roach and the other absconders had taken a substantial amount of their loot with them. On 1 June, Joseph Dudley, the colonial Governor, said that 'every good man will do his duty … to discover the pirates and their treasure'. With that last magic word, the colonists needed no further urging.

However, Roach and his shipmates knew a few good men as well. Amid drenching rain, they assembled at a safe house in desolate Cape Ann, and persuaded a friendly captain to spirit them away. Roach and another pirate failed to make the rendezvous, and were soon captured.

The escape ship headed north to the Isles of Shoals, a remote island group six miles off the coast, intending to bury their treasure. Meanwhile, from the Massachusetts mainland, a gung-ho Army major named Stephen Sewall set sail in pursuit. His vessel sailed through the night and arrived at the islands at dawn, posing as a fishing boat. When his concealed soldiers rose from the deck in unison, they took the runaway pirates completely by surprise. Seven were seized on the main island, another three on Star Island, and four on the ship. Major Sewall also retrieved forty-five ounces of the gold. Since that was only a fraction of their share, there is a local tradition that an even greater stash remains buried on the islands.

Peter Roach and his pirate shipmates soon discovered that they were dealing with officials who outmatched them in venality and corruption. Crammed into airless cells at the height of summer, the prisoners begged for fresh air in the open yard. One outraged clergyman complained that, for this basic right, 'there was extorted from them £30'. That sum – €5,000 or more today – bought them only three days, after which 'they were again confined to their former wretched circumstances'.

The trial that began with undue haste on 30 June was a mockery of justice, even by the harsh standards of the 1700s. One legal analyst was later to describe it as 'judicial murder'. Admittedly, Roach and his shipmates *were* guilty of murder and piracy. That said, there were many legal grey areas that could have saved them from execution. The colonial authorities went to outrageous lengths to ensure they did not benefit from these loopholes.

If Roach had been tried in London, his fate would have been decided by a jury. Here in Boston, it was a civil case, in which many checks and balances did not apply. All matters of law and fact were decided by the presiding judge and court President, Governor Joseph Dudley, who stood to gain a substantial 'royal bounty' if the pirates were convicted, and nothing if they weren't. The prosecution case was led by his son Paul, who would be paid a large slice of the treasure on conviction.

THE

Arraignment, Tryal, and Condemnation,

OF

Capt. John Quelch,

And Others of his Company, &c.

FOR

Sundry *Piracies, Robberies,* and *Murder*, Committed upon the Subjects of the King of *Portugal*, Her Majesty's Allie, on the Coast of *Brasil*, &c.

WHO

Upon full Evidence, were found Guilty, at the *Court-House* in *Boston*, on the Thirteenth of *June*, 1704. By Virtue of a Commission, grounded upon the Act of the Eleventh and Twelfth Years of King *William*, *For the more effectual Suppression of Piracy.*

Convicted of 'piracies, robberies and murder': this newssheet from 1704 tells how Cork buccaneer Peter Roach was hanged in chains on the banks of the Charles River in Boston, alongside his captain, John Quelch. The pirates never revealed where they had hidden their treasure.

Dubliner John Clifford, the loyal seaman who became the main prosecution witness, was the first to feel the pressure. Although the authorities recognised his innocence, he was forced to plead guilty to piracy before testifying: if he did a good job, he would be pardoned; if he didn't, he could face the gallows. The pirates' defence lawyer protested vigorously, but Joseph Dudley impatiently swatted his objections aside.

The trial proper began on Monday, 19 June. Paul Dudley, the Attorney General, said the pirates had been given a sword to fight Queen Anne's enemies, but instead had 'sheathed it in the bowels' of her friends, the Portuguese – not once or twice, but nine times, 'till they were glutted'.

The defence counsel, James Meinzies, tried desperately to save his clients, who were accused of 'horrible crimes, that all the world must needs detest and abhor'. Even today, the transcript reads like a tense legal drama, with Meinzies battling heroically against impossible odds. He produced several legal arguments, and was repeatedly slapped down by the President, Joseph Dudley.

Joseph Dudley, controversial governor of Massachusetts: he was more interested in getting his hands on the buried treasure of Peter Roach and his fellow pirates than presiding over a fair trial.

When the legal arguments were exhausted, John Quelch himself cut in. The prosecution could not prove the origin of the gold dust, he protested.

The response from Joseph Dudley was an insight into his true motives. 'If you would say anything to that purpose,' he thundered, 'you should acquaint the court where you took those quantities of gold ... let us see some of them here.'

Similarly, when Scudamore was led to the bar, the President's main question was: 'Where is your gold?'

As the trial neared its end, the three pirates from Ireland – Peter Roach, John Carter and Dennis Carter – changed their pleas to guilty, 'hoping for the Queen's mercy'. The judge was unimpressed. 'This court can make no bargain with you,' he said. 'You have pleaded guilty.' And with the utmost gravity, Joseph Dudley ordered them all to hang.

> *Friday, the 30th of June 1704. Pursuant to orders in the Dead Warrant, [six] pirates were guarded from the prison in Boston by forty musketeers, constables of the town, the Provost Marshal and his officers … being allowed to walk on foot through the town, to Scarlet's Wharf, the Silver Oar being carried before them; they went by water to the place of execution, being crowded and thronged on all sides with multitudes of spectators.*

A 'broadside' newssheet published in Boston describes the last, mournful journey of Peter Roach and his shipmates to the gallows on the Charles River. Walking with him, to the solemn beat of a lone muffled drum, were Quelch, the murderer Peter Scudamore, and three other ringleaders.

The execution drew a huge crowd. A local diarist wrote that crowds thronged the hillside: 'But when I came to see how the river was covered with people, I was amazed. Some say there were 100 boats.'

Mounting the scaffold, Quelch doffed his hat and made an elaborate bow. 'I am condemned only upon circumstances,' he told them. The only reason he was being hanged, he said, was that he 'brought money into New England'. Another pirate protested that 'so many men's lives were taken away for so little gold'. Others pleaded their innocence and begged forgiveness.

However, Peter Roach, the last to be given an opportunity to speak, maintained a stoic silence. 'He seemed little concerned,' the broadside reporter wrote, 'and said but little or nothing at all.'

A prominent clergyman preached from a boat as the ropes were fastened to the men's necks. 'When the scaffold was let to sink,' wrote the diarist, 'there was such a screech of women that my wife heard it ... a full mile from the place.'

All the other pirates, including John Carter and Dennis Carter, eventually had their death sentences revoked and were put to service in the Navy. Clifford got his pardon.

As the citizens shuddered over the caged corpses that were left to twist in the wind, the Boston authorities began an unedifying scramble to divvy up what was left of the pirates' haul. They were obliged to give the gold to the Treasury in London, but first they could skim their fees and charges off the top. They did so unashamedly, with Paul Dudley getting £36, Major Sewall getting £132, the prison keeper getting £30, the militia captains sharing £27, and even the local tavern keeper earning £28 for 'entertainment of the Commissioners during the sitting of the court'. And so it went on, until the purses that were eventually sent to London contained less than 800 ounces of the original 1792 ounces of gold dust. Court President Joseph Dudley received an unspecified 'royal bounty'.

By my calculations, the Boston officials skimmed ten per cent of the original haul and London got some thirty-five per cent, leaving fifty-five per cent unaccounted for. The only crumb of comfort for Peter Roach as he stood on the gallows was that the Dudleys and their cronies had failed to get their hands on the bulk of the treasure. Wherever the *Charles*'s gold lay hidden, it was a secret that the silent Corkman took with him to his eternal rest.

No matter how hard we search ... we will probably never know the precise location of Roach's stores.

Before we leave Cork City, we have to mention another pirate with whom Peter Roach is sometimes confused – his near-namesake Philip Roche. Roche was born into a Cork seafaring family around 1693 and, according to the eighteenth-century pirate biographer Captain Charles Johnson, was 'a brisk, genteel fellow', whose affable manner concealed 'an inhuman monster' with a 'black and savage nature'. Today, we might call him a psychopath. Certainly, the brief and brutal career of the Roche gang reads like a Quentin Tarantino saga of ultraviolence. (Sample: 'They beat out their brains … [They were] all over as wet with the blood that had been spilt, as if they had been dipped in water or stood in a shower of rain.')

Roche began by operating a marine-insurance scam and, when it all went wrong, hitched a ride on a French merchant ship leaving Cork for Nantes. While the captain and mate were asleep, Roche, together with a Corkman named Richard Neal and two brothers named Pierce and Andrew Cullen, took over the ship. They pitilessly slaughtered two crewmen as they climbed down to deck from their duties at the rigging. A boy who fled to the topmast in terror was grabbed by the arm 'and tossed into the sea'. A fourth crewman had his skull smashed in as he tried to escape. Then Roche tied up the captain and mate and threw them screaming into the ocean. Roche doctored the stolen ship to conceal its origins and sold its cargo in Rotterdam, where they took on more goods and sailed off again.

After a heavy drinking session on St Patrick's Day, the Roche gang threw the cargo's owner into the sea, where he stubbornly refused to drown. 'He swam about the ship … calling out for life,' but the pirates callously sailed on. Roche finally abandoned his stolen ship in France and headed for London, where he foolishly tried to claim some back-money from his insurance racket. He was rumbled and jailed for fraud, and when he tried to smuggle a letter to his wife back in Ireland, he was rapidly identified as the prime suspect for the Cork–Nantes sea massacre. Philip Roche was convicted of piracy and died, unlamented, at the end of a rope at Execution Dock in 1723.

8

PIRATE PILGRIMAGE THE EIGHTH

Berehaven, Leamcon, Baltimore, Valentia Island

At six in the morning, we are awakened by the sound of a noisy swimming party. Close at hand, we can hear the sounds of heavily built bodies splashing in the water and grunting indelicately. It is as though a bunch of Wimbledon tennis players are practising early-morning aqua aerobics.

We rub our eyes and emerge into the bright, fragile light of a perfect west-of-Ireland morning, wondering who could be inconsiderate enough to have such a clamorous revel at this unearthly hour.

Dolphins. At least fifteen of them, just a few yards offshore, diving and surfacing and leaping in arcs, hunting for the shoals of fish that streak through this Atlantic sea-inlet in their thousands.

It's just a typical morning in Bere Island, West Cork. As we discover later when we excitedly tell the story to locals, such sights are pretty much routine in Bantry Bay, where the six-mile-long Bere Island guards the ancient mainland seaport of Castletown Berehaven, in the shadow of the bruise-coloured rise of Hungry Hill. Situated on the remote Beara Peninsula, at the extreme southwest of Ireland, Berehaven is one of the key pirate locations on my list. As a near-perfect deep-water port, it has always been a blessing to mariners – and, it follows, a godsend to pirates as well.

For centuries, the formidable O'Sullivan clan operated out of nearby Dunboy Castle. They claimed jurisdiction over the local seas, and operated a protection racket on passing shipping. Captains who refused to pay would have their ships attacked and seized.

But it was much more than that. The Elizabethan general Sir Peter Carew complained that he couldn't suppress pirates here because the O'Sullivan clan leader protected them, 'covering their vessels with his ordnance [guns], and mustering a fleet of small craft and a sufficient number of men to bid defiance to the Queen's authority'. A leading corsair of the era, Captain John Callis, testified that O'Sullivan was the district's principal 'maintainer' of pirates.

The O'Sullivans lost their base in Dunboy after they backed the doomed Spanish invasion of 1601. Of course, when the law-abiding English colonial administrators moved in to the area, they soon called a halt to all this piracy nonsense.

And if you believe that, you'll believe anything.

In fact, their corrupt officials worked hand in glove with the new breed of pirates who invaded West Cork and Kerry in the early 1600s. As this chapter will show, the very men who were supposed to suppress piracy were the ones who did most to foster and encourage the trade. These officials didn't just turn a blind eye to the buccaneers. They were, to coin a phrase, Bere-faced criminals.

The Hellhounds of Dog's Leap and the Pirate Armadas of West Cork

The young African woman shivered in the chilling Irish wind as the pirates forced her into the rowboat and ferried her ashore. Then, as she stood on the strand at Berehaven and looked up at the sombre swell of Hungry Hill, she must have wondered what further horrors fate held in store for her in this cold and unfamiliar land.

Hadn't she suffered enough already – ripped away from her African homeland by slavers, force-marched in irons to the coast, stuffed into a stinking hold, and swapped back and forward between slavers and merchants until, finally, she had ended up as just one more item of stolen property aboard this pirate ship bound for Ireland?

The pirate captain, a man named Lording Barry, led her up through the village to the Big House. As she stood mutely at the door, other pirates carried packages of fine cloth and lace from their ship and deposited them beside her.

Eventually a man came out. His bearing and attitude made it clear that he was the person in charge of this village. The pirate leader talked to him urgently, cajolingly, in a language she did not understand. He pointed at her. The man in the Big House looked her up and down, and finally nodded. The African woman did not understand his words, but she knew exactly what was going on. Just like the lace and the fine cloth, she was being offered as a gift to this man – to use as his servant, his cook, or whatever other duties he felt like demanding of her.

It was only later that she discovered that his name was Humphrey Jobson, that he was from England, and that he had been sent by the King's Admiralty to suppress piracy in this region. She was essentially a bribe to Jobson – a payment for his silence, the price for his looking the other way as Barry and the pirates unloaded their stolen goods, and a fee for his friendly intervention if they ever needed a pardon.

This obscene transaction between outlaw and lawman actually happened in Berehaven in 1615. In financial terms, the bribe was substantial. The package had an all-in value of £100, which equated to nine years' wages for a labourer, or five years' salary for a professional man. However, the records tell us absolutely nothing about the young woman, who was described in the doubly insulting parlance of the time as 'a negro wench'. What was her name? Which part of Africa did she come from? And what eventually became of her?

Most fascinatingly of all, was she still around these parts sixteen years later? And, if so, what thoughts went through her mind when she heard the news that slave traders had sailed all the way *from* Africa to the village of Baltimore in Cork and spirited away 107 villagers for sale on the slave markets of Algiers?

We will never know the answers to any of these questions. What we do know is that, in the turbulent quarter-century from 1606 to 1631, Africa and southwest Ireland were closely connected in a way that they were never connected before, and never have been since. And what linked them could be summed up in one word:

Pirates.

They came here to West Cork in their thousands, and at the height of their power they were untouchable. They sailed not in individual ships, but in fleets that vastly outnumbered and outgunned the English Navy. They didn't just have captains, they had so-called admirals, who ruled over their Confederacy of the Sea. They regarded themselves not as outlaws, but as kings and princes of the ocean.

The astonishing story of the pirate armadas of southwest Ireland has been almost totally forgotten by a public who are besotted with their later counterparts, the Pirates of the Caribbean. Yet, with up to twenty-seven ships and anywhere from 1,000 to 2,000 fighting seamen, the pirate fleets of Cork and Kerry were certainly in the same league. This may not have been the Golden Age of Piracy (roughly 1680 to 1730), but in Olympic terms it certainly qualified as the 'Silver'.

Up until this point, piracy had mostly consisted of small-time coastal raiding. You had the great pirate families – the O'Driscolls in Cork, the O'Flahertys in Connaught, and of course Gráinne O'Malley in Mayo. In the 1580s, the Kerry town of Tralee operated as a pirate haven with the blessing of the Denny family.

But in 1604, the pirate business suddenly went into hyperwarp. There was a new breed of pirate, mostly commanded by Englishmen or maverick Dutchmen, but also including Irish captains and – surprisingly – one lieutenant of African ethnicity. Huge pirate armadas – bristling with guns and weaponry – descended on southwest Ireland and took control of the coasts. The authorities were powerless to resist them.

There were many factors behind this explosion, but the catalyst was a peace deal in 1604 that ended the long war between England and Spain. The English Navy was run down, and many fighting mariners suddenly found themselves out of a job. Meanwhile, in a double whammy, King James I also banned licensed piracy. Suddenly, there were hordes of angry young seamen, resentful and anti-authoritarian, not to mention hungry, hanging around the coasts and drifting into piracy.

Ireland's southwest was almost tailor-made for their needs – ideally positioned beside major shipping lanes, and featuring many lonely harbours, inlets and islands. It was the natural jumping-off point for the New World, so it was a perfect location to take advantage of the rise in Atlantic trade that resulted from the same peace treaty. Although this area had been devastated by conflict, it was on the verge of a post-war economic boom: the world demanded more preserved food, and West Cork could provide it in the form of salted fish. Newly-rich merchants began to covet the sort of wines, spices and exotic goods that the pirates could bring ashore. The buccaneers also had a 'get out of jail free' card – the fact that piracy was not a capital offence in Irish law. Pirates who were caught had to be sent to London for execution. Some claimed an archaic legal loophole known as 'benefit of clergy', which could save them from the hangman. All in all, it was simpler for the authorities to pardon them and bring them onside. Essentially, being a pirate in West Cork was a bit like being a rogue financier in Wall Street in the early 2000s: you could enjoy jaw-dropping profits if everything went well, and avoid any penalty if it didn't. What was not to like?

And the profits were indeed huge. Cargoes of prize ships were routinely sold for around £3,000, or well over two million euro in labour-value today. One pirate kept a £2,000 slush fund stashed away to buy his freedom if he were ever caught. Others could afford to build fine houses, and even palaces in the sun.

So from 1605 onwards, thousands of English and Irish pirates began to congregate in areas like Berehaven, Baltimore, Leamcon and the appropriately named Schull. They formed their own 'Confederacy' under so-called admirals – charismatic figures like Richard Bishop and Peter Easton.

Yet, while their flotillas were enormous, they could also scatter widely at the first hint of trouble. That didn't happen too often, because with up to 250 big guns at their disposal, they could laugh at the Navy's lone patrol ships.

These people could almost have invented the term 'international terrorism', because this was only one arm of their operation. They *owned* the North Atlantic, moving easily and fluidly across a triangular zone that had Newfoundland at its top-left tip, and southwest Ireland at its top-right. And at the bottom tip lay the Barbary states of Africa.

It seems like a crazy idea – pirates from the chilly states of northern Europe flocking like migrating swallows to the blazing sun of Africa. Yet it happened, and somehow it worked so well that this intercontinental pirate alliance was destined to terrorise the world for the next two centuries.

When we talk of the Barbary, or 'Berber', states, we mean Tripoli, Tunis and Algiers – roughly, present-day Libya, Tunisia and Algeria – and a small area on the Atlantic coast of Morocco. The first three were on the Mediterranean and were nominally part of the Ottoman Empire. However, they were semi-detached and were under the effective control of the Barbary corsairs – pirates who had become heroes after taking Algiers back from the Spanish, but who were kept in check by the Ottoman Sultan's militia. This arrangement suited the Sultan just fine: he could benefit from the pirates' raids on Europe while simultaneously tut-tutting at their outrages. Similarly, in Morocco, pirates were allowed to operate freely in seaports like Sallee and Mamora.

A new phase began when renegade Dutch privateers drifted down to Barbary, where their mastery of ocean-going ships gave an adrenaline shot to the corsair business. From their secure bases in Africa, the Barbary pirates and their northern allies could now roam the Atlantic, capturing lucrative cargos and enslaving thousands of Europeans. Since every captured ship could be converted into another oceangoing pirate vessel, the business expanded exponentially. Later, English and Irish pirates joined the Dutch freebooters. Not all of them were cynical opportunists. Many converted to Islam and some became religious zealots. For instance, the Dutch convert Morat Rais – who was later to raid Baltimore – was an evangelical firebrand who constantly harangued his European colleagues to convert. For Morat, an essential part of any raid was the ritual burning of a Christian church and the execution of a priest.

However, these new-style corsairs needed secure bases in northern waters to stock up on meat and fresh water, and to service their ships. Southwest Ireland ticked all the boxes.

Once the English realised what was happening, they appointed officials to live in the key harbours. However, the lure of pirate gold was irresistible. Almost to a man, they went over to the dark side.

The case of Humphrey Jobson, stationed in Berehaven, was typical. Jobson had been a model of rectitude before he came to Ireland. He was something of an Admiralty hatchet man, regularly sent to English piratical centres to curb the buccaneers. Once, when despatched to Plymouth to clip the wings of the formidable Hawkins family of freebooters, he resisted their intense intimidation and stood firmly until they backed down. We don't know what finally turned his head in lonely Berehaven, but we can guess.

This was the only recorded case in southwest Ireland in which pirates offered a live human being as an inducement, but there were plenty of other cases of corruption. In Baltimore, the pirate Captain Boniton gave the local landlord the ultimate 'sweetener' of sixty chests of sugar. Nearby, pirates bought off a naval officer named Captain Williams with sugar and coral. When a pirate named Baugh brought in a haul worth £3,000 and went to negotiate for pardon with one Sir William St John, the official responded by 'embezzling Baugh's goods while his ship was in custody'. Even the naval admiral who was in overall charge of hunting down these pirates, Thomas Button, was taking backhanders.

The English coined a new term for the shore-based accomplices without whom the buccaneers could not exist: they were called 'land pirates'. And of all these land pirates, one name stands out. His name was William Hull, and he controlled the infamous freebooting haven of Leamcon.

On the next leg of my trip, I decide to approach Leamcon from the sea, which is how people usually approached it in those days. Its appeal to pirates was not its accessibility from land, but the opposite: its remoteness and relative inaccessibility. For sailors, it was an ideal port – a clean anchorage in a sheltered bay, further protected from bad weather by the skinny barrier of Long Island. On our trip today, we sail from Baltimore on the other side of the bay, passing some of 'Carbery's Hundred Isles' – islands with delightful names like Spanish Island, Hare Island, Horse Island and the Calf Islands. Before me, to my left, lie Sherkin Island, Clear Island and the Fastnet Rock. Ahead, high on a hill to my right, a squat and somewhat sinister dark tower of stone lets us know that we are approaching Leamcon. This was the castle of William Hull.

Leamcon (Irish for 'Dog's Leap') is situated just southwest of Schull, on the peninsula that ends in Mizen Head. Outside the immediate area, few people even know it exists. That is not surprising, for apart from the tower house, and apart from the wild and excitingly rugged beauty of the terrain, there is nothing remarkable about it. In fact, it is hard to imagine that this innocuous bay was once the second capital of a vast pirate empire, or that it was an anarchistic, freebooting haven that defied the might of England's Navy for two decades.

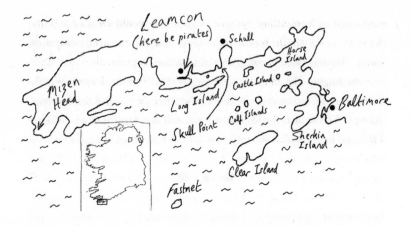

Yet, if I were offered one trip on a time machine, this is the era and the place I'd choose to visit. It must have been a fascinating experience to stand on the shore, right here, and watch the great corsair ships roll in, filled to the gunwales with pirate plunder. To see the merchants' eyes widen with greed as the freebooters unload their sweet-smelling hauls of nutmeg, cinnamon, ivory tusks, fine wine and lace. To watch returning mariners hug their temporary girlfriends, and to hear the women giggle with delight as they hold up a gold necklace that lately hung around the neck of some Spanish *doña*. To see the piles of exotic goods auctioned to clamouring merchants. And all of this happening under the benevolent gaze of William Hull, the Deputy Vice Admiral of the province of Munster, who is supposedly there to suppress the freebooters, but who has, instead, turned Dog's Leap into one of the world's greatest havens for sea-dogs.

For instance, if we were to set our time machine to July 1611, we'd find an admiralty officer called Captain Skipwith standing on the shore, desperately pleading with the English pirate Peter Easton not to disappear to Florence with his latest capture, a 'richly laden' London ship named *Concord*. (Easton was a remarkably successful pirate who, during his career, would rake in 'two million pounds in gold' and would eventually retire to live in a palace.) On his arrival at Leamcon, the awestruck Skipwith found thirteen pirate ships, each with its own captain, all under Easton's command. The fleet had 500 men and 250 guns. Easton was in the process of converting the *Concord* into another buccaneer warship, tuning it for speed and adding guns. He told Skipwith, almost casually, that he himself had just narrowly escaped death – a number of captured merchants whose ships he had seized had attacked him in bed in his cabin. Easton and his men, although wounded, had fought them off, and three of the attackers had jumped overboard. This was normal life aboard a pirate ship.

That same summer, an English report complained about the pirates they nicknamed 'Easton's Hellhounds'. They were 'well provided with victuals by land-pirates that dwell here'. The pirates had been in Leamcon for so long that 'they have wives and children in these parts', and these families were rich with cash. Together with Baltimore across the bay, Leamcon operated its own independent financial zone, with its own money system. English money was rarely seen – the only acceptable coins were pieces of eight and Barbary ducats. And with no banks around, the buccaneers had stashed their cash in the time-honoured manner: 'It is thought some treasure is buried on land by these pirates.'

When a Captain Jennings brought a Spanish ship worth thousands into Roaring Water Bay in 1609, English naval officer Captain Williams was sent to tackle the pirates of Leamcon. He found himself completely outgunned, and instead accepted a bribe of nineteen chests of sugar and four chests of coral, in a transaction that his superiors drily described as 'too much familiarity'.

Let's reset our time machine to 1625 – by which time Leamcon has operated as a freebooting haven for nearly twenty years – and watch William Hull preside over one of his greatest piratical auctions. An English ship taken by the Dutch pirate Claes Compaen has sunk in the local channel, and its salvaged contents are up for grabs, alongside other stolen goods. Hull himself successfully bids for 'forty horseloads of pepper', and a prominent English attorney named Sir Lawrence Parsons also grabs a share. A merchant from faraway Waterford buys 'one chest of camphor ... tobacco, fourteen rolls, pepper 1000-weight, cloves 212 weight, elephant teeth, three, Muscovy hides five dozen', while another buyer snaps up fine bed-covers from the Canary Islands. A military man named Lieutenant Jacques of Cork buys '16 pounds weight in massy gold'. At the end of it all, a colourful caravan of stolen goods trails out of Leamcon, headed eventually for various points in Ireland, England and France.

The man behind all this was, unsurprisingly, an ex-pirate himself. William Hull began life as a humble seaman in Devon – although his father was at one stage Mayor of Exeter. He obtained a licence to go privateering, but turned pirate. When he was caught, his dad had a word in the right ear, and young William escaped the noose. Disgruntled by King James's crackdown on piracy, William set up business in Leamcon, where the authorities were less pernickety. He leased his own castle – that tower on the hill – and made all pirates welcome. Soon, sea-rovers of all nations were queuing up to avail of this pirate paradise. Hull's profits were astronomical – one expert reckons that a single pirate haul was worth seven million dollars in today's money. And because the pirate captains were often in a hurry, they would swap high-value exotic goods directly for beer and beef. Hull invested his cash bonanza in legitimate businesses like fish processing plants to safeguard his future. Throughout all this, he kept his position as the Admiralty's watchdog, and he was even knighted in the 1620s.

Under Hull, the buccaneering business thrived. English officials complained that there were two main bases for piracy in the known world

– the notorious Barbary Coast, and southwest Ireland. In Leamcon, the local vicar was a pirate collaborator. In Sherkin Island, off Baltimore, pirates even served on juries. Pirate rule was, almost literally, set in stone in places like Dutchman's Cove near Baltimore, and in nearby Crookhaven, where the freebooters sculpted secret stone stairways to help them land their goods. No wonder the English viceroy, Lord Chichester, complained that the pirate plague was like a mythical hydra, with multiplying heads. Another official claimed, colourfully, that the pirates would even rip open the gates of hell – a phrase that has always struck me as a great title for a Meat Loaf album.

The pirates loved booty, in both the new and old senses of the word. Soon the area was attracting prostitutes from all over Scotland and England as well as Ireland. Seedy establishments known as 'alehouses' sprang up like noxious weeds all over the area: they operated as brothels and thieves' kitchens as well as pubs. They were quite often run by pirates' wives or widows. One official report said the area had become a refuge for 'desperate and dishonest men' and 'shameless and adulterous women'.

With no real law and order, places like Baltimore and Leamcon became every bit as wild as Port Royal and Tortuga in the Golden Age. For instance, a report from Baltimore complained that one pirate crew offloaded their money 'in a most riotous manner'. In another incident, a stolen Spanish ship arrived in Baltimore harbour amid rumours that it had £6,000 hidden somewhere in its hull. The local people had to be physically restrained from tearing it apart plank by plank.

Amid all the chaos, some pirates tried to do a runner with their shipmates' treasure. Historian John Appleby has recorded some amazing examples from the records of the Admiralty Courts. One involves a pirate named Baptist Ingle or Hingley, who came ashore at Baltimore after a successful mission in 1613 and fell for a woman in Schull. After 'making merry' with her (to quote the records), he jumped ship with £100 of his shipmates' money.

Appleby also cites the case of another crewman, one Henry Orenge, who deserted the same pirate ship in Baltimore with a stash of stolen diamonds and other precious stones sewn into his trousers. He fled to England, but on the voyage from Dublin to Chester was rumbled when he tried to sell the gems to an aristocratic lady he met on the ship.

For many people in the locale, piracy was a part-time business. In an area where people barely scraped by, it was something you had to do to survive. A bit of farming, a bit of labouring work in winter, a bit of fishing in summer – that's a common pattern in the west of Ireland today, and in the 1600s you could also go 'on the account' with pirates.

There were also unwilling pirates – mariners captured at sea, or landlubbers who were abducted by buccaneers. There are plenty of recorded instances in which men visited Baltimore to sample the delights of the 'alehouses', drank themselves stupid, and were rudely awakened next morning by some pirate bosun shouting at them to swab the decks. In other cases, pirates simply smashed their way into homes, pulled respectable citizens out of their beds, and frogmarched them aboard.

At the other end of the spectrum, there were the hardcore pirates. These were often criminals on the run, looking for double or quits, one last throw of the dice. But while some pirates could get rich and retire, others weren't so lucky. Drunken crewmen, suddenly wealthy, could blow or lose their money in the taverns. They would gamble away their cash ('they play continually for Barbary gold' said one witness) and fight over the outcome. They would steal from one another, and sometimes murder their shipmates. One pirate captain, John Ward, made a rule that any man who killed a shipmate should be strapped to the corpse and buried at sea, still alive, along with his victim.

However, the stories of the leading figures in this pirate armada had extraordinarily happy endings. Of the three main buccaneer 'admirals' of the era, two ended up retiring to palaces in the sun and the third built himself a plush home in Cork. All three died peacefully in their own beds, which is not how pirate stories are really supposed to end. In order to take a closer look at these three admirals, let's hit the road again, this time to the furthermost point of the Iveragh Peninsula in County Kerry and a beautiful island called Valentia.

Even the name Valentia Island sounds exotically Hispanic and piratical, although it has nothing to do with Valencia in Spain – it is Irish for 'sea-mouth island'. Protruding into the warm Gulf Stream, Valentia has its own unique microclimate, damp yet mild, which encourages many sub-tropical plants. Those other exotic creatures, pirates, have also thrived there. Nowadays, the island is accessed by a bridge from Portmagee, whose very name celebrates an eighteenth-century smuggler and sea-rover, Captain Theobald Magee.

One autumn morning in 1612, the people of Valentia awoke to find their island surrounded by a massive pirate fleet of more than two dozen vessels, carrying easily a thousand fighting men. To put the size in context, this was nearly the same number of ships with which the Spanish invaded Kinsale in 1601.

This formidable flotilla was led by the phenomenally-successful Peter Easton from Somerset. Easton was the third man to hold the title of Admiral of the Irish pirate fleet. He had just taken over the title from his predecessor, Richard Bishop, and was the number one thorn in the flesh of the English. Known as 'the Arch-Pirate', Easton had started life as a licensed privateer, but had turned rogue in Newfoundland. (In Canada, tradition claims that he rescued a distressed Irish princess – one Sheila na Geira – from Dutch buccaneers. She married his lieutenant and, supposedly, gave birth to the first European baby in this new colony of Newfoundland. Sadly, however, there is no evidence that Sheila or her royal father, the oddly-titled 'King of County Down', ever really existed.)

Operating in the classic Atlantic triangle, Easton put the fear of God into the English when he blockaded Bristol with forty ships. He spurned an offer of a royal pardon, claiming: 'I am a kind of king myself.' When his men landed in huge numbers in West Cork in 1610, the authorities admitted their forces were 'too weak to grapple with them'.

The English tried to turn him, but never succeeded. On one occasion their efforts were stymied when Easton attacked a rival pirate and 'threw him overboard', leaving him to drown. It didn't help when the Queen of France complained about his attacks on her shipping after a French vessel was captured and brought into Kinsale.

At age forty, Easton decided, wisely, to cash in his two million pounds and retire to southern France. He bought a palace, and ended his life as 'Marquis of Savoy'.

Valentia may have witnessed one of the high points of Irish piracy – the gathering of Easton's enormous and defiant fleet – but it was also the backdrop for one of the buccaneers' greatest defeats. In the early 1620s, an Irish pirate named David Burke terrorised the waters off the west of Ireland until a courageous naval officer named Captain Rice captured his flagship, the *St Michael*, in a sea battle just off this island. (I am indebted to the researches of historian John Appleby for the facts behind this story.)

David Burke led a small but effective force of forty-eight Irish pirates, who exploded on to the scene when they captured the merchantman *St Michael* five leagues off the Lizard rock. He converted the vessel into a man-of-war, with 'eight murdering-pieces' – devastating blunderbusses mounted on pivots – and four anchors hanging on the bow. After transferring the captured crew into his own inferior ship, he callously wrecked it against a rock. The seven men on board were lucky to escape with their lives.

Not so lucky were the crewmen of the *Paragon*, a Scottish ship taken by Burke off Clare Island. Posing as a friendly merchant-mariner, Burke befriended the ship's master, who invited his crew on to the *Paragon*. Once on board, the pirates ruthlessly killed their host and his first mate, and forced five crewmen to jump overboard. Two of them drowned. By this 'detestable treachery and murder', they gained the ship and its rich cargo of Canary Island wines.

Burke rampaged through the local waters, capturing ships from Holland, England and France, until he had amassed a fortune in stolen goods. His haul included wines and hides, as well as exotic goods such as cochineal, sarsaparilla (a medicinal root) and bezoar stones (digestive blockages extracted from the stomachs of Levantine goats and believed to counteract poison). The list demonstrates, once again, the wide and often bizarre range of pirate plunder.

The pirates split up, with Burke heading for a friendly port to dispose of the cargo, while his Irish sidekick Egmont Mallio set course for Valentia. But as Mallio approached the island, Captain Rice appeared on the horizon with his navy ship *The Phoenix* in full pursuit. The two ships clashed in a deadly sea-battle, and despite the effectiveness of the pirates' 'murdering-pieces', the navy men emerged as the victors.

Twenty-eight of the pirates were hanged at Cork, and another seven killed on land as they tried to escape. David Burke's piratical reign of terror was over.

In 1634, Valentia Island was a base for a prominent Barbary corsair named John Nutt (not one of the Confederacy admirals, but a lone wolf). John Nutt was one of the most notorious pirate captains to haunt southwest Ireland.

Born in Devon in England, he shot to prominence when he saved hundreds of mariners from a mass Navy press-ganging expedition. They formed the nucleus of his pirate fleet. Initially operating off Newfoundland, he became so rich on plunder that he could afford to offer £500 for his pardon. Once he joined the pirates of the African–Irish network, there was no stopping him. An English captain who was sent with three gunships to capture Nutt found him lying off the Irish coast with a fleet of twenty-eight Barbary pirate ships – as far as I'm aware, the greatest single pirate fleet ever recorded in Ireland. The navy man had to run for his life. Nutt was 'incomparably the greatest nuisance in His Majesty's dominions,' wrote one historian. 'Nothing in the seas was safe from him.'

He was also a thug and a rapist. One of his Irish victims, a sailor named Hugh Baker, told in 1623 how Nutt's crew seized him at the mouth of Youghal Harbour. Nutt had so many guns that he had ten cannon mounted and another eighteen spares in the hold. The pirates were 'very rich', and the ship was full of Barbary gold, with which they gambled all day and night. At one stage he heard Nutt boast that, if he were caught, he could afford to buy off the authorities with £2000 – an extraordinary amount, equal to 100 years' wages for a professional man.

During that time, Nutt attacked a Cornish boat, whose captain made a desperate dash to escape but was caught, after three warning shots, at the very entrance to Dungarvan Harbour. They freed all but one of the male passengers, but kept over a dozen female passengers, 'all of which were ravished by the pirates' company, but only one, Jones's wife, a saddler from Cork, whom Captain Nutt took for himself into the cabin, and there had her a week'. Baker himself escaped at that point, and knew nothing more of the fate of the unfortunate Mrs Jones and the other victims. No doubt they ended their days as slaves in North Africa.

Presumably, Nutt did not mention this incident to his wife, when he later invited her on board his flagship at Crookhaven.

The squalid incident certainly disproves any Hollywood myth of pirates as romantic figures, whose attitude to women captives was a mix of good-humoured arrogance and gentlemanly courtesy. True, women in this unique pirate society could become rich, and rise to positions of power as innkeepers and suppliers of goods, but these were mainly the pirates' wives and girlfriends. Women like Mrs Jones, not to mention the unfortunate alehouse prostitutes, represent the grubby underside of the same coin.

Nutt continued his trail of destruction around the Irish coast, culminating in an incident in the 1630s, in which he relieved the incoming Viceroy of Ireland, Lord Wentworth, of his silver, his furniture, and even his clothes. No-one was safe, indeed.

The very first Admiral of the Irish Confederacy fleet was a Kentish man named 'Little John' Ward. Short, bald and plain-spoken, Ward was a courageous fighter and an inspiring leader, who once took a prize against three-to-one odds, charging in 'as though he had the courage to outbrave death'. As the townspeople of Ireland no doubt found out, his men were notoriously badly behaved when they blew their piratical earnings on land. '[Their] habit and carriage on shore [was] far more detestable and uncomely … than their thieving at sea,' wrote one contemporary, with '… swearing, drinking, dicing and the utmost enormities'.

From his African base in present-day Tunisia and his northern base in Munster, Ward created havoc. He converted to Islam, changed his name, and ultimately retired as a very rich man in Tunis, where he built a palace of alabaster and 'lived like a Bashaw in Barbary'.

Ward was replaced as pirate Admiral by his lieutenant, Richard Bishop from Yarmouth, 'a man of … experience in that profession'. The pragmatic Bishop took things to a new level by entering into a robust commercial alliance with the corrupt Admiralty official William Hull in Leamcon, and introducing a new era of 'institutionalised' pirate commerce.

Under Bishop, the pirate fleet was 'well manned and shipped and [with] good mariners', and there was 'a continual clamour from poor people that are daily spoiled and robbed'. At one point in 1609, he could summon twenty-one ships and well over 1,000 men. Bishop regarded himself as a patriot. He was disgusted both with Ward's transformation into an African 'Bashaw' and Easton's defection to France. 'I will die a poor labourer in mine own country,' Bishop protested, 'rather than be the richest pirate in the world.'

He made Leamcon his second home, accepted an English pardon and built himself a fine mansion nearby. He never went 'on the account' again, although the English suspected that he still directed pirate operations from the safety of his new home, and raided him every so often just to make a point.

Ireland's golden age of piracy could not last for ever. A combination of factors ultimately forced the buccaneers out of their comfortable havens, their Land of the Lotus Eaters, in Leamcon and Baltimore.

Firstly, an infamous freebooter named Henry Mainwaring turned legit and – as the price of his pardon – produced a tell-all book that blew all the pirates' secrets. He told how they used ports and inlets in Ireland, where 'a pirate may trim his ships without affront' and obtain 'all commodities and conveniences' with the blessing of corrupt officials. He explained how the buccaneers faked cattle raids to get supplies of beef from willing accomplices ashore. He revealed the secrets of the pirates' playbook for sea attacks. When the pirates sought R-and-R, he explained, ports like Baltimore and Leamcon offered a 'good store of English, Scottish and Irish wenches … [who] are strong attractions'. Mainwaring summed up southwest Ireland, in his now-famous phrase, as 'a nursery and storehouse for pirates'.

Secondly, the English, stung by rebukes from the Venetians and the Dutch, began to build up their navy. Thirdly, Mamora, one of the pirates' main bases in Morocco, fell to the Spanish. Fourthly, the Munster fish business prospered, and those same merchants who had previously welcomed pirates were now demanding safe seas. (Even William Hull saw the writing on the wall: in 1625, he captured eight pirates on Leamcon's Long Island and had them executed.) But mainly, the pirate boom ended because the exasperated Dutch Navy tore into the Irish havens and did a serious cleanup job. The era's most prominent Irish pirate, Patrick Myagh, was cornered by the Dutch captain Moy Lambert in Crookhaven in 1614. Myagh and his son jumped into the sea and tried to escape, but were slaughtered on reaching the shore.

The final nail in the coffin, though, was the sensational slave raid carried out in Baltimore by the Dutch convert and religious zealot Morat Rais in 1631. This was definitely a shifting of the gears. It was not simply a pirate raid, although renegade pirates played a leading role: with a large number of Ottoman soldiers on board, it was, in the furious words of King Charles I, an 'invasion' by a foreign power. This second wave of pirates did not want to trade with the residents, or cosy up to the local authorities. Like the early Vikings, they wanted to sack, burn and enslave. In my experience, this distinction is not always appreciated by some modern commentators.

Many of the remaining Irish-based pirates drifted away – to Africa, to the European free ports, or across the Atlantic. But a large proportion simply stayed ashore, married their girlfriends and merged into the fabric of southwest Ireland, where the population presumably still includes the several-times-great grandsons and granddaughters of pirates. If you want to see their monument, just look around you.

Where did the pirates' money go? There's a fascinating theory that at least some of it ended up funding settlements in the New World, laying the foundation stones of modern America. Jamestown and Bermuda have been cited as examples of colonisations that were made possible by the rich flow of money that washed into the Irish pirate enclaves and travelled like a tidal wave across the Atlantic.

Some historians view the English settlements in West Cork in the early 1600s as trial runs for later, more successful, colonies in what is now the USA. For instance, the settlement in Cork's Baltimore was founded by English Protestant dissidents seeking freedom from Anglican domination. (They had leased the village fairly and legally.) One of the main driving forces was a Puritan family, the Winthrops. A man named John Winthrop was a leading figure in creating what was intended to be a brave new world in Baltimore, but which ended up becoming economically enmeshed with the pirate economy.

In 1630 – just before the devastating raid by Morat Rais – this man's nephew, also named John Winthrop, set sail from England in the flagship *Arabella* with 700 Puritan followers, in a bid to re-try the same experiment in Massachusetts. He had spent some time in the Cork settlement before embarking on this venture. Nephew John eventually became the first Governor of Massachusetts, and his band of pioneers founded the community that would become Boston.

On the voyage out, this same John Winthrop delivered his now-famous 'City on a Hill' speech, setting out his vision of a free society. In 1961, President John Kennedy said: 'I have been guided by the standard John Winthrop set before his shipmates on the flagship *Arabella* 331 years ago, as they, too, faced the task of building a new government on a perilous frontier.'

So, amid all their wheeling and dealing with pirates, we should not lose sight of the freedom-seeking ideals of those coastal settlers in southwest Ireland – ideals that withered in the darkness of the pirate era, but which would ultimately find their fruition thousands of miles away in America, in pioneering expeditions that may have been made possible by the family funding that came from pirate gold.

Not all the treasure of the West Cork buccaneers made its way to the New World colonies, nor filled the pockets of English opportunist merchants. There is a persistent local tradition that some of the treasure that was 'buried on land by these pirates' (to quote the official English report of 1611) still remains concealed beneath the boulders and gorse bushes of these rugged headlands. One spooky legend claims that the pirate John Nutt – who, in reality, did keep a huge hoard of gold stashed away to bribe his way to freedom – buried his wealth at several points along this coast. As a local historian recorded in 1869: 'It was customary with him to bury his kegs on various headlands, at then at each place to sacrifice a black slave, whose spirit, it is believed, even still keeps watch over the hoarded treasure.'

So beware. Do not hunt for buried treasure in these parts … unless you want to risk incurring the curse of John Nutt and the ghostly guardians of his gold.

9

PIRATE PILGRIMAGE THE NINTH

Castleisland

It has just stopped raining and the sun is breaking through, bright and brittle, as I walk through the north Kerry market town of Castleisland – described by its most celebrated native, the late writer Con Houlihan, as 'not so much a town as a street between fields'. He was referring to Castleisland's most famous feature – an extraordinarily wide main street that looks broad enough to cope with a Russian Mayday Parade. In a town of around 2,500 people, it seems delightfully out of proportion, almost as though Paris's boulevard designer Baron Haussmann came here on a weekend trip, had a few Guinnesses and went a bit mad with a local bulldozer.

The town sits at the mouth of the Vale of Tralee, with the dark-green-and-dun slopes of the Glenaruddery Mountains to its north and the Stacks Mountains to the northwest. Tralee town, to the west, is a former buccaneering haven – they even have a street named after the Denny family, who were pirates in Elizabethan times – but I haven't time to visit it on this journey. Maybe next trip.

As I wander along the pleasant riverside walk, I find it hard to imagine that Castleisland was once a key frontier outpost in a bitter and bloody war between the feisty native Irish of South Kerry and the Norman conquerors who'd established themselves in the north of the county.

In the early 1200s, the Normans decided to erect a line of castles along the River Maine, with this point as its main fortress. It was their version of Hadrian's Wall. They noticed a particular river-island whose waters provided a natural moat, and here they erected the 'Castell on the Island' that gives the town its name. This became the centre of power for the invaders in Munster for the next three-and-a-half centuries.

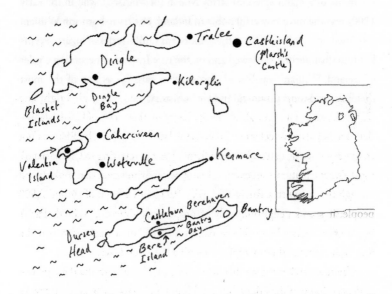

Only a tiny part of it survives today – an unfriendly-looking grey stone tower that stands incongruously near the back gardens of modern terraced houses. High up in the structure, two gaping blank windows stare out over the landscape, as though perpetually on the lookout against another attack. To the side of the tower, the amputated fragments of a once-enormous wall protrude in an odd curve, as if the stone were swelling with some sort of organic growth. Meanwhile, real organic growths, in the form of ivy and creepers, slither up to the very top of the sheer walls like ninja invaders.

Looking at this stunted ruin, it's hard to get a sense of the original scale. According to local literature, at one stage Castleisland Castle was 'a massive structure, stretching northwards from the bank of the river to the foot of Maum Hill, a distance of well over a mile, and the same distance east along the bank of the Maine'.

Why am I here, miles inland? Because this castle was the creation and the home of a man named Geoffrey Marsh (or Marisco), who in the early 1200s was the most powerful noble in Ireland. His Irish-born son William was lined up to follow in his father's footsteps until a series of bizarre events left him disinherited, outlawed and on the run. Instead of becoming a ruler of Ireland, William was forced into another career – as one of the most infamous and most successful pirates in history.

The Framing of
William Marsh

Almost eight centuries ago, a Benedictine monk named Matthew Paris sketched a gruesome drawing in the margin of his vellum manuscript. It shows a notorious Irish pirate being dragged through the streets behind a prancing horse on the way to his execution in London in the year 1242.

If we can believe the dimensions in the sketch, the victim is a tall man, a good nine inches taller than the horse's rider. Taut red haulage ropes are tied to each of his raised ankles. They stretch forward to either side of the horse's collar. The youngish, curly-haired man seated on the horse doesn't look like a sadistic executioner – at first glance, he seems like any one of a dozen affable lads you might meet in a modern sales office. The artist captures him as he glances over his shoulder to check his prisoner, his attitude of professional concentration interrupted only by an oddly self-conscious half-smile. This seems curiously at odds with the ghastliness of the image until you remember that the artist has filtered out the surroundings – the baying, ugly mob of spectators, the kicking clogs, the hundreds of dirty fists hurling stones and rotten fruit at the victim. If the man on the ground is the villain, the horseman is one of the stars of this macabre public spectacle. He is revelling in his fifteen minutes of fame.

The victim, aged perhaps in his late thirties, is dressed in a green, knee-length tunic and a white hood. He seems barely conscious. His open eyes stare vacantly skywards as his head bumps along in the mud. This is not surprising, for he has already been dragged by horseback after his initial arrest, has been tortured in the Tower, and is now about to suffer the most dreadful death his tormentors can devise. He has been sentenced to be hung, drawn and quartered.

Irish pirate William Marsh, who became notorious as 'the Night Hawk', is drawn through the streets of London as part of a gruesome execution ritual. Although guilty of piracy, he was almost certainly innocent of plotting to assassinate the King.

Many readers will be familiar with this sadistic practice from Elizabethan dramas and from modern movies such as *Braveheart*, which showed the Scots rebel William Wallace suffering an identical fate around sixty years later. I am not going to describe it in detail. It is inventively awful and creatively grotesque. Yet this penalty did not appear out of nowhere. At some stage in history, someone in authority must have said: This offender is so evil, and his deeds so appalling, that we must dream up a brand-new form of prolonged, agonising death that will send out a dreadful warning to others.

That's why this drawing is so extraordinary. Because this form of execution was originally, and specifically, custom-designed for this particular victim. He is a pirate-admiral named William Marsh, and he is the first man ever to die this awful death. 'He was very odious to the King,' explains Matthew Paris, perhaps unnecessarily.

William Marsh was a high-born Irish nobleman, the wealthy son of a viceroy, who was outlawed and deprived of his inheritance by an autocratic king for reasons of political expediency, and who reacted by turning pirate and conducting a ruthlessly efficient naval campaign against a harsh and intolerant regime. The story of the young noble who turns to piracy after being cheated of his birthright has become a regular cliché of pirate fiction, but Marsh was perhaps the original of the species. From his almost-impregnable base on a rocky island between England and Ireland, the man they called 'the Night Hawk' harried ships all along the Irish Sea, terrorising both coasts with his fearsome war-galleys, all the way from Wexford to Dublin and Drogheda, and as far north as Scotland. He proved almost impossible to capture, but in the end he was taken by treachery, caged in the Tower of London, and convicted of high treason.

Marsh was certainly a political rebel, and undoubtedly a pirate and a criminal. But of the crime for which he was actually sentenced – that is, sending an assassin to murder the King in the royal bedroom – he was clearly and obviously innocent.

William Marsh was set up.

It was a right royal stitch-up, involving almost every layer of the English Establishment, from the King downward.

First, a bit of background. England was ruled at the time by Henry III, a weak and indecisive monarch who was constantly under pressure from the same class of noblemen who had cornered his father, King John, and forced him to sign away some of his powers in the Magna Carta. Henry's relationship with these barons was fractious. A portrait shows the weak-chinned, long-nosed man looking resentful and bemused, like some frustrated modern geography teacher who can't keep control in class. Henry would have loved to rule as an absolute monarch, but he didn't have the muscle and he didn't have the money. And Henry needed a *lot* of money. He was personally extravagant, and he had grandiose plans for empire-building. He relied on the barons for cash, and in exchange they wanted more power for themselves.

Henry III of England: he wanted William Marsh dead, and was prepared to frame him for murder.

According to the monk Matthew Paris, Henry had a ferocious temper. But his arrogance hid a spineless and irresolute nature. As one historian put it: 'He earned the contempt of Englishmen and foreigners alike by the instability of his purpose.'

Among the many aristocrats to suffer at Henry's hands were the Marsh family of Ireland. And of the Marshes, the man who suffered most was William.

William Marsh is described in two contemporary annals as 'an Irishman by nation'. He was born somewhere in Ireland's southwest, but I cannot find any document that tells us precisely when or where. It was probably in one of the many castles built or owned by his powerful father Geoffrey – perhaps at the castle he constructed at Castleisland in Kerry, or at his majestic family base at Adare Castle in Limerick. The surname Marsh, or its variants de Marisco, Marais or Moreys, means exactly what it says – 'from the marshes'. William was the archetypal bogman.

And yet … has any future pirate ever come from such a grand background? The Marshes were, in the early 1200s, among the most dominant and influential families in the country. From 1215 onwards, William's father Geoffrey served several times as Lord Justice of Ireland, and was – according to Paris – 'one of the most powerful men in Ireland'. Another biographer went further: he said Geoffrey was among the most dominant and influential individuals in Europe.

The nephew of an archbishop, Geoffrey made good alliances through marriage and worked his way up the ladder of power. His young son William grew up well used to the high life: grand banquets in castles, jousting contests, hunts for stags in the dense forests. He rubbed shoulders with the greatest nobles in the land.

In 1220, Geoffrey was appointed as Ireland's Viceroy – literally, a man who stood in for the King. He ruthlessly crushed a major rising in Connaught, where he 'slew and made prisoners to the number of 20,000'. Yet he bemused many with his insistence on justice for the locals. When an

Irish king under Geoffrey's protection was attacked and killed by a Marsh supporter – an offence usually treated with a small fine – Geoffrey insisted that the guilty man should be executed.

Meanwhile, his son William was earmarked for great things. He was received into the King's service. He married the Archbishop of Dublin's niece and received a substantial dowry.

So up until that point, the Marshes had been enjoying their place in the warmth of King Henry's affections, and William was being groomed as a major player for the future. But it was all about to go horribly, irreversibly wrong. And it was all caused by the arrival in Ireland of one man.

His name was Richard Mareschal, the Earl of Pembroke, grandson of the famous Strongbow. Pembroke was rebelling against the King, and when his troops arrived in Ireland, Henry wrote to the Irish barons with clear orders to defeat the traitor. If they succeeded, he pledged, they could share out his substantial lands between them.

Geoffrey Marsh defeated Pembroke by trickery, and the rebel Earl was fatally wounded in battle on a windswept Kildare plain. When word reached London, there was widespread public outrage. Pembroke was a popular figure, and it was generally agreed that he was the victim of foul play. There were violent protests. King Henry vigorously back-pedalled. 'Forgetful of his own orders,' says one account, '... he accused [the Irish barons] of treachery.'

Geoffrey and his son William were fined a total of six thousand marks, and they spent most of the year 1234 in prison. Finally released, they travelled to London in an attempt to clear their names, unaware that they were blundering into a hornet's nest of political intrigue. Instead of receiving a reward for obeying the King's orders, the Marshes were about to be set up for murder.

The murder victim was a civil servant named Henry Clement. It's not clear whether he was a pawn in the King's game, callously sacrificed, or whether his murder was one of those fortunate coincidences that happened just at the right time to play its place in a grander design. Whatever the truth, for Henry it was definitely a murder of convenience.

Clement was a high-level envoy who ran messages between England and Ireland. He was also a bit of a braggart, who annoyed a lot of people. According to the monk Matthew Paris, he spent much of his time in London, bad-mouthing the late rebel Richard, Earl of Pembroke, and boasting that he himself played a key role in Pembroke's death.

After nightfall on Sunday, 13 May 1235, a large band of riders galloped up to the house where Clement was lodging, near the gates of Westminster Palace. Armed men jumped off their horses, smashed their way into the lodging-house, and stormed upstairs by torchlight. The landlady thrust her head out of the window and screamed for help, but nobody came to her aid – even though there were royal guards nearby. The assailants attacked and wounded the main tenant, a surgeon, while his guest Henry Clement tried to scramble to safety out of a window. But there was no escape – the street was full of hostile riders. Clement was dragged back and brutally murdered. The killers doused their torches, clattered down the wooden stairs, and grabbed the reins of their horses from waiting accomplices. They spurred their mounts and thundered off into the darkness of a nearby graveyard.

The King, who was in residence in the palace at the time, was outraged at this 'dishonour' and 'scandal' outside the very gates of his home. He demanded a full investigation. Although several people witnessed the attack, nobody could identify the murderers. The main suspect was one Gilbert Mareschal, the brother of the late rebel Richard, who had every reason to seek revenge on a man who claimed to have killed his brother. He was directly accused of the murder, and a lengthy inquiry began.

Then something very strange happened. Inexplicably, the focus shifted to William Marsh. Even though the case against him was flimsy, the prosecutors piled up the circumstantial evidence. Two witnesses claimed to have heard William complain a few weeks earlier that the murder victim, Henry Clement, was blocking his career. Others said that William's friends threatened Clement, and that William himself tried to find out where Clement was staying. But there wasn't a single witness who could connect William with the murder.

Why did suspicion shift so quickly from Gilbert, the initial suspect, to William? Probably because Henry had cut a deal with the aggrieved Mareschal family: they would remain loyal and quell the protests, provided Gilbert walked free and their enemies the Marshes were framed for the murder instead.

The Marshes went on the run. Geoffrey vanished into the Priory of St John, pleading for sanctuary from the monastic knights. William galloped off to Devon, with some similarly accused friends, determined to lose himself in England's wild west. Father and son were also excommunicated by the Church. The family had been outlawed both from this world and from the next.

One early historian sums up the entire shoddy episode: '[Geoffrey] … having crushed the insurrection and slain Earl Richard, awaited at the King's hands the highest reward his fidelity and valour entitled him to; yet the fickle Henry showed himself quite otherwise disposed … Lord Geoffrey was deposed and banished, and his lands seized into the King's hands.'

As Geoffrey headed north to Scotland, his son William began a new career as a pirate. He had every reason to seethe with resentment, for he was almost certainly innocent of Clement's murder. (Years later, just before his execution in Tyburn, William Marsh would make a final Confession to a religious friar. He freely admitted all his crimes, but protested his innocence of the Clement murder to his last anguished breath.)

If Henry thought he had heard the last of Geoffrey's family, he was very much mistaken. His problems with William Marsh were only just beginning.

William Marsh, son of Geoffrey Marsh, took up his quarters on an island near Bristol, called Lundy, a place impregnable by the nature of its situation, where he lived like a pirate ... indulging in plunder and rapine, and, attended by his companions, traversed the places on the neighbouring coast, despoiling the inhabitants of their property, especially wine and other provisions. By sudden incursions he frequently carried off vast booty ... and in many ways injured the Kingdom of England both by land and sea, and caused great loss to the native and foreign merchants.

The words of the monk Matthew Paris, written in the mid-1200s, reveal how William had exacted a bitter revenge on the King who betrayed him. This was an era when hundreds of small-time pirates operated around the English and Irish coasts. One more would hardly rate a mention. But Marsh was something much more worrying than that. With his own flotilla of galleys, he was more a fleet commander than a pirate captain. And judging by the scale and scope of his operations, his campaign was more than just piracy. It was war. It was insurrection at sea.

William's new home of Lundy Island was a perfect base for a pirate. It was crucially situated about eighteen miles from England and over 180 miles from the southeast coast of Ireland. Its position off the mouth of the Bristol Channel meant it could dominate the busy sea-route between the English ports of Bristol and Barnstaple and the main southern Irish ports of Wexford, Waterford, Youghal and Cork. Tidal currents and hidden dangers meant that passing vessels found it difficult to avoid Lundy

– they had to sail close by. The island had a large population of rabbits and pigeons, so if times became hard, the pirates would still have plenty of meat for the pot. But the most attractive thing about Lundy was that it is a natural fortress, and almost unassailable. 'An impregnable retreat,' said Matthew Paris. An English courtier elaborated: 'It has only one approach, where two men can scarce walk abreast. The steep and frightful rocks on every side forbid entrance.' So long as William could place guards on this pathway, it seemed that no-one could ever take him by surprise.

The Marisco Castle on Lundy Island, as sketched by an artist in the 1800s. Named after the Irish buccaneer William Marsh, it marks the spot where the 'Night Hawk' built his piratical eyrie. It proved impregnable until he was betrayed by a comrade.

For much of the time, fog and sea-mist lent Lundy a cloak of invisibility. 'After the jealous clouds have shrouded it for weeks,' writes one observer, 'they drift away, and the grand and lonely Lundy Island rears its scarred and riven-granite cliffs from the fretted sea ... a lofty table-headed rock, surrounded by steep and occasionally perpendicular cliffs, with grisly seams and clefts and … fantastic coves and grottoes … Sea-birds whirl like driven clouds, cluster in the crannies, and balance themselves upon the waves, filling the air with hoarse screaming.'

This was the pirate island that William selected as his base. His father Geoffrey may have thrown up grand castles in Ireland, but William's 'castle' would be made of sea-rock, seaweed and shingle. This tiny island, shaped on the map like an elongated seahorse, would be his home for the next seven years.

William created an eyrie on a hilltop above a perpendicular cliff-face. He gathered around him a force of hardened fighters – 'outlaws and fugitives' like himself, who had nothing left to lose – and began to build up his empire of the sea. Merchant craft were captured and converted into warships. Some new galleys were built from scratch, using the remnants of wrecks.

At first, he stayed close to Lundy, targeting merchantmen on the Ireland–Bristol route. This in itself created a major headache for the Kingdom, but William was only just beginning. He extended his operations to 'plunder and rapine' on land, sweeping down suddenly on defenceless coastal settlements and making off with large hauls of stolen property. Terrified villagers dubbed him 'the Night Hawk', because no-one could ever tell when or where he would strike next.

As William Marsh's confidence grew, his area of operation expanded – from Wales, Devon and Cornwall to Ireland's southeast coast, then further north to Dublin and Drogheda, and finally as far away as Scotland. The waters between the two great islands of Britain and Ireland – from chilly Galloway to balmier Cornwall – were his to plunder at will. He targeted high-demand goods that were easily resold. Wine was a favourite, but one source says that during his 'desperate ravages' he preferred to steal 'beef and biscuits'.

One writer talks of 'the poor Bristol traders, hugging close the Welsh or English shore, preferring the risk of being cast upon the cruel slate reefs of Hartland or the sand flats of Carmarthen Bay to falling into the clutches of the corsairs of Lundy'.

He created alliances with powerful locals on both coasts, and before long, Lundy became just one of his many pirate havens. He dominated ports like Drogheda, on Ireland's east coast. He became more ambitious, more political. He captured wealthy merchants and held them to ransom. This not only earned him a fortune, but fulfilled the classic terrorist objective of destroying confidence and destabilising trade. The luckless captives were cast into dank prisons until their ransoms were paid. And the rewards were enormous: one group of merchants was freed for £120, perhaps a million euro today.

At one stage, citizens in Irish districts as far removed as Ulster, Drogheda and Dublin were ordered to raise cash for a fund to compensate for William's depredations. Tensions rose even further when the pirate forged an alliance with the King of Scotland and assembled a joint fleet. There were fears that the allies were considering an invasion of England, with William lined up to replace Henry as King. But the plot never translated into reality.

Actually, William would always deny that he ever showed disloyalty to King Henry. In his view, it was the other way around. He believed he was forced to flee, as one writer puts it, 'to avoid the ignominy [of] an unjust suspicion … [He] turned pirate only for the purposes of filling his belly'.

It didn't matter, because by this stage Henry and William were nursing a bitter and implacable mutual hatred. Henry felt powerless and humiliated. William was burning with resentment, not only because of his original banishment, but also because Henry had been taking out his anger on William's wife Matilda back in Ireland. Even though she owned her property in her own right and was innocent of any wrongdoing, her lands were confiscated. This had become personal. There was no going back.

Henry longed to capture and execute his nemesis, but more than that – he dreamed of putting him to a prolonged, excruciatingly painful and ignominious death. Yet he couldn't risk the displeasure of the other barons. To ensure that William would deserve this grisly end, he needed proof that the Irish pirate had been plotting the assassination of the King himself.

Suddenly, in the autumn of 1238, the ideal opportunity landed in Henry's lap. A disturbed individual was caught, raving nonsense, acting irrationally and wielding a knife, in the royal holiday home. Could he have been sent as an assassin by William Marsh? Was this the sort of man Marsh was likely to choose for such a crucial mission? Of course he was. With the right sort of persuasion, the poor dupe would say anything Henry wanted him to say.

The incident happened at the royal hunting lodge in Woodstock, Oxfordshire, where Henry was relaxing with his young bride Eleanor of Provence (they had married two years previously, when he was aged twenty-seven and she was aged twelve). The estate of Woodstock, which has since disappeared, was a garden of exotic wonder. A century beforehand, the first King Henry had created a walled park where lions, leopards and camels roamed. The second Henry used the lodge as a secret love-nest for his mistress – according to tradition, she was quietly murdered after Henry's wife surprised the two secret lovers there. It was here, too, that the same Henry had his first blazing confrontations with his troublesome Archbishop, Thomas Becket. Woodstock was no stranger to drama and even bloodshed.

The current King Henry made his own contribution by adding a chapel. He would have been better off installing extra safety measures, because on that September night, the security at Woodstock seems to have been surprisingly lax. A stranger, well-educated and with a military bearing, somehow made his way into the royal court and walked right up to the unprotected monarch.

—I have the mark of royalty upon my shoulder, he announced grandly to the King. Give me back the kingdom that you have unjustly usurped from me.

Guards rushed the intruder and roughed him up, but Henry ordered them to stop. 'Let the madman rave,' he ruled. 'Such people's words have not the force of truth.'

But later that night, the man returned and sought out the King's bed-chamber. He stole in through an open window, bolted the door against the guards, and dived towards the King's bed-couch with dagger upraised to strike. But there was nobody there.

'By God's providence,' says Matthew Paris, 'the King was sleeping with the queen [in her bedchamber].'

The noise alerted a maidservant, who, despite the late hour, was still awake and praying by candlelight. 'When she saw this madman searching all the private places in a bid to kill the King, she was greatly alarmed … at her cry the King's attendants awoke, and leaped from their beds with all speed … [and] broke open the door.' They quickly overpowered the intruder.

The contemporary historian Thomas Wikes had a different take on the story. The man had inveigled his way into Woodstock by acting as an enter-taining simpleton, 'making sport among the domestics in the manner of a fool'. But that night, the intruder was 'found under the King's bed, lying hid in the straw, intending to kill him with a very long knife'. A third version says he had posed as a clergyman.

Whatever the truth, Henry rapidly re-evaluated his early opinion that the attacker was irrational and mentally disturbed. The unfortunate man was put to torture with one aim in mind – to persuade him to say that he was a professional hitman, sent by William Marsh. Unsurprisingly, the assailant gave his interrogators the right answer. 'After a while,' says Paris – with a world of dark subtext in those three words – 'he confessed that he had been sent to kill the King by [William Marsh], son of Geoffrey.' The furious King 'ordered him to be torn limb from limb by horses'.

Another early historian, Raphael Hollingshead, claimed that the prisoner died defiantly, glorying in his crime and 'not caring what had become of himself so he might have despatched his purpose'.

Henry lost no time in getting the word out: William Marsh was 'a traitor against the King'. Anyone who aided him would be made to suffer. Authorities in every port were ordered to search and apprehend.

It took another four years, but they finally got him.

During those four years, William had continued, and even stepped up, his piratical activities. According to another source: 'The King, fearful that another attempt would be made [on his life], urged on by his nobles, and moved by the complaints of merchants whose cargos were seized, as well as by the lamentations of the people … ordered the capture of the island stronghold by fair means or foul.'

In the spring of 1642, the King summoned a war council.

—This island cannot be assaulted by force, his military advisers warned him. It can be taken only by treachery. Your Majesty must act not forcibly, but cautiously, to catch this robber.

—Do whatever it takes, Henry snapped. Use every diligent endeavour to take this man and free the country of him. There will be a great reward if you capture him, for he is most hateful to me. He sent a villain to cut my throat.

Suitably motivated, the nobles got to work. They captured one of William's associates, turned him by whatever means, and sent him back to Lundy with secret instructions. Next they drew up a plan. Since a full-on naval assault on Lundy was unlikely to succeed, they opted for what we would today describe as a special-forces raid. But who would lead it?

A young Kentish man named Richard Chilham, a baron's son, stepped forward. He was the heir of war hero Richard Fitzroy, a love-child of the late King John (and therefore the current King's half-brother), and he was eager for action. It was agreed that he would lead the midnight assault on William Marsh's lair. Chilham created a team of fourteen hand-picked warriors – two knights and twelve veteran sergeants – and received a sub-stantial war-chest of forty marks to fund the mission.

On a cold May night, Lundy was enshrouded in its usual miasma of mist as Chilham's men stole ashore on rowboats and formed up on the shingle. A quick reconnoitre confirmed the island's fortress status. There was only one pathway, 'where two men can scarce walk abreast', and that was heavily guarded by Marsh's men. William's fortress sat on top of a sheer cliff, which was scalable using a series of ladders, but which had a guard stationed on top. At a word from this guard, says one writer, 'flights of arrows or boulders rolled down from above would have discomfited or overwhelmed any scaling force.'

That night, William Marsh was seated comfortably at dinner with his entourage of sixteen lieutenants. He had no reason to fear an attack, because nothing could get past his guards.

There was only one problem.

The lone guard at the top of the cliff was the man who had turned traitor.

The assault team negotiated their way to the rocky base of the cliff and began scaling the sheer rocks. The guard saw them and remained silent. Within a few minutes, they were standing by his side on the clifftop, drawing their swords ready for the climactic phase of the mission. Thanks to the traitor, they knew the fortress's layout. They stormed the building. One concerted rush, a brief scuffle, and the whole affair was over. The Night Hawk of Lundy was tethered and hooded at last.

Richard Chilham took no chances with his captive. His team ferried William to the mainland, where – according to one account – the pirate was dragged behind a horse on the road towards Bristol. There was great rejoicing in Severnside at the news that the town's tormentor had been caught. Marsh was thrown into the most secure dungeon in the city's prison, 'so loaded with irons' that he could hardly move.

A few days later, they arrived in London. 'On the eve of St James,' writes Paris, 'William and sixteen accomplices were legally convicted and sentenced to death with particular ignominy by the King's express command.'

Paris continues: '[He was] first dragged from Westminster to the Tower, and thence to that instrument of punishment vulgarly called the gibbet … horrible to relate, he suffered not one but many deaths.' The monk then goes on to describe the world's first case of hanging, drawing and quartering. After William 'breathed out his wretched soul', the quarters of his body were 'sent into four of the principal cities of the realm, so that his lamentable spectacle might inspire fear in all beholders'.

William's last confessor, a friar named John of St Giles, was later interrogated by the eager authorities. Did the condemned man admit his guilt? They were disappointed. Despite the torture, William remained adamant that he was innocent. 'Invoking the judgement of God, [Marsh swore] that he was free from and utterly guileless of the crime of high treason … and the same of the death … of Clement,' writes Paris. However, William did come clean about all his genuine crimes.

And then: 'With soothing words of consolation, the confessor dismissed him in peace, exhorting him to suffer his punishment with patience, as a means of penance.'

The King's men secured the forbidden island and seized William's galleys as trophies for the King. Richard Chilham was hailed as a hero by the long-suffering coastal dwellers of Ireland and England, and received a bonus of forty shillings. This was a man who would never have to pay for a drink in Bristol or Dublin again.

William's father Geoffrey Marsh died shortly afterwards, an outlaw and a fugitive to the end. 'After the ignominious death of his son and the loss of all his friends, [Geoffrey] was himself taken from amongst us,' Paris writes, 'thus finally ending so many deaths by his own.'

Back in Ireland, William's wife Matilda courageously fought a prolonged legal battle with Henry. The King had snatched her substantial properties because her husband was a traitor. Matilda hit back hard, by proving that she received them in her own name from her uncle, the wealthy Archbishop of Dublin. She refused to be intimidated, and eventually Henry backed down.

How do we classify William Marsh? It's difficult. He was undoubtedly a pirate – several contemporary chroniclers use that word to describe him. But he was certainly no small-time coastal robber. He was a political revolutionary, who courageously challenged a despotic King in the only way open to him at the time – in other words, he was first and foremost a rebel, who was forced to operate as a pirate, rather than a pirate who was declared a rebel.

William himself claimed that he was forced into extreme measures to survive after losing everything he owned and unjustly being declared an outlaw.

Yet, had the dice rolled differently, he would probably have followed his father to become a viceroy of an English-dominated Ireland. William Marsh was simply unlucky.

'The Night Hawk' was certainly no angel, but today he gets a bad press that he does not deserve. He is sometimes accused of 'plunder and rape', which seems to be a misunderstanding of Matthew Paris's phrase 'plunder and rapine' – that is, robbery by force. It is also often stated as fact that he tried to assassinate the King, even though the charge does not stand up to the least scrutiny. Why would Marsh choose a clearly deranged individual for this crucial task? And why would a trained assassin who got close to the King waste time in an incoherent rant instead of simply finishing the job? If Marsh had really wanted Henry dead, he would have made a better stab at it (so to speak) than that. 'The accusation of treason ... is extremely improbable,' says the *Oxford Dictionary of National Biography*, adding that the charge was trumped up amid the political backlash over Richard Mareschal's death.

Another historian has analysed all the facts in the case and concluded: 'The evidence incriminating William [Marsh] was clearly worthless. If the would-be assassin had not been insane, he would not have ... drawn attention to himself before making the murderous attempt. [Marsh] had nothing to gain from the King's death.'

I agree completely.

William Marsh has left no historical legacy, yet there is an interesting coda to his story. Henry's sadistic execution of Marsh was a clear message to the fractious barons: look what I can do to any one of *you* if I choose. If it was a warning, it backfired. Because a decade later, a group of barons backed the weakened King into a corner at Oxford and dictated their terms to him, forcing him to grant fairer legal trials and to cede some powers to a fifteen-man council. The 1258 'Provisions of Oxford' were an important baby-step towards democracy, and are now regarded as England's first written Constitution. It was a pity that neither of the two Marshes, early martyrs to this process, lived to see it.

Today, there are few concrete reminders of the William Marsh saga. The royal lodge at Woodstock, scene of the assassination attempt, was levelled in the 1700s by an aristocratic lady, apparently for no other reason than that it spoiled her view. In Ireland, Adare Castle and the Castleisland fortress remain in ruins as memorials to the Marsh empire that crumbled into dust. On lonesome Lundy, there are remains of a castle fortress on a clifftop – it is known locally as the Marisco [or Marsh] Castle, and, although it was actually built after William's death, it stands on the spot where the Night Hawk had his lofty piratical nest. Another reminder of William Marsh is the Marisco Arms – the island's only pub. As an Irishman, William might well have approved.

Three years after ordering William's execution, the pious King Henry began building a new cathedral for the greater glory of God. Most of us are familiar with it, if only through television images of royal weddings. It is a magnificent structure, whose gracile stone arches and airy vaulted ceilings seem to soar heavenward in defiance of the laws of gravity. Next time you visit Henry III's Westminster Abbey and stand in awe of its humbling beauty, consider this: the same mind who conceived this celestial work of art also dreamed up the hellish torture known as hanging, drawing and quartering. And that is indeed a disturbing insight into the unfathomable paradox of the human psyche.

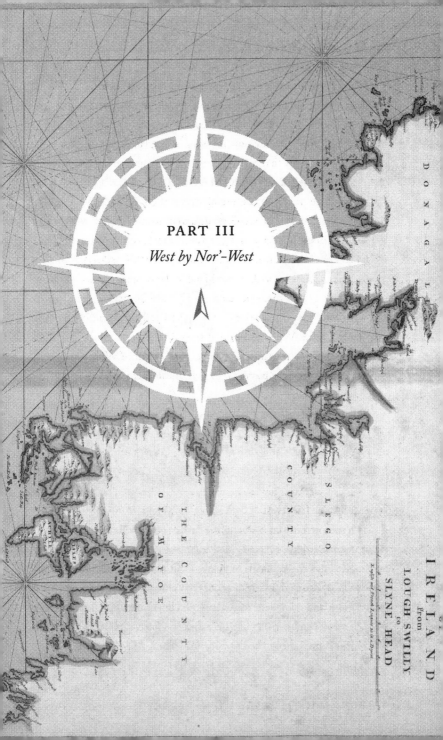

PART III

West by Nor'-West

10

PIRATE PILGRIMAGE THE TENTH

Clare Island

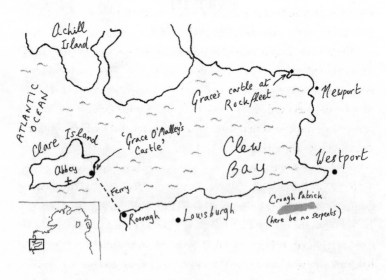

On this perfect May morning, the surface of Clew Bay is a deep Mediterranean blue, reflecting and intensifying the robin's-egg shade of an almost cloudless sky. Drifts of mauve thrift tumble chaotically down the stone walls of Roonagh Harbour as our ferry chugs off towards Clare Island. Ahead, the island's silhouette looms large and imposing, the 460-metre bulge of Mount Knockmore rising like the rump of a kneeling pilgrim with head lowered and arms outstretched towards the County Mayo coastline.

That's not such an inappropriate simile, because some of the tourists on board are, in a sense, pilgrims: they have travelled from all over the world to worship at the shrine of a famous female pirate named Granuaile. Grace O'Malley was, of course, the sixteenth-century buccaneer who has become famous as 'the Pirate Queen'.

'This was her home, Clare Island,' says a young American woman in a pink windcheater. She tells me she's a huge fan, and has read everything about her online. 'She was born here; she grew up here. This is where she went to school and where she got married. And this is where she's buried, in a canopy tomb at the old abbey.'

The ferry docks at the island jetty, beside a beach where the parchment-coloured sand transmutes the sea into a sort of toothpaste aqua, and we all negotiate the slippery steps to the pier. The visitors – a mixture of daytrippers, overnighters and serious hikers who have come here for the famous cliff walks – disperse within minutes, and it seems that we have this paradise entirely to ourselves.

On a clear spring day like this, being on Clare Island is like getting a day trip to Eden. Well, without the serpent, because – as the looming purple mass of nearby Croagh Patrick constantly reminds us – St Patrick got rid of all the snakes a long time ago. The light here is preternaturally clear, yet infused with just a hint of turquoise, as though the entire world has been cleansed through a dishwasher with some greeny-blue sparkle-adding ingredient, and then buffed and polished to translucent perfection. The colours shock the senses. At one point, I pass a bank of wild irises, just coming into bloom, and look up to see a line of clothes on a washing-line, dancing in the wind against the butter-yellow backdrop of a gorse-covered hill. The vivid reds and blues and greens and whites of those everyday garments strike the eye like a mobile artwork, and for the first time I realise just why so many artists love to work in this light. Their paintings are not exaggerating those colours: this is genuinely how they appear.

The clear air intoxicates as we walk through the boreens, savouring the heady marzipan smell of the yellow gorse blossom and listening to the nasal cries of new lambs in the fields all around. Swifts dart across the canvas of the blue sky, silhouetted in dramatic shapes, like Matisse cut-outs. At one point a fat pheasant, disturbed by our approach, stands up from its bed of wild iris and waddles off in disgust.

We reach the twelfth century Cistercian 'abbey' – a misnomer, since this building was never more than an out-chapel to a mainland parish church. We enter with reverence, not just because it is a place of worship, but also because it is a little-known artistic treasure. Above our heads, faded but clearly visible, are paintings reflecting the mediaeval mindset. They charm and disturb in equal measure. Stags are hunted across the ceiling. A mounted earl holds a spear upraised, poised to strike as he gallops, stirrup-less, across the wall. An angel weighs the souls of the dead before assigning them to Heaven or to Hell.

Along one wall is the famous canopy tomb that is reputed to hold the remains of Grace O'Malley. Curiously, the sober archaeological leaflet in the church says nothing at all about the Granuaile connection. It says the tomb is the last resting place of an O'Malley lord. There may be a clue in the fact that the plaque alongside, bearing the family coat of arms and cited by eighteenth-century sources as proof of her burial there, actually post-dates Grace by nearly a hundred years.

Emerging into the sunlight, we stroll down to O'Malley's Shop and Post Office, where we buy tea and cakes and sit outside in the warmth of midday. At length, we take a circuitous hike back to the harbour, and approach a grey stone structure overlooking the bay. Even in this kindly light, it looks grim and forbidding. It is widely known as Granuaile's Castle, but to be honest, it looks more like Kafka's. That's understandable, since it was remodelled as a police barracks in the 1800s. Yet you can still see sections of the old tower fortress, including the garderobes

– the uncomfortable, long-drop toilets in the upper rooms.

The pink American woman is there already, taking selfies. 'That window up there?' she points. 'That was the bedroom where Granuaile slept. Every night, she tied a long silken thread from her big toe to her ship, so she'd know if anyone tried to steal it.'

I look up dutifully, smile and mumble my appreciation through a mouthful of cake. But by this stage, I have spent the best part of a year researching the story of Grace O'Malley, and I haven't the heart to tell her that the big-toe story is – like the silk thread itself – just another flimsy, far-fetched and very, very tenuous yarn.

It's one of many legends about Grace. Wonderful, colourful stories that are impossible to verify or falsify, and are calculated to drive any researcher crazy.

'Good luck trying to write about Granuaile,' a historian friend once warned me. 'You'll find that all the interesting stories aren't true, and all the true stories aren't interesting.'

That's not quite accurate – the real Grace was a fascinating character – but by now, I know exactly what he was getting at. So in this chapter I've decided not only to tell the remarkable true story of the real Grace O'Malley, but also to devote a section to the most common and colourful Granuaile myths, together with my own views on their origins and their reliability. That's called having your cake and eating it.

Grania Mania

The story of the female pirate Granuaile – Grace O'Malley – has always held a particular fascination. For a start, it has an amazing cast of characters. Not only will we meet 'Gambling Grace' herself, but we will also encounter names that even the scriptwriters of *Pirates of the Caribbean* could never imagine in their wildest dreams. Names like Black Oak O'Malley, Iron Richard Burke, Battling Donal O'Flaherty, and – my personal favourite – 'Satan's Slash-hook' Burke. And, may I point out, these are names that predate World Wrestling by about 400 years.

Grace herself has been dubbed 'the Pirate Queen', although she was not literally a royal queen (even under the generous Gaelic system), or a queen among pirates in terms of her buccaneering accomplishments. Really, Grace 'the Pirate Queen' O'Malley is much more like Elvis 'the King' Presley. Her royal title is more fanciful than literal; she began life as a rebel, but ended up as a compliant figure of the Establishment; and she became far more successful *after* her death than she had ever been before.

For the benefit of those who aren't familiar with her story, 'Granuaile' was a notorious sixteenth-century Irish pirate, whose plundering exploits off Ireland's west coast infuriated not only her neighbours, but also the English colonists. 'The affrighted natives trembled at her name,' wrote one early historian, and an English viceroy agreed, saying she was 'a terror to all merchantmen that sailed the Atlantic'.

When she died in the early 1600s, it was the best career move she ever made. Grace, who's also known as Grania, Gráinne and Granuaile, is now at the centre of a phenomenon you could describe as 'Grania Mania'. Devoted followers – I like to call them Graniacs – come from all over the world to venerate the shrine of her supposed home on Clare Island. She has become internationally famous. Her name is a franchise worth a small fortune. She has been the subject of books, plays, a full-length movie, a one-woman show, TV documentaries, a Broadway musical, a song-cycle, poems, ballads, rock songs and even 'Pirate Queen' T-shirts. There is a festival dedicated to her. In short, since her death, she has become a major money-spinner. Not bad, for someone who ended her days living 'a farmer's life, very poor' in the craggy outcrops of Connacht.

Now here's the strange thing. Details of Grace's actual piracy – the basis of her fame – are scant and sketchy. This is no surprise, because, overall, we have only the shakiest notion of the basics of her life story. We don't know precisely when or where she was born, where she spent her childhood, or when, where and how she died.

We've no idea what she looked like. No contemporary descriptions survive. A search of Google Images shows a bewildering variety of appearances, from a *Cosmopolitan*-style beauty with sculpted eyebrows and coiffed, flame-red hair, to a dark-haired sea-rover in a pirate hat. Some show her in dresses with plunging necklines; others have her in punkish tattoos and nose-rings. Some writers rave about her flawless beauty, but one (female) historian in 1877 reports a popular tradition that she was ugly, adding with a shudder: 'Her ugliness must have been remarkable.'

While many imagine her with red hair, one scholar states confidently that she was 'a dark lady, tall and commanding', and another writes that she was 'swarthy'. Yet her son reputedly had golden hair, so they may all be wrong: Grace could have been as blonde as her namesake Grace Kelly.

The real Grace O'Malley – as opposed to the legendary heroine we know today – was more intriguing than her mythical counterpart. Born into wealth and privilege, she climbed to greater status not only through her skills as a pirate, but also through two strategic marriages. Her formidable buccaneering abilities gave her an advantage over the relentless English invaders who set out to destroy her in the late 1580s. They tried to drive her into the sea – but they didn't realise that the sea was her natural element.

Sometime around 1530, an Irish chieftain's wife named Margaret O'Malley took a deep breath and forced a baby into the world. She was probably lying on a straw bed in her husband's stone tower house, gasping from her labour and coughing from the swirling smoke of an open fire. Through the narrow windows, she could almost certainly glimpse the waters of Clew Bay, a wildly beautiful inlet of the Atlantic Ocean. Word spread rapidly across the nearby fields and hills that Black Oak O'Malley had just fathered a girl-child.

No-one could have predicted that this baby would grow up to upset all the rules and shatter all the conventions of her community. Although the actual title of chieftain would forever be denied to her because of her gender, she would become the de facto leader of her clan, commanding the loyalty of hundreds of fighting mariners who were prepared to die at her command.

She was born into a seafaring family. 'A good man never was there, of the O'Malleys, but a mariner,' wrote one poet, and the family motto claimed they were 'powerful by land, powerful by sea.' Emerging from hideaways in Ireland's most hazardous passages and sounds, the fearsome O'Malley galleys would roam the seas from south Kerry to Donegal and Scotland. Yet romantic accounts of a buccaneering life under the Jolly Roger are far from the truth. Although they would attack passing ships and pillage neighbouring towns, the O'Malleys' main income came from levying fees for protection and putting the squeeze on English fishing boats. They also acted as mercenaries.

It was a hazardous life. An old adage claimed that while a rival family was famous for strength, and another for healing, the O'Malleys were famous in those days for 'dying like pigs'. One O'Malley chieftain drowned with his fleet off the Arans in the 1100s; another lost six of his seven ships in 'a whirling storm' in the 1400s; and in 1513, an Eoghan O'Malley, who had sacked Killybegs, was pursued by his victims and killed while sheltering from a storm.

In her late teens, Grace married a neighbour whose name, Battling Donal O'Flaherty, says it all in terms of his personality. Donal was heir-apparent to a pirate clan who ruled most of Connemara, and who posed such a threat to the merchants of Galway that they had erected a prayer in stone: 'From the Ferocious O'Flaherties, Good Lord Deliver Us.' The marriage was a political alliance between two warring tribes. Two centuries beforehand, the O'Flahertys had slaughtered several leading O'Malleys during a peace conference. The O'Malleys had retaliated with a punitive raid, plundering all their rivals' riches, but their ship was wrecked on its way home, and both the raiders and their spoils went to the bottom of the sea.

Donal and Grace had three children together, and when he died in the mid-1560s, she returned to Clew Bay, taking with her some galleys and scores of discontented O'Flaherty mariners. On the death of her father, for all practical purposes, she became leader of her clan.

Grace began to harry and pillage shipping all along the western seaboard. As she explained later, her 'maintenance by sea' – meaning piracy – was a case of survive or die, in a brutal world where 'every chieftain for his safeguard and defence ... took up arms by strong hand to make head against his neighbours'.

She was now in her thirties, at the prime of life. She controlled a fleet of galleys and a force of hundreds of men. A string of fortresses around Clew Bay made her base secure. She was finally in control of her own destiny.

An evocative poem from the 1800s, taking a creative guess at her state of mind, may not have been too far from the mark:

She ploughed with unfatiguing toil / the fluent rolling furrow / Delight-
ing on the broad backed deep / To feel the quivering galley / Strain up
the opposing hill / and sweep down the withdrawing valley /… And
from the winds that tossed the crest / Of each wide-shouldering giant /
The smack of freedom, and the zest / Of rapturous life defiant.

A typical O'Malley force was amphibious, comprising sixteen cavalry-men on land and 200 fighting mariners in 'long galleys' which could easily be carried ashore. There were around forty men to each ship, although the larger ones could carry seventy. Oarsmen with extraordinary powers of endurance would haul up to fifteen oar-blades on either side. '[They] depended more upon the physical exertions,' writes one expert, '… than upon their ordinary rig of a single mast with a square sail.' Their shallow draughts, combined with local knowledge, allowed them to escape from pursuit into the trickiest of inlets.

Exactly how many galleys did Grace command? Nobody knows. Typi-cally, the O'Malleys had used about half a dozen. Estimates of Grace's fleet have varied from three ships to twenty at most. (By comparison, the pirate Fineen O'Driscoll in Cork had up to eighty.)

Her pirate ships raided the coast all the way from Valentia in the southwest to the Ulster seaports in the northwest, and across the sea to the Hebrides. '[She] soon surpassed [her father's] plunderings by the extent and magnitude of hers,' says one account. Another adds: 'The coast was plundered of cattle and other property, and many people were murdered.'

In the late 1560s, as she entered her forties, Grace married 'Iron Richard' Burke, a deputy for chieftainship of another neighbouring clan, and around 1567 they had a son, Toby. Richard's superior fortress of Rockfleet Castle at Carrigahowley, at the head of Clew Bay, became Grace's main base and her personal home. More than two centuries later, in 1793, a correspondent for the Dublin academic publication *Anthologia Hibernica* visited Rockfleet to write an article about the castle and its famous owner. He claimed: '[Grace's] larger vessels were moored in Clare Island, where she had a strong castle, and her smaller craft she kept at Carrigahowley'.

He said that Grace's bedchamber had a hole cut through the outer wall: 'A cable was run from a vessel, and fastened to her bed'. (Another version claims it was 'a silken thread' and that it was tied around her toe. Other versions claim this was in Clare Island or Achill.)

More credible is the story that she became one of Ireland's first lighthouse-women. There is a relic of a miniature wooden ship in a museum in Mayo: Grace was said to have filled it with tallow, placed it in the castle's upper room, and lit rush-lights to guide friendly ships safely home.

The tomb of a Burke family chieftain. Granuaile married 'Iron Richard' Burke in the late 1560s – but did she really divorce him permanently after just one year by seizing his castle and shouting: 'I dismiss thee' from the ramparts?

Granuaile's new base proved a magnet for footloose freebooters. As the *Anthologia* writer reports, 'Her fame attracted many desperate and hardy mariners from distant parts.'

In 1576, Grace makes her first grand entrance to the historical record. An English viceroy named Henry Sidney wrote: 'There came to me a most famous feminine sea captain called Grany O'Malley, and offered her service to me ... with three galleys and 200 fighting men ... this was a notorious woman in all the coasts of Ireland.' He praised her seafaring abilities: 'She was, as well by sea as by land, more than master's mate with [her husband].'

Another English administrator, Munster President William Drury, encountered her two years later. He referred to 'Grane-ny-Maille ... governing a country of the O'Flahertys [*sic*], famous for her stoutness of courage and person, and for sundry exploits done by her at sea'.

By this stage, according to *Anthologia Hibernica,* 'her piracies became so notorious, and her power so dangerous ... that £500 was offered for apprehending her'.

She was captured while on a sea-raiding expedition to Kerry, and incarcerated in Dublin Castle. Drury spluttered that she was 'a woman that hath impudently passed the parts of womanhood,' adding only as an afterthought that she was 'a great spoiler and chief commander and director of thieves and murderers at sea'. I wonder what Queen Elizabeth, female sponsor of privateers, thought of the first sentiment?

On her release, Grace resumed her sea raiding. On 8 March 1579, the Galway merchants despatched a force under Captain William Martin to seize her fortress at Rockfleet. It was the greatest military threat Grace had ever faced, and she rose to the challenge. 'So spirited was the defence made by this marvellous woman,' wrote one historian, 'that the beleaguers were compelled on the 20th to retreat.'

Richard Burke was knighted in 1581, and so, with a couple of deft diplomatic moves, the outlaw Granuaile had become Lady Burke. The long-suffering citizens of Galway were left to seethe silently as their tormentor swanned airily around their town. The President of Connacht, Nicholas Malby, observed that Grace mingled among the gentlewomen, and 'thinketh herself to be no small Lady'.

The tyrannical English general Richard Bingham: when he threw Granuaile's son Toby into prison, she dashed to London to plead her case to the court of Queen Elizabeth.

However, English petty officials saw another side of the sociable Lady Burke when they tried to collect rent. One collector described Grace as particularly aggressive: '[She] would have fought with me before she was half a mile near me.' Eventually, she paid up.

When Iron Richard died, she returned to Rockfleet with her forces and 'a thousand head of cows and mares'. She embarked upon a new phase of piracy in alliance with her son-in-law, Richard 'Satan's Slashhook' Burke (literally, 'Devil of the Reaping Hook'). They imported Scots mercenaries and asserted their power.

The new President of Connacht, Richard Bingham, reacted ruthlessly, and the next few years were bitter and bloody. When Grace's son Owen O'Flaherty – who was never in rebellion – was murdered by English troops, she accepted an English assurance of safe conduct in order to protest this injustice. Instead, she was arrested and thrown on to a scaffold with a dangling rope. Grace later complained about how Bingham had 'caused a new pair of gallows to be made for [my] last funeral'. She was reprieved at the last minute.

She escaped with her galleys to Ulster – 'fear made me fly by sea,' she explained – where she eventually obtained a royal pardon. She told the English that she had lived peaceably since 1586. 'Utterly did [I] give over [my] former trade of maintenance by sea and land.' Since then, she said, she lived in rural Connacht as 'a farmer's wife, very poor'.

Well, not quite. Her galleys raided English settlements on the Aran Islands after an English carpetbagger with the wonderfully moustache-twirling name of Sir Thomas Lestrange tried to establish a colonist settlement. In a second raid in 1590, she took two or three cargo-boats 'full of knaves' to Aran Mór, razed the properties, and stole twenty marks' worth of goods.

Grace fell out with another of her sons, Murrough O'Flaherty, when he allied himself with Bingham in 1591. She 'manned her navy of galleys ... burned [Murrough's] town, spoiled his people of their cattle and goods, and slew three or four of his men'.

By the time Grace entered her sixties, Bingham had taken over much of her territory. She wrote directly to Queen Elizabeth asking for a pardon and a pension, in return for a pledge to 'invade with fire and sword all your Highness's enemies'. Bingham turned the screw: he arrested her son Toby and threw him into prison. 'Gambling Grace' bet everything on a trip to London to plead her case.

What happened in London is the stuff of legend (see 'Myths'), but the real story of political brinkmanship is just as exciting. While she tensely awaited the Queen's verdict, news of Bingham's savagery was reaching the capital. He knew that Grace's disclosures could destroy him. She needed to be silenced. He wrote to London, lying that Grace had been behind every uprising in the area for four decades – 'the nurse of all rebellions' – and demanding her execution.

Unconvinced, the Queen gave her verdict on 6 September. Referring to Grace as 'this aged woman', she told Bingham she should be left in peace with her pension. Elizabeth was confident that Grace would 'fight in our quarrel with all the world'.

Back in Ireland, Bingham simply ignored Elizabeth's order, and Grace reverted to piracy. One report says she built three new warships and assembled 300 marines. As late as 1601, when she was around seventy, one of her great galleys was sighted off Donegal. It carried thirty oarsmen and a hundred crack musketeers. The galley sneaked in among the rocks, but the English opened fire and the pirates were captured. Grace herself was not on board.

In the early 1600s, Grace passed away – we don't know exactly when, or how, or where. The date of 1603 is often suggested. If that is correct, she probably missed news that would have gladdened her old heart – that her beloved son Toby was knighted by Elizabeth's successor, King James. He was later created 'Viscount Mayo' by Charles I, and became exactly what Grace herself always sought to be – a powerful player in the new colonial order.

Tradition claims that Grace left all her pirate gold to the Cistercians, and now lies buried in the old abbey on her fabled birthplace of Clare Island – supposedly the abbey where she was also baptised and married. Every year, pilgrims come to worship at this shrine to the 'Pirate Queen'.

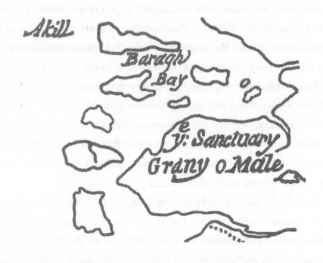

'Ye Sanctuary of Grany O Male': this simplified detail from a map of Ireland of the early 1600s shows the territory ruled by the pirate Granuaile in her heyday.

But are they coming to the right place? In the nine-volume *New Survey of Clare Island* (1992–2009), archaeologist Conleth Manning wrote that, despite her name today on the local castle, and despite the strong tradition that she is buried at the abbey, 'there is no historical record connecting her with the island'.

Combing through my research material, I find nothing to contradict this conclusion. All the popular accounts of Grace's baptism, education, marriage and burial on Clare Island are, at the very least, open to question. Hubert Knox's detailed *History of Mayo* (1908) says that the mainland castle of Rockfleet is 'the only castle known to have been [her] dwelling-place'. As historian Paul Gosling writes in Volume Five of the *New Survey*: 'The popular view of Clare Island as a mediaeval pirate's stronghold is far removed from the reality.'

However, one aspect of Granuaile intrigues me more than any other. How did Historical Grace – the beleaguered clan leader who generally collaborated with the English colonists – become transformed into Legendary Grace, the symbol of national freedom?

As I discover, the elevation to patriotic icon happened almost overnight, not in the mid-1500s, but around two centuries later – in 1753. That was the year that Ireland was rocked by a major constitutional drama that threatened London's domination over its first colony – and the spirit of Granuaile was first invoked.

It almost became Ireland's version of the Boston Tea Party – a simple row over tax revenue that blew up into a crisis and challenged England's King. Over this howling gale of political fury, the name of Granuaile was shouted as a rousing war-cry.

The 'Money Bill Crisis' of 1753 was a serious threat to English rule. Let's summarise the story quickly: the Dublin Parliament, seeking more power for itself, passes an important tax vote without reference to the King. The English Viceroy, the Duke of Dorset, reprimands them. He says the money itself isn't a problem, but they *must* recognise the King's authority. There is a tense standoff. The dispute becomes a challenge of self-determination. There is a huge split between the 'court' faction (in favour of London direct rule) and the 'patriot' faction (wanting more local powers). Patriotic pamphlets are circulated. The interior of a Dublin theatre is demolished by an angry crowd.

In this explosive atmosphere, an anonymous singer in an unknown location – perhaps a tavern, perhaps a coffee house – launches into a newly-composed political ballad that becomes the patriots' anthem. It is called *Granu-Weal*, and it transforms the pirate heroine, for the first time, into the embodiment of Ireland.

> *A courtier called Dorset, from Parkgate did sail*
> *In His Majesty's yacht, for to court Granu-Weal;*
> *With great entertainment he thought to prevail,*
> *And rifle the charms of Granu-Weal.*

Note the heavy-handed pun on 'court'. The Duke of Dorset wants Granu-aile to submit to London. Granuaile stresses her loyalty, but warns: 'No foe shall invade me in my liberty.'

It was at that moment that Grace the Icon was born. From then on, the name of Granuaile has been used as propaganda in almost every Irish disturbance. Like the French icon Marianne, this imaginary Grace is always there with her flag, leading the insurgents at every barricade – no matter how different or disparate the actual cause. The Jacobites sing a ballad in which she plots to put Bonnie Prince Charlie on the throne. She later embraces the 1798 rebellion, and Padraig Pearse includes her in a poem presaging the 1916 Rising. Today, she is also portrayed as a proto-feminist.

Like most pirates who roamed the ocean, Grace left hardly a ripple on the surface of history. None of the Irish annalists mentions her. In 1684, an historian named Roderic O'Flaherty published a 400-page family history, yet gives her only a passing mention as the wife of the 'powerful and opulent' Donal. He lists none of her achievements, and says nothing about a meeting with the Queen, but simply writes that she was 'celebrated in after-times by the name of *Grauna Weale*'.

Today, the figure of Grace O'Malley attracts an almost religious devotion that is difficult to explain except as a resurgence of some ancient Irish goddess culture. Indeed, some poems in her honour read almost like hymns to a deity. This religiosity, with all its pilgrimages and shrines and festivals, makes it difficult for any researcher to find the real Granu-aile. Any 'tradition' or 'oral history' is impossibly muddied by the popular ballads of the 1700s and the romantic tales and novels of the 1800s, yet today, these stories are often given the authenticity of holy writ.

Was she, as commonly depicted, a lifelong rebel, a brave heart battling for national freedom? Not really. The true Grace, who promised to fight England's enemies with fire and sword, and who pledged to 'pray continually for Your Majesty's long life and prosperous reign' does not sit easily with the image of Grace the Freedom Fighter. Professor Mary O'Dowd states in the *Oxford Dictionary of National Biography*: 'With the exception of the Bingham era of the late 1580s, the strategy of O'Malley … appears to have been one of negotiated co-operation with the English administration in Ireland.' Her tactic paid off, because, as the writer points out, her son emerged as Viscount Mayo and the greatest landowner in the county.

But this is a book about piracy. What was Grace's record in this area? In my view, it was very significant. She was a remarkable sea-warrior, and the scale and range of her operations, together with the ferocious defiance she showed towards Bingham and the armed forces of Galway City, placed her in the top echelon of pirates operating in Ireland. Her seaborne campaign could also be regarded as political, in the sense that she harassed the newly arrived English colonists in the Aran Islands.

But compared to William Marsh, who terrorised the entire Irish Sea? Compared to the Baltimore O'Driscolls, whose eighty-ship navy brought mighty Waterford to its knees? Compared to the Three Privateers, who captured a total of 114 vessels? Compared to the West Cork 'Confederacy of the Sea', which blockaded ports for weeks and made the English officials afraid to venture out of harbour? I'm afraid there is no contest. A monarch among pirates she was not.

As long ago as 1860, an academic complained that so many 'silly stories' were circulating about Grace O'Malley that people regarded her as a character of fiction. The situation has not improved since.

Any attempt to question these myths is sometimes interpreted as an attempt to denigrate the achievements of a remarkable woman. But really, all it does is challenge the eighteenth- and nineteenth-century *construct* of Granuaile, which is a completely different thing. I believe that the real, historic Grace O'Malley would have been truly horrified to think that she would be remembered as a cynical schemer who married purely in order to grab a property, or, even worse, as a psychopathic child-abductor. Refuting these myths does not damage her reputation – it restores it.

Here are seven of the most popular Granuaile myths, with my own fallible opinions about their reliability:

Myth One: The Haircut

THE STORY: As a child, Grace asks her father (or sometimes her mother) to let her come along on a piracy trip. The amused parent pointedly tousles her long hair and tells her that this is not her place as a girl. She disappears and returns with her hair closely cropped to fit in with the menfolk. This earns her the nickname Granuaile, from 'Gráinne Mhaol' or 'bald Grace'.

THE REALITY: This was an invented story, reverse-engineered to explain the unflattering nickname of 'bald Grace'. *Granuaile* actually derives from 'Gráinne Uaile', with 'Uaile' meaning the O'Malley territory. Besides, it's an inconvenient fact that most *male* mariners had long hair in those days. To sixteenth-century sailors, a cropped head actually signified criminality and disgrace.

MY VERDICT: Doesn't make the cut.

RELIABILITY INDEX: 0/10

Myth Two: Grace Was a Royal Queen

THE STORY: Grace was, literally, a royal queen or princess.

THE REALITY: This is rarely claimed nowadays, but up until the 1900s, such fanciful titles as 'Queen of the West' and 'Queen of the Western Ocean' were bandied around. One writer claimed in 1872 that she was Princess of the 'independent Principality' of Clare Island.

The independent Principality of Clare Island is just five miles long. I can't help recalling the words of modern American humorist PJ O'Rourke when told that he was descended from Irish kings: 'It seems we were all kings in the olden days. But who wasn't? ... "I'm the King, from this rock down to the creek, and from that cow to the tree. And this is my wife, the Queen, and our dog, Prince."'

That's an exaggeration, but not by much. In the 1500s, Ireland had around ninety rulers, including five dozen kings.

More recently, the rigorously academic *New Survey of Clare Island* (1992–2009) threw cold water over the royal dream. In this survey, the archaeologist Conleth Manning states flatly: 'She was never a queen or leader of the O'Malley family.'

MY VERDICT: Grace was probably of royal blood, descended either from the King of Connacht, Brian Orbsen, or his brother. But she was never a royal Queen or Princess.

RELIABILITY INDEX: 2/10

Myth Three: 'I Dismiss Thee!'

THE STORY: Grace married her second husband, Richard Burke, on a sort of temporary, test-drive basis, using a Gaelic law that allowed her to divorce him after one year by saying: 'I dismiss thee.' Exactly twelve months after moving into his castle, she locked the gates against him, shouted the declaration from the ramparts, and kept his fortress.

THE REALITY: Grace and Richard did not divorce then, or ever. It is a matter of record that they remained a married couple until his death in the early 1580s. Throughout the 1570s and 1580s, official documents describe her as Richard's 'wife'. They attended functions as a couple. When he was knighted, she became his 'Lady'. Writing in 1593, Grace describes herself as Richard's widow. The early *Anthologia* account of 1793 reports the marriage, but says nothing about a divorce.

Besides, as historian Theresa D Murray has pointed out in *History Ireland*, no evidence has been found in the Gaelic legal system for any type of one-year provisional marriage. Indeed, it's difficult to imagine how such a law could ever have been workable.

This story is sometimes used to establish Grace's credentials as an early feminist. It's true that she was an indefatigable battler for her rights as a woman in a male-dominated world, but this story does not illustrate it. To my mind, it's less Gloria Steinem and more in the style of Zsa Zsa Gabor, who famously declared: 'I'm a marvellous housekeeper. Every time I leave a man, I keep his house.'

MY VERDICT: Divorce story, I dismiss thee. However, the couple might have had a temporary tiff along those lines.

RELIABILITY INDEX: 1/10

Myth Four: She Met Queen Elizabeth as an Equal

THE STORY: In London, Grace meets Elizabeth I face to face, as an equal monarch. Despite Grace's initial defiance, the two 'sister queens' get on well together, conversing in Latin and negotiating an Anglo-Irish peace agreement.

THE REALITY: This is the Grace story that has excited the imagination like no other. 'A long mantle covered [Grace's] head and body,' writes *Anthologia Hibernica* (1793) in the earliest version I can find. 'Her hair was gathered on her crown, and fastened with a bodkin; her breast was bare ... the court stared with surprise at so strange a figure.'

The image that turned a pirate into a national icon: an artist in the 1700s imagines the legendary encounter between 'sister queens' Granuaile and Elizabeth I of England. Yet it is unlikely that they ever met face to face, and they certainly did not meet as equal queens.

One historian has claimed Grace visited Elizabeth as a 'sister sovereign'. Another said she arrived in pomp like a European head of state: '[O'Malley] patronised the Great Queen … graciously.'

In the *Anthologia* version, a lady lends Grace a fine lace handkerchief. She blows her nose and throws it into the fire. She tells the protesting lady that in Ireland, 'they were much cleaner than to pocket what came from their nostrils'. In a later version, it's the famous Sir Walter Raleigh who reprimands her, and Grace reacts with an obscenity. When offered a lapdog by Elizabeth, she snaps: 'Keep it to yourself, Queen of the English, it is only fit for such idlers as you.' However, the two women eventually bond, chatting lengthily in Latin by the fireside.

It's not until the early 1900s that we see the first flickers of doubt. One authority concedes that 'there is no authentic account of this famous interview'.

And there lies the problem. As far as I can establish, there is no documentary proof that Grace and Elizabeth met in person. I have in front of me four separate modern-era accounts of their supposed meeting. Each writer names a different royal palace. Hampton Court, says one. Greenwich, says another. Lambeth, says a third. Most likely Richmond or Nonsuch, says the fourth.

Based on the available evidence, it's clear that Grace did indeed go to the royal court in London in 1593 to put her case. We have no idea how she got there. She may indeed have sailed her galleys up the Thames, drawing gasps of astonishment from Londoners, but alternatively she may have taken the faster, safer route, mostly overland, via Chester on England's east coast. Two historians in the Victorian and Edwardian eras state, as fact, that she took that route.

She had more sense than to present herself as a rival queen – her deferential letters make that clear. For her part, Elizabeth had endless problems on her mind, from the threat of Spanish invasion to plague and public disorder in London. Besides, Grace was just one of many, many beseeching petitioners. In all likelihood, the case would have been handled by senior ministers, with Elizabeth taking the final decision after advice, dictating the verdict to a courtier.

Discussing this subject in his essay 'Elizabeth I and the Government of Ireland', Professor Ciaran Brady, a specialist in early modern history, writes: 'There is in fact, no sound evidence that such a private interview ever took place.' He adds that the popular story, with all its stereotypes, derives from 1700s ballads and antiquarian accounts based on 'highly questionable folk memories', supplemented by later poetic imaginings.

He says that, on the face of it, such a meeting seems 'highly improbable'. Grace was never perceived as enjoying 'anything like the status of the queen of England'. Besides, Elizabeth rarely allowed such personal interviews, especially in her later years, because of security concerns.

In my view, this solves the mystery of why Elizabeth pityingly described her contemporary Grace as 'this aged woman'. Obviously, Elizabeth was relying on the written petition in which the canny Grace had fudged her age and depicted herself as a frail widow at death's door. Had they actually met, one glance at this hale and hearty sea warrior would have rapidly changed her mind.

MY VERDICT: This is probably a propaganda story dating from the 1700s, a time when the Irish Parliament wanted more power, and Grace, symbolising Ireland, was portrayed as England's equal. It is extremely unlikely that Grace ever met Elizabeth, and we can be certain that they did not meet as equal queens.

RELIABILITY RATING: 2/10

Myth Five: Her Lover Hubert de Lacy

THE STORY: Grace falls in love with handsome knight Hubert de Lacy after he is shipwrecked on a Clare Island beach. She marries him (or takes him as her lover). But Hubert is murdered by the dastardly McMahon clan, and Grace exacts a dreadful revenge.

THE REALITY: If you were a novelist, you'd introduce a character with a Mills & Boon name like Hubert de Lacy to lend some sparkle to Grace's rather dull love life. So it would come as no surprise if Hubert actually *were* an invention, a character of literary fiction, dreamed up by one W.H. Maxwell in his wildly popular Gothic novel *The Dark Lady of Doona* (1833).

Maxwell, with a nod towards classic myths like *Dido and Aeneas* and *Calypso*, tells how Hubert is found unconscious on the strand and adopted by his Dark Lady, Grace O'Malley. 'His bearing bespoke a noble lineage,' explains the author. 'His dark eye and small moustache gave him a bold and martial character.' They fall in love. They marry. When the rival McMahons murder Hubert, Grace inflicts bloody retribution like a heroine in a Tarantino revenge epic.

Does Hubert make any recorded appearance before 1833? If he does, I can't find it. Could Maxwell have based de Lacy upon an existing legend? Unlikely, since the author seemed to have had no interest in Grace's real history and did zero research. His previous work on west-of-Ireland legends barely mentions her. In *Dark Lady*, he uses characters from other eras and claims de Lacy was her first husband. Even at the time, an indignant magazine reviewer pointed out that de Lacy had no basis in reality since Grace already had two real-life husbands. In 1860, a university academic eviscerated *Dark Lady*: 'It is neither good furbished-up fact nor pleasing fable, but a gallimaufry of third-rate romance phrases, caricaturing historic personages who were so little contemporary that some of them died before the rest were born.'

Today, de Lacy is variously described as Scottish, English, Irish and even Norwegian.

MY VERDICT: The dark-eyed, small-moustached de Lacy was never a real person, but a literary invention. However, I could be proven wrong.

RELIABILITY RATING: 1/10

Myth Six: The Howth Kidnap

THE STORY: Grace is turned away from Howth Castle, and retaliates by kidnapping the Lord's little son and heir.

THE REALITY: I used to believe this story, because it featured in the weighty *Dictionary of National Biography* (1897). Its source was the 1838 *History of Dublin* by John D'Alton. Here is D'Alton's version:

'About the year 1575 ... she landed at Howth, and proceeded to the castle, but it being dinner time, the gates were closed. Indignant at what she considered a dereliction of Irish hospitality, she seized the young heir of St Lawrence [i.e., the Lord of Howth], then playing on the shore, carried him on shipboard, and sailed with him, a prisoner, to her own castle, in Mayo. Nor was he restored until his father entered into an express stipulation that his gates should never again be shut at dinner hour.' That tradition supposedly survived throughout the centuries.

The earliest version of the tale that I can find is in the 1793 *Anthologia Hibernica*. Locked out, Grace 'discovered that Lord Howth had a child nursing not far off ... it was a boy, and heir to the title. Him she carried on board ship.' Both these versions, together with a third account in 1830, are clear that the victims were Lord Howth and his eldest son and heir, who was either a nursing baby or a small child.

I checked *The Peerage of Ireland*, and found that in (and about) 1575, the Lord of Howth was Christopher St Lawrence, known as 'the Blind Earl', whose son and heir Nicholas was then a seasoned soldier in his twenties. So if *The Peerage* is correct, the incident could not have happened as described by D'Alton. The *Anthologia* version can be refuted too, because there was no time during Grace's adult life when a sitting Lord of Howth had a male heir in infancy.

The lord who preceded the Blind Earl between 1549 and 1558 had no children at all. And when Christopher's successor, Nicholas, took over in 1589, *his* eldest son was aged around twenty-one.

Grace myths tend to shape-shift into new forms when they're disproven. Refuting them is like playing whack-a-mole. So a different version emerged in the late 1800s, maintaining that Grace kidnapped the Blind Earl's *grandson*, also called Christopher. But that's not the original story, and in my view it was simply a late nineteenth-century invention intended to make the facts fit a good yarn.

That's not the only thing that changed. The *Anthologia* version, and several 1800s versions, say Grace demanded 'a large ransom' for the child. This inconvenient ugliness was quietly dropped in the early 1900s.

None of this matters, because here's the clincher that refutes the myth once and for all: *The same story was told about a Lord of Howth who lived in the late 1400s – long before Grace was born.*

In this earlier-placed story, the kidnapper was the great-great-great grandfather of Grace's husband: Richard 'Bent Shield' Burke, chieftain from 1469 to 1479. It was recorded in the mid-1600s by the annalist Duald MacFirbis, writing within living memory of Grace, and thus risking ridicule if he were wrong. He says that this 1400s Richard 'carried off the Lord of Howth … and naught else was required for his ransom but to keep the door of his court open at dinner-time'.

Historians have been aware of this for at least a century. In fact, one early writer tried to get around the problem by arguing – more heroically than convincingly – that Grace may have deliberately staged a re-enactment of the 1400s kidnap, presumably as a kind of homage or performance art.

I believe that both stories are myths, echoing a universal folk tale (*Baucis and Philemon* for example) in which a wandering monarch or god reacts badly when refused hospitality.

The main evidence for the Grace kidnap is that it appears in the Howth Castle records. But up until the eighteenth century, the castle's record-keepers were enthusiastic tellers of tall tales. Debunking the kidnap myth, the eminent historian Lord Walter Fitzgerald – an expert on the family dynasty – concluded in 1907 that the story was among several 'unreliable' family legends. There was 'no reason to believe that this warrior-queen ever set foot in Howth'. He believed the legend arose from an enigmatic family painting showing a female figure carrying a child on horseback. Other historians have cited this picture as confirmation of the legend, but to the more analytic Fitzgerald, it was the other way around: 'This story was made to fit [the] oil painting in Howth Castle – a glance at which makes the whole thing absurd.'

It remains a popular story, yet few people seem to pause and think just how disturbingly creepy it is. In one 1830 version, Grace finds the toddler wandering alone. She lures him away by asking if he likes ships and if he'd like to see inside her galley. Substitute the words 'puppies' and 'camper van' and suddenly it doesn't seem like such a jolly tale.

As a footnote, I decided to drop in to Howth Castle to check out whether the doors-open tradition still holds true. Its official website stated: 'All [visitors] must make appointments well in advance.' At first I thought this was ironic – but on reflection, I have to admit it's just plain good sense. MY VERDICT: The 1400s tale was obviously transferred to the more famous Grace, in much the same way as all good quotes are attributed to Oscar Wilde. RELIABILITY RATING: 0/10

Myth Seven: The Algerine Pirates
THE STORY (based on the original 1838 version): Grace gives birth to her son Toby at sea, sometime in the late 1560s. That same day, as she's nursing him in her cabin, Barbary corsairs from Algiers attack her ship. The Irish captain panics. Grace storms on deck half-dressed, opens fire, and repulses the invaders with a pithy quip worthy of Arnold Schwarzenegger. Then she calmly resumes feeding her baby.
THE REALITY: The Algerine corsairs could not have been there at that time. The nineteenth-century source for this story places it off County Mayo, but the African corsairs did not arrive in the wild North Atlantic until the early 1600s, when Dutch renegades like Simon Danser gave them the necessary ships and technology. According to Philip Gosse's classic *History of Piracy*, they first ventured out of the Straits of Gibraltar in 1585 – nearly two decades after Toby's birth – and even then, only to Morocco and the Canaries.

Another problem is that this tale has suspicious similarities with the true story of Anne Bonny (see Pirate Pilgrimage the Sixth). Both heroines are maternal figures – Anne is pregnant and Grace is a nursing mother – who curse their cowardly male shipmates when left alone to battle off attackers.

Thirdly, the Algerine attack story does not feature at all in *Anthologia Hibernica*, whose correspondent collected stories about Grace in Mayo in 1793. He heard a completely different tale: that Toby was born while Grace was on her famous voyage to meet Queen Elizabeth in London. At the royal palace, the new-born baby was 'brought in the Queen's presence and knighted'. That story was generally accepted until it was refuted in the early 1900s.

The origins of the Algerine story are interesting. In 1838, the distinguished scholar John O'Donovan was collecting traditional stories in County Mayo. He encountered a colourful figure named 'Old Hennelly' and the two got on famously. O'Donovan would fondly refer to Hennelly as a 'Professor of Literature' or a 'Professor of Mathematics and Ancient Traditional Lore'. In fact, Hennelly was a hedge-schoolmaster and (in the words of one modern academic) 'a Mayo character', whom O'Donovan delighted in encouraging. When Old Hennelly offered some 'traditional accounts' about the O'Malley family, O'Donovan tidied up his confused prose and published them as oral history.

Most of Old Hennelly's stories are, essentially, jokes, with a build-up and a punchline, usually in the form of a pithy quote. Some are risqué and misogynistic. You get the definite sense that they were meant to be told with a chuckle, for the benefit of a male audience of porter drinkers.

One tale depicts the adolescent Toby trying to shelter from gunfire by crouching behind his mother's rear. Grace asks him in salty language whether he is trying to hide in the place from which he emerged as a baby. In another story, Grace gains a castle from a marital dispute. The castle owner had complained that the marital bed was too long. His wife replies: 'I wish there was miles in it.' The husband, enraged, takes this as a reference to his brother, named Miles. He tries to kill Miles, but Miles kills *him* instead, and Grace takes his castle. A third story involves Grace's son Toby as an adult. When Toby's wife suggests that her brother could cut up meat quicker than he could, Toby disappears for a while and returns to slam the brother's severed head on the kitchen table. He demands: '*Now who is the better man?*' But Toby's triumph doesn't last for long, because the wife's other brother, a dwarf who likes to wear women's petticoats, gets his revenge by knifing Toby in the groin while pretending to run playfully between his legs. Clearly, all this hokum is far more useful to students of Freud than to students of history.

Amid these tall tales, Hennelly's original version of the Algerine attack emerges as an almost farcical anecdote.

Grace is nursing newborn Toby when the 'Turkish corsairs' strike. She curses her crew: 'May you be seven times worse this day twelve months, who cannot do without me for one day!' Wrapping a quilt loosely around herself, she emerges on deck. But instead of going on the attack, she performs a sort of lunatic polka, 'dancing and capering about'. The Algerine attackers fall around the place laughing, surprised at 'her monstrous size and odd figure' in the flapping quilt. As they double over, helpless with mirth, she produces two huge blunderbusses from under her bedsheet and opens fire, exclaiming: 'Take this from unconsecrated hands!'

Never mind that it would have been difficult to pull that stunt with the type of firearms available in the 1560s. What on earth is that punchline all about? It's clearly a reference to the belief that new mothers were spiritually unclean until they could be 'churched', but why should the Muslim Algerines care? Any intended humour has been lost with time.

Incidentally, the scholarly O'Donovan seems to have noticed, even then, that the corsairs could not have been around Ireland in the 1560s.

He queries, in brackets, whether the Algerines should be substituted by Frenchmen. I won't comment. I think our work here is done.

MY VERDICT: Great story (I used it myself in a 2006 book), but I now believe it's based on a shaggy-dog tale that was never meant to be taken seriously. In my opinion, anyone who tells this story in future should be required by law to clarify that it comes from the same source that gave us the cross-dressing, crotch-stabbing dwarf.

RELIABILITY RATING: 0/10

11

PIRATE PILGRIMAGE THE ELEVENTH

Broad Haven

After returning to the mainland, I drive north and west along the Mayo coast towards my next destination – the remote Mullet Peninsula. Just north of Newport, however, I take a detour down a grass-choked laneway to check out another remarkable relic to the pirate Grace O'Malley.

I negotiate a tight bend and, abruptly, there it lies directly ahead of me, emerging with as much suddenness and surprise as an O'Malley pirate attack. Now *this* is much more like a Granuaile castle, as one would imagine it. Rockfleet – the only castle that's definitely known to have been Grace's home – is a perfect tower-fortress from the mediaeval era. It is squat, square in profile, and somehow powerful with latent energy. The mere sight of it is calculated to put the fear of God into any potential attacker.

It sits right on the edge of a lonesome estuary, with water lapping at its lower stones, and a mass of dark bladder-rack seaweed writhing around its base. Today it basks in tranquillity, a silence disturbed only by the complaints of sheep and the cawing of crows that fly in and out of its upper ramparts. But if you stand quietly for a moment, it is easy to imagine the scene on 8 March 1579, when Grace and her pirates repulsed a full-scale attack from Captain Martin and his marines from Galway. Arrows and spears would have rained from those arrowslit windows, boiling water from those ramparts. I can almost hear the blasts of muskets; the screams of the wounded; and finally the shouts of triumph from the O'Malley defenders as the attackers retreat in ignominious defeat.

A sign on the door warns visitors to keep clear of the castle because of 'health and safety' concerns. So, no change there: people would have needed to do much the same in Granuaile's day.

The coastal road past Achill (which will feature in Pirate Pilgrimage the Thirteenth) is a joy to drive, but once you pass Bangor Erris and head out west, the landscape becomes blanket bog, as flat and featureless as Kansas. It adds to the sense of remoteness and isolation as you approach the market town of Belmullet, which guards the skinny isthmus leading to the almost-island that is the Mullet Peninsula.

Years ago, when communications were much worse, I drove to Belmullet to write a feature article. When I asked about the problems of such remoteness, one local representative endeared himself to me with his positive attitude. He argued that Belmullet wasn't remote at all. It was everywhere else that was remote from Belmullet.

Four centuries ago, such inaccessibility was a real advantage to the pirate trade. In the early 1600s, an English source wrote that Mayo people were 'the most barbarous and dangerous people in all Ireland', and that their 'only dependence is upon the depredation and spoils of pirates'. And of all the pirate-friendly harbours in Mayo, the place that attracted most freebooters was right here: in the inner-bay known as Broad Haven Harbour.

I stop for a coffee in Belmullet. It is a friendly, laid-back sort of place, and today it is sparkling cheerfully in the sunshine, but I have to leave it to travel further into the heartland of the peninsula. The winding road to Ballyglass is a starkly beautiful reminder of an Ireland of long ago. The bogland is torn by dark-brown gashes of turf beds, but softened by bog-cotton. Stacks of turf dry out in the fields. Reedy inlets

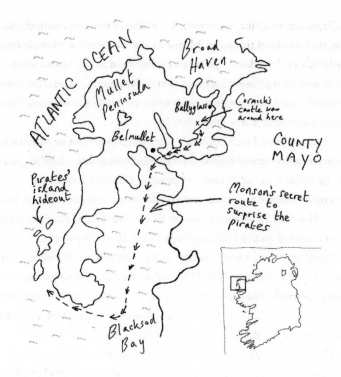

appear on either side, projecting deep into the peninsula. You can see people harvesting the turf, although today they load it into car trailers instead of donkey carts.

The road stops abruptly at the working port of Ballyglass Pier. The sea is a deep bottle-blue, dotted with orange lobster pots. Far off to my left, where Broad Haven Bay opens north into the Atlantic, I can see a lighthouse, the jagged rocks known as the Stags, and a range of near-white cliffs. To my right is Broad Haven Harbour – the inner section of the same bay – with its pleasant green-yellow hills and sandy beaches. Apart from the occasional shout from a fishing boat at the pier, it is almost spookily quiet.

It was around here, somewhere on this coast just south of Ballyglass, that an Irish chieftain named Michael Cormick owned a pirate-friendly castle. He laid on lavish feasts for visiting buccaneers, treated them to music sessions and even, I suspect, offered 'honey traps' of amiable young women in order to persuade them to bring their stolen goods in to Broad Haven rather than to any other port.

So in the year 1614, Michael Cormick was elated when he heard that a notorious pirate named Captain Henry Mainwaring had arrived in Broad Haven, hoping to sell a cargo of plunder. Cormick slaughtered an ox, ordered his harpist to tune up, and told the young women to dress in their finery. However, 'Mainwaring' was not all he seemed to be. He was actually a naval admiral named William Monson, and he was determined to clean up Broad Haven, which he regarded as 'the well-head of all pirates'. There was only one real trap in Broad Haven that day ... and it was about to be sprung upon Michael Cormick.

The Admiral, the Pirate, the Chieftain and his Daughters

Sir William Monson was a pirate-hunter extraordinaire. He was himself a former privateer, who had run away to sea at the age of sixteen and had seen action almost immediately when his ship captured a Spanish vessel after a night-long battle. On his first command, he had become so lost in storm and fog in the Atlantic that his crew narrowly avoided starvation, limping into Dingle Bay with one single biscuit left in their stores.

He had fought the Spanish Armada, had survived two years in a prison in Lisbon, and had earned his knighthood during the English raid on Cadiz. Now aged forty-five, he had been entrusted with the unenviable task of clearing out pirates' nests in Scotland and the west of Ireland.

On his way to Mayo, Monson was caught up in a terrible storm, in which one of his four ships was wrecked and another two were hopelessly lost. Left with only a fraction of his firepower and manpower, the admiral remained doggedly determined to complete his mission, using guile instead of gunpowder. He sailed right into the pirates' lair and announced through messengers that he was Captain Henry Mainwaring (a well-known corsair captain), and that he wanted to dispose of a large cargo of stolen goods.

The man who controlled the action at Broad Haven was Michael Cormick, a clan leader who owned a castle near Ballyglass. (Monson refers to him as 'Cormat'.) Although he was probably not a seafaring corsair himself, Cormick certainly filled a role then known as 'land pirate' – he facilitated the buccaneers and shifted their goods. When a messenger told him that the famous Henry Mainwaring had chosen Broad Haven as his offloading point, Cormick must have felt that Christmas had come early. He sent the messenger back with an eager invitation and a summary of his own credentials.

—I have facilitated many pirates in the past, often putting myself in great danger from the authorities, he said. I would be happy to do the same for the famous Captain Mainwaring.

One of Monson's officers, a Captain Chester, went ashore to get supplies of beef, and was invited to visit Cormick's home. He found himself the object of extreme attention, even flirtation, by three adult women who were introduced as Cormick's daughters, and who were obviously well used to keeping visiting pirates happy. 'He was welcomed and friendly entertained by the daughters, whose desire was to hear of their [pirate] sweethearts and to receive their tokens,' Monson wrote. He referred to the daughters as 'hackneys', a word usually used to describe everyday workhorses. We can only guess at his meaning, but we can be sure it wasn't complimentary.

The daughters were especially keen to see the main man, Captain Mainwaring, whom the villagers 'confidently believed would enrich them all'. After making sure that no-one in the village had actually met Mainwaring face-to-face, Monson decided to assume his persona and oblige.

'The time approached that Sir William had promised to visit them,' Monson recalled, referring to himself in the third person, 'and for his greater honour they had drawn down 400–500 people to attend on the shore side … three of their principal men ran up to their armpits in water, striving who should have the credit to carry him ashore.'

A later engraving captures the colour of the scene. Monson's rowboat, carved with decorative fishes, punts towards the shore through the shallows, with crowds thronging excitedly on the strand. One man, chest deep in seawater, is wading towards the boat while another is clinging on to the side, inviting the admiral to climb on to his shoulders. Monson, a long-nosed, bearded figure dressed in doublet and plumed cap, looks down with the air of a sad but stern judge.

The three greeters turned out to be a London trader, a local schoolmaster and a Galway merchant, who formed a sort of troika of land pirates working under Cormick. 'These three gallants, like gentlemen-ushers, conducted Sir William to Michael Cormick's house; and the meaner sort followed with acclamations of joy … no man was ever so welcome.'

The reception was so enthusiastic that few people noticed a curious boatload of timber that followed the honoured guest onshore and remained under guard during the festivities.

Monson found Cormick's house in full party mode. 'The three hackney daughters rose to entertain him, and conducted him to the hall newly strewed with rushes … in the corner was a harper, who played merrily.'

Typically, a feast like this would have taken place in the castle's Great Hall, an upstairs banqueting room with a giant fire in the middle and one to the side. 'They put rushes a foot deep on their floors, and on their windows,' reported one French visitor to Ireland. 'The great hall was commonly strewed with marrowbones, and full of hawk perches, hounds and other dogs.'

Suspended above the side-fire on stakes, like a hammock, was an ox-skin filled with beef broth. Once boiled, the chunks of beef were roasted on spits. Another guest at a Celtic feast said he was offered 'no less than a whole beef, boiled and roasted, and what mutton I know not, so profusely did they lay it on the table.'

Drinks were generously served. To refuse to drink, or to leave early from the feast, was considered a deadly insult. 'Go up, and you come not down until the morrow,' wrote another guest.

The chieftain usually sat at the centre, his sword lying on the table before him. A contemporary woodcut shows a harpist kneeling in the corner, his instrument to his shoulder, his eyes closed in concentration as his fingers fly over the strings. A dancer steps and sways, cloak swirling in time to the music.

The feast at Cormick's house was no exception. 'The women offered to dance; one chose Sir William, which he excused, but gave free liberty to the rest of his company.' Cormick's three daughters wanted news of pirate boyfriends at sea, but above all they expected gifts.

The London trader buttonholed 'Mainwaring', and offered to supply ten seamen for his crew. When the honoured guest accepted, he wrote a note to them: '[We] are all made men, for valiant Captain Mainwaring and his gallant crew are arrived in this place. Make haste, for he flourisheth in wealth.'

The sting had gone on long enough. Monson rose to his feet, silencing the musicians with a wave of his hand.

—I am no pirate, he thundered. I am a scourge of pirates, sent here by the King to suppress them and their abettors. Since you have condemned yourselves out of your own mouths, we have no need of a trial. We will proceed directly to the execution.

He pointed to the timber that was being transformed, as he spoke, into a full-sized scaffold down by the shore. There had been much merry dancing, he said, but the next set would be a 'mournful dance' at the end of a rope.

He clapped the ringleaders in irons, announcing that they would be hanged at dawn. They remained overnight, 'lamenting, bewailing and repenting', as the solemn clinking of their shackles was gloomily counterpointed by the hollow thud of the carpenters' hammers.

At daybreak, the townsfolk were marshalled to witness the executions and the condemned men were brought forth in irons. But Monson was in generous mood.

—I am prepared to pardon your wrongdoing, he told the community, if you will give your solemn promise never again to have any dealings with pirates.

The traumatised villagers agreed, and the culprits endured nothing worse than a night in irons. Monson's principal aim was to entice some real pirates into the harbour, and the tactic paid off within twenty-four hours. A corsair ship made to enter Broad Haven, but hastily fled when its captain spotted the naval vessel. The newcomers retreated to the Inishkea Islands and waited. Soon afterwards, Michael Cormick received a letter from the pirate captain.

'Dear friend … I was frightened by the King's ship … I pray you send me word what ship it is, for we stand in great fear.' The pirate asked Cormick to light a fire on shore if it was safe to come in.

Monson instructed him to play along, and to write back to assure the pirates that the ship was harmless. The next step was obvious – to light the fire on the mainland facing Inishkea and surprise the pirates as they came ashore – but Monson knew that some 'piratically given' sympathiser would tip them off in advance.

So instead, he concocted an elaborate plan. First, a brief scene-setter. Imagine the setting, schematically, as a capital letter 'H', with the left-hand upright as the near-island of Mullet Peninsula; the crossbar as the isthmus to the mainland; and the right-hand upright as the regular Mayo coastline. The space below the crossbar is an estuary, Blacksod Bay. Above it is the separate estuary of Broad Haven Harbour, where Monson's ship lay at anchor. The pirates were waiting at the Inishkeas, at the outer base of the left upright. To get to the campfire spot, Monson would be expected to sail upwards, past the top of the 'H' and then down its left-hand side. Instead, he left his ship there, idling at anchor.

He told no-one of his real plan, which was to wait until darkness fell and then row two small boats *southwards* to the isthmus. The crew dragged the boats onshore, raised them to their shoulders, and carried them two miles across land before relaunching them in Blacksod Bay and rowing for many miles around the bottom of the 'H' – that is, to the south of the peninsula – to arrive secretly at the rendezvous point. The entire operation was conducted at high speed in great secrecy, and in foul weather. It was a remarkable feat of human endurance that left the locals 'in astonishment'.

'The scourge of pirates': Admiral William Monson poses as a famous buccaneer in order to spring a trap on the unwitting folk of Broad Haven in Mayo. Welcoming him, 'they ran up to their armpits in water, striving who should have the credit to carry him ashore'.

The navy men lit the campfire and waited as the pirate boat loomed out of the darkness. 'The pirates had not the power to resist,' Monson wrote, 'but yielded like so many wolves caught in their own snares.'

The admiral claimed that his visit freed the bay of buccaneers. 'Pirates ever after became strangers to that harbour of Broad Haven,' Monson recorded. This was a slight exaggeration, because the notorious pirate Claes Compaen arrived in 1626, to service two of his ships. Michael Cormick stayed true to his word and detained six of Compaen's men, who were later released on the orders of the English. So Monson's main point holds true – in 1614, he had achieved, with a little cunning and trickery, what generations of English gunships had failed to do in similar pirate havens such as Leamcon and Baltimore.

Monson's report is invaluable, because it provides a rare and fascinating insight into what life was like in pirate enclaves like Broad Haven, Baltimore and Leamcon in the early 1600s: the crowds flocking to the shore to greet an incoming pirate ship; prominent townsfolk competing for the honour of plunging shoulder-deep into the icy seawater to carry the captain ashore without so much as a splash on his clothing; the warm reception in the rush-strewn great hall with toasts in smuggled claret and dances to the music of harpists.

Especially intriguing is the role of the three daughters, who (Monson strongly implies) were provided by Michael Cormick as part of his hospitality package. He refers to 'the relief [pirates] find by a gentleman there dwelling, who spared not his own daughters to bid them welcome'. It is possible that the straitlaced Monson overreacted to the warm and open Irish hospitality shown by the three women, and mistook it for a sexual overture. On the other hand, we know from other sources that Gaelic chieftains sometimes allowed guests to become intimate with their womenfolk as part of the hospitality tradition. One visitor at another feast recalled: 'Towards evening, when the chief began to grow mellow, he called in his favourite girl to sing, which she did very well and was a neat handsome jolly girl … he stipulated with his guests that they were welcome to any liberties with her from the girdle upwards, but he would not permit any underhand doings.' The claim by Cormick that the three women were his 'daughters' sounds about as believable as a Russian pimp offering his 'sister'. Were they professionals, provided for visiting freebooters and passed off as daughters to maintain some shred of decorum? Were they, in essence, a honey trap to attract pirates? We can only speculate.

Monson's tale illustrates the awful dilemma that such remote seaboard communities faced every time they spotted the approach of a strange sail. They were on their own, far from help, and they had to live on their wits, instincts and – above all – on their tradition of unquestioning hospitality. If the visitors turned out to be lawmen, they professed loyalty. If they turned out to be pirates, they would stress their discretion and their willingness to look the other way. In either case, they would kill the bullock, uncork the wine and bewitch the newcomers with their *céad míle fáilte*, their hundred thousand welcomes. This was not deception or hypocrisy – simply something they needed to do in order to survive.

12

PIRATE PILGRIMAGE THE TWELFTH

Killybegs

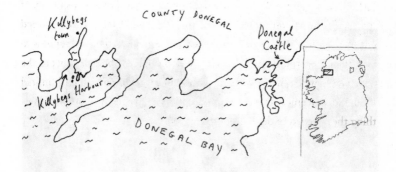

I have left Mayo in my rearview mirror and I'm passing under the shadow of massive, purple-hued Ben Bulben mountain on my way north through Sligo. I find it incredibly frustrating to drive through Yeats Country, past iconic locations like W.B. Yeats's grave and Lisadell House, without even slowing down. But I am on the pirate trail, not a literary tour, and I am determined to reach my next destination, Killybegs, before nightfall.

Eventually I see signs for Donegal Town, where I divert from my route to take a look at one of the key locations featured in this chapter's pirate tale.

Donegal Castle, ancient home of the fiery O'Donnell family, was long coveted by the English. It was one of the 'greatest' and 'fairest' fortresses in Ireland, said one colonist, where 'a boat of ten tons may come within twenty yards of the castle'. After the Flight of the Earls, the last of the great Irish chieftains, in 1607, they seized their chance to take over the fort. The new owner was Sir Basil Brooke, a soldier and adventurer who was soon to face one of his greatest challenges – not from Irish insurgents, but from pirates.

Donegal Castle: it was here that English enforcer Basil Brooke seethed in impotent fury as pirates rampaged through nearby Killybegs, drinking and wenching in an epic buccaneering blow-out. 'Twenty good men could cut their throats,' he urged the authorities as he hatched a plan to murder them in their cups.

I wander around the stately Jacobean castle, looking at the upper windows and imagining the days in 1627 when Brooke wrote increasingly frantic and angry letters to his superiors, complaining that pirates had completely taken over the nearby port of Killybegs and that he was powerless to stop them. Flush with plundered gold, the buccaneers were running amok in the streets, swilling back wine and having a great time with the tavern women. It was like a real-life version of those scenes in the original Disney 'Pirates of the Caribbean' theme ride, in which scary-looking buccaneers fight, drink with buxom wenches and rampage around the town.

We'll tell the story in a moment, but first ... onwards and westwards to Killybegs. As I approach town, stretching before me is a wide blue inlet; a busy harbour packed with fishing trawlers; and, in the distance, guarding the harbour entrance, the lighthouse of Rotten Island. The newly constructed pier is loud with industry, because Killybegs, with a population of only around 1,300, is one of Ireland's major fishing ports.

This place is steeped in history. King Philip of Spain sent his envoys here to plot his ill-fated 1601 invasion. Pirates, too, were attracted to this deep, safe and yet remote western harbour. But whenever they attacked, the tough locals often gave back as good as they got – as I learned when I visited the town's fascinating maritime museum.

'In 1513, Galway pirates attacked Killybegs when the defenders were absent,' says one poster, 'But they were overrun by local farmers and boys who killed over a hundred of them.'

In a separate incident in the early 1500s, the O'Malley pirates sacked this town, but the Donegal men caught up with them on their way home and killed their leader, Eoghan O'Malley, as he sheltered from a storm.

Lesson: you don't mess around with the people of Killybegs.

As I wandered around town, I had to remind myself that modern Killybegs, with its state-of-the-art fishing harbour, would be unrecognisable to those who lived in the seaport in the 1500s and 1600s. A 1622 chart in the maritime museum shows a quiet, underpopulated village, with just over a dozen buildings and about six sailing ships in the harbour. Everything else is open hills and countryside.

This was the scene of bucolic serenity that locals would have experienced as they went about their work on the morning of 29 April 1627. It didn't last for long, because later that day, the notorious pirate Claes Compaen roared into town … and for the next few days, all hell broke loose.

'Twenty Good Men Could Cut Their Throats'

On a spring night in 1627, a pirate ship of 500 tons steals silently into Killybegs Harbour, displaying a formidable array of forty brass and iron cannon. The buccaneers carry out a quick and expert reconnaissance, to establish that there is no threat from the English Navy and no visible sign of an army presence on land, before giving the all-clear to their comrades who are skulking in the cover of a nearby bay.

As the hours pass, the flagship is joined by two more heavily armed vessels, each bristling with thirty cannon. Finally, another four craft arrive, to complete the pirate war-fleet of seven ships.

The people of Killybegs have never seen anything quite like this before. The word spreads, although at first it is only a rumour: this is the much feared war-fleet of the infamous Dutch pirate Claes Compaen, one of the most successful buccaneers in history, with a total of more than 300 captured ships to his name. For the last few years, he has been using Ireland as a clearing-house for disposing of stolen goods, commandeering remote southern ports like Leamcon in County Cork and acting as a sort of bad Santa Claes for the eager merchants who queue up to buy his exotic wares at bargain prices. In order to stay one step ahead of the frustrated royal revenue collectors, Compaen has been playing an irritating game of cat-and-mouse with the English – he repeatedly promises to pledge allegiance to King Charles, so long as he can just dispose of one more cargo or have just one more season at sea.

The fleet of pirate Claes Compaen in action: the Dutch pirate would auction off his stolen booty in Leamcon in West Cork. When Basil Brooke went aboard his ship at Killybegs, he found a vast treasure hoard containing 'chests of gold' and 'Spanish silver'. Compaen himself was dripping with bling.

In Killybegs, the response to Compaen's arrival is a strange mixture of apprehension and avarice. On the one hand, Dutch seamen have a reputation for behaving wildly on shore leave. Yet, on the other hand, these pirates are capable of transforming the local economy overnight as they purchase new gear, buy supplies at inflated prices, and toss around their ill-gotten ducats and dollars in the hostels and alehouses.

No-one can foresee the extent to which both of these scenarios are about to materialise. Compaen's visit to Killybegs will go down in history as an epic buccaneering blow-out, one of the most drunken and debauched sprees of pirate shore leave ever recorded in Ireland. And yes, the pirates would spend a fortune – equivalent to hundreds of thousands of pounds today – on feasting, wine and 'loose women', all under the approving and tolerating gaze of the local police chief and the minister of religion.

Standing on the sidelines, fuming, through all of this is the County Constable, a former soldier and adventurer named Sir Basil Brooke. As a lifelong man of action, he is aching to drum up an army of volunteers to drive the pirates out of his territory. But his hands are tied by his superiors, who are still hopeful that they can convince Compaen to give up his old sins and ally himself with the English. Brooke is under no such illusions. He regards the pirates as so much vermin, who must be eradicated. He is about to draw up a secret plan to enlist 'twenty good men', who will wait until the pirates are dead drunk, and then swoop down and massacre the lot of them.

By this stage, Claes Compaen had chalked up a brief pirate career, but an astonishingly successful one. He claimed to have captured 350 ships of all nationalities. He roamed far and wide, from his native Holland to his alternative buccaneering bases in Ireland and in Morocco. He was also, arguably, the world's first celebrity corsair. A book about his adventures became a bestseller during his own lifetime, enhancing his reputation as a sort of popular anti-hero. It is thanks to his biographer – an anonymous schoolteacher from Compaen's home village – that we know so much about his life and his remarkable exploits.

Claes Gerritszoon Compaen was born in the quiet village of Oostzaan in North Holland and, so far as we can tell, enjoyed a staid and decent life until, on a whim, he decided to go to sea as a privateer in 1621. Privateers were highly respected at the time: one band of mariners known as 'the sea beggars' had played a major role in Holland's liberation and were regarded as folk heroes. The freebooters, as they were called, were quietly encouraged by the merchant class, so long as they confined themselves to attacking the country's hated enemies, the Spanish and Portuguese. For a while, Compaen thrived in this role, and everyone prospered. However, he soon fell out with his financiers over money. Like so many privateers before him, he crossed over to the dark side into outright piracy: but he did the transition in style. He invited his financial backers to a lavish dinner, where, after encouraging them to eat and drink their fill, he left them holding the bill. Then he disappeared over the horizon in a 200-ton gunship with seventeen cannon, cheered on by his equally eager crew of nearly seven dozen men. From that point on, he attacked the ships of his homeland with the same furious intensity as he attacked her enemies.

Compaen was a charismatic figure. Described as blond, fair-featured, well-built and politely spoken, he was mercurial and infuriatingly unpredictable: some of his victims were greeted with a joke and treated kindly, while to others he behaved in a 'resolutely evil' manner. To his crew, he was a hero. His generosity in sharing his ill-gotten wealth made him so popular that volunteers were soon queuing to join his force. To his fellow Dutchmen, he became a figure of fascination, a sort of mix of gentleman-highwayman and Great Train Robber.

Before long, he commanded a pirate flotilla of seven ships and 400 men, and his appearance struck fear into seamen of all nations. His zone of operation stretched from Morocco to the northernmost points of Europe, and, like so many of his Dutch pirate colleagues, he fostered links with the Barbary states in North Africa. (The ruler of Morocco described him as 'the master of the sea'.)

One island enticed Compaen more than any other. It was an island with wild, lawless, unpatrolled inlets where a pirate could safely hide from the authorities, yet blessed with tranquil coves where he could beach and service his ships; an island with deep, safe harbours where stolen goods could be offloaded and sold in full view of corrupt lawmen who would not only allow the auctions, but join in the bidding themselves. An island with piracy laws so lax that, even if he were to be captured, he would usually receive a soft rap on the knuckles rather than a hard drop from the gallows. That island was Ireland.

In the mid-1620s, he sailed into the west Cork pirate haven of Leamcon, and established a financial understanding with local landowner and Deputy Vice Admiral of Munster, Sir William Hull. As we saw in Pirate Pilgrimage the Eighth, Leamcon was famous to merchants, and infamous to the frustrated authorities, as a kind of bargain basement for pirated goods. In 1625, the authorities compiled an intriguing list of 'people who bought goods of the pirate Campane at Leamcon' after one of his ships had partially sunk in the harbour. The list gives an insight into the range and quality of Compaen's stolen cargos. Buyers travelled from many miles away to bid for stolen hauls of Brazilian timber, Asian nuts and spices, African ivory and Canaries wine.

But while Hull and Compaen facilitated each other, they did not appear to trust, or even to like, one another. Once, Hull invited Compaen to stay overnight in his home. The Dutchman agreed, but brought ashore a private army of eighty men, whom he insisted should stand guard over his bedroom all night as he slept.

The English attitude to Compaen could be summarised in a remark allegedly made by Franklin D. Roosevelt about a Central American dictator: 'He may be an S.o.B., but he's *our* S.o.B.' So long as Compaen agreed to attack everyone else's shipping and to leave English vessels alone, he could be regarded as an English asset. On 1 October 1624, Sir Henry Cary, the highly acquisitive Viceroy of Ireland, issued Compaen with 'an absolute protection', allowing him to operate freely around the Irish and English coasts, despite the furious protests of the Dutch, who were trying to hunt him down. Hearing that a Dutch naval fleet was closing in on Compaen in Leamcon, Cary ordered William Hull to 'allow him the best part of the harbour for his defence, and if they [the Dutch navy] should land, Hull can bring whatever force he has to his succour'. He explained that all of this was a preliminary to pardoning Compaen and keeping him onside.

Compaen seemed content to let the English remain under this illusion. By December that year, Cary was telling Hull that '[he] desires to submit himself, his ship, and goods, to the King's mercy'. But by February 1625, the amnesty had expired. Compaen demanded that Cary extend his protection and 'give him leave to sell, and so to revictual and begone to sea to look for more booty', after which the pirate might deign to return to renegotiate. Understandably, Cary thought these terms were 'neither honourable ... nor safe'. He put a naval vessel from Waterford on standby to attack.

Then he sent Compaen a message that revealed his real priorities. He wanted Compaen's loot. If Compaen were to write to Cary personally, 'stating where his wealth lies, and that he will make a voyage to sea to fetch it, and return hither again by midsummer next', then a pardon could be considered, for a fee of £10,000 payable by the pirate. In the meantime, as a gesture of good faith, Compaen was to leave a deposit of £500 worth of goods in William Hull's hands, and promise to take away no more than £200 worth of the gold and silver he had brought into Leamcon.

The impending crisis was averted when Compaen swore that he was honestly intending to submit to the King. The naval ships were called off, and Cary wrote out another free pass.

In May 1625, a certain Captain Harris – the Waterford-based naval officer who had been told to hold off on pursuing Compaen – warned the authorities in some frustration that the Dutch pirate was 'still hovering about these parts'. The following February, Cary gave a thirty-day pass to Compaen and his men to visit Dublin, provided they 'behaved orderly'. Later that same month, a curious receipt appears in the records: for just over £684, 'from monies found upon dead bodies of one of Compaen's pirates from sums paid for goods part of the Turkish prize at Dublin'. Since it gives no further details, we can only speculate about the colourful tale that must lie behind this dry ledger item.

Compaen's cosy relationship with the English turned sour when a stolen cargo discovered in Devon was traced back to an English ship that had been attacked by Compaen. The English authorities declared him an outlaw, and seized a sizeable haul that Compaen had landed at Leamcon.

The incensed Compaen retaliated by capturing the son of an English official and threatening to hang him if his goods were not returned. The authorities refused point blank. Compaen gave them two 'last chances' to save the boy and when they stood firm, he backed down, impressed by their resoluteness. These were 'devils', who would rather lose a much-loved relative than lose money, he declared, half in disgust and half in admiration. The hostage was freed and Compaen contented himself with burning down a castle instead.

Later in 1626, Compaen came to Broad Haven in Mayo with two ships. Captain Harris wanted to 'take him in the harbour', but Cary was under orders from his boss, the powerful Duke of Buckingham, to open new negotiations with Compaen. Cary ordered local army officers to entertain the Dutchman, and when local chieftain Michael Cormick detained six of the pirates, he was ordered to release them. Compaen went south to Kerry, then set his course northwards for Killybegs in Donegal.

Compaen pulled in to Killybegs Harbour in late April 1627. First one ship appeared, presumably to scout out the harbour. It was then joined by two others, and finally a further four, making a formidable fleet of seven heavily armed pirate vessels. A local observer didn't know what to make of the incursion. 'They are all invaders from abroad,' he wrote.

Word soon reached the County Constable, Sir Basil Brooke, in his castle in Donegal Town. Brooke was among a class of people who often cropped up in that era: opportunists who arrived in Ireland with virtually nothing, and who were transformed, almost overnight, into wealthy squires controlling large estates of confiscated land. Brooke had fought the Irish insurgents Hugh O'Neill and Red Hugh O'Donnell as a captain of 100 troops. When he was discharged in peacetime in 1604, he was rewarded with a large area of the O'Donnells' land. He moved into Red Hugh's ancient castle, and tore it apart for renovations. However, he overstepped the mark when he grabbed some lands belonging to the Church, much to the annoyance of the local bishop. Eventually, after an acrimonious row, he was ordered to hand them back.

Brooke's main job as County Constable was to maintain law and order, but it wasn't easy. The English plantation did not prosper, and by 1617, Brooke was having to negotiate with a rebellious clan leader who had kidnapped his young son. The last thing he needed was more trouble on his doorstep. So when one of the world's most infamous pirates arrived in Killybegs with an armed fleet that could easily outmatch the royal ships, he had every reason to worry.

As soon as the fleet appeared, Brooke wrote to Cary, warning that there were '[seven] full ships at Killybegs … of Captain Compaen the pirate'. He added ominously that he would send an update of news 'no matter how bad it is'. There was still total confusion over the pirate's status. 'He claims to have got the King's protection,' Cary reported vaguely to London. 'If he does not adhere to this, I have given orders to try and effect his capture … [although] the lack of ships here is serious.'

Brooke, meanwhile, was dealing with the threat in real time. He reported that the first three ships comprised a flagship of 500 tons armed with forty brass and iron cannon, and two escorts, each bearing about thirty big guns. He was highly sceptical of Compaen's claim to be under royal protection.

—If you have really come for the King's pardon, Brooke wrote to him, you will do no damage here.

Compaen knew that he had enough firepower to level the town of Killybegs and that Brooke was powerless to resist, but he preferred to get what he wanted without any trouble. 'I will do no damage,' he promised Brooke, 'but merely require provisions for which I will pay largely.'

He backed up his message by using a trick that pirates often used in the age of slow communications: he claimed he had received his amnesty in a distant location, and that word hadn't yet reached Ireland.

Compaen had been a regular visitor to Sallee in Morocco, where his goods were shifted by the Dutch pirate Morat Rais. (Four years later, Morat would achieve lasting infamy as the man who carried out the slave raid on Baltimore in Cork.) Both pirates were friendly with the English envoy and spy John Harrison. Now, in Killybegs, Compaen maintained that 'I have a protection from the King of England, which came lately to my hands upon the coast of Barbary by one Captain Harrison.'

It was all smoke and mirrors, but Brooke had no way of checking. As Compaen's crewmen, flush with money, began to drift ashore in search of drink and diversions after months at sea, he wrote to High Constable James Hamilton of Killybegs, ordering him to arrest the pirates as they landed. Hamilton not only ignored the command, but tipped off the buccaneers in advance.

What happened next was quite astonishing, but by no means rare in the small coastal communities frequented by pirates. Constable Hamilton enlisted the aid of his brother William, the local vicar, and between them they showed the visiting pirates a good time. 'They entertained Compaen and his men,' Brooke spluttered, 'and supplied them.' He added, and not incidentally: 'Compaen and his men spent £1,000 to £1,500 there, all in Barbary ducats and Spanish silver.'

This equates to at least €180,000 to €270,000 in today's money, and it demonstrates how the arrival of a pirate ship could set a local economy roaring in the course of a few days. However, there was a downside. The cash-flush pirates went on a riotous bender, scandalising the locals as they staggered drunkenly from tavern to bawdy house. '[They] are always drunk,' Brooke complained. 'His men drink ... on the shore with loose women.'

As the drunken Dutchmen cursed and roared their way around the town, Brooke could take solace only in the fact that they weren't carrying guns. 'Compaen's men do not come ashore armed, except with knives to cut their meat.'

Brooke coldly hatched a plan to murder the crewmen in their cups, and in that way, end the Compaen threat once and for all. If he could assemble a hit squad, less than two dozen Englishmen could surprise the buccaneers and take advantage of their vulnerability. 'Twenty good men could cut all their throats,' he pleaded to his superior, Lord Conway. 'I believe this is to be done, and indeed, it is the only way to act.'

But Cary would not agree, so Brooke had to look on in impotent frustration as the freebooters rampaged through the town, drinking and wenching, in full view of the police chief and religious minister. To his disgust, he was even instructed to re-open negotiations with Compaen.

When he boarded the buccaneer's flagship, Brooke was astounded to see a vast haul of treasure in pirate chests. 'They are very rich, with chests of gold hammered down tight, and Spanish silver,' he reported later. '... He is said to have £6,000 or £7,000 on board in gold, silver and jewels.' That sum would be equivalent to perhaps €1 million to €1.2 million today.

Other witnesses confirm that the pirate was, indeed, fabulously wealthy. One Dutchman who met him in Ireland reported that Compaen's pockets were bulging with gold coins and that every visible part of his anatomy was covered with portable gold wealth of the sort that we would now describe as bling.

Compaen received Brooke in the great cabin, and confided that he was afraid to leave his own ship because he might never get back on again. He was facing the threat of mutiny from one faction in his crew who thought he should be seeking a pardon from their home country, Holland, instead of England. Now, as soon as his men had blown off some steam, he planned to sail to Amsterdam to start negotiations.

—I just wish I had got a pardon from the King of England first, he told Brooke ruefully. But for now, the matter is out of my hands.

Brooke's account has the ring of truth, because we know from other sources that Compaen lived in constant fear of being deposed and murdered by his own men. He kept himself armed at all times, and even slept with a gun by his side. He paid a fortune to hire personal bodyguards, but he couldn't trust them completely, either. The threat of mutiny was always at its worst when – as in Killybegs – the men were driven wild by alcohol.

According to his contemporary Dutch biographer, there was once an incident when Compaen's men seized a large cargo of wine and proceeded to drink themselves into a mutinous frenzy. Compaen went to bed that night with a loaded gun by his side and a second firearm hidden under the mattress. But when the drunken mutineers stormed into his cabin, he knew he was outgunned. He used his legendary charm to calm them down, promising that he would answer all their grievances. The mutineers changed tack in an instant, cheering for Compaen and turning their fury on the ringleaders of the revolt instead.

In Killybegs, however, the wild party ended without serious incident. Eventually, the pirate admiral gathered together his hungover crew, hauled anchor and turned his back on Donegal forever. The following month, Henry Cary reported that 'the danger is blown over for the moment'. However, Brooke still seethed with fury over his missed opportunity.

—If you had just given me the power, he wrote angrily to Cary, I could have captured the pirates and their ships.

However, poor old Brooke was out of the loop on this one. He was unaware of machinations taking place in high political circles. Viceroy Cary was worried about another Irish rebellion, and had a secret plan to transform Compaen's fleet into a mercenary navy, which would use the pitiless techniques of the pirates to crush any dissidents. For as long as this remained a possibility, Cary was never going to approve of the massacre plan.

The pirate invasion of Killybegs was over – but there are three small footnotes to this colourful episode in Irish pirate history. Sir Basil Brooke, the man who drew up the pirate massacre plot, died in 1633. His family later moved to Fermanagh. Just over 300 years later, Sir Basil's descendant and namesake, Sir Basil Brooke (Lord Brookeborough), became Unionist Prime Minister of Northern Ireland, a job he held for thirty years, during which he is chiefly remembered for his 'not an inch' policy on social reform. He was finally ousted as leader just three years before the eruption of the Ulster Troubles, a tragedy that a man of greater vision, or even slightly more tolerance, might have been able to forestall.

Claes Compaen returned to Amsterdam, and actually did negotiate a pardon for himself and his crew. Under the deal, he returned a quantity of his stolen wealth and kept the rest. (Poor Henry Cary never did get his hands on any of it.) By now legitimately wealthy, Compaen was able to return to his home village of Oostzaan, buy a fine house and resume a life of staid middle-class respectability. He lived for another three decades, long enough to see the schoolmaster's book about his life become a publishing phenomenon, and he died in his own bed in 1660. Whoever said that crime does not pay had obviously never heard of Claes Compaen – although you can't help feeling that he got out of piracy at just the right time.

't Begin, Midden en Eynde

Der Zee-Rooveryen van den Aldersamieusten Zee-Roover

CLAES G. COMPAEN,

Van Ooſtzanen in Kennemer-landt.

VERVATTENDE

Sijn wonderlijcke / vreemde en Landtsschadelijcke dyyf-tochten.

Waer in verthoont wordt, hoe hy met weynigh Schepen de Zee onveyligh ghemaeckt, een ongelooffelijcken Buyt, en groot getal van ſchepen van alle Landen gherooft, enaf-geloopen heeft.

Ghedruckt by een Liefhebber van alle Nieuwigheden / 1659.

Celebrity corsair: This book about Claes Compaen's exploits became a bestseller in his own lifetime. For years, Compaen played cat-and-mouse with the English, who wanted to enlist his pirate fleet as a mercenary navy to repress Irish insurgents.

The final footnote relates to a recent discovery, and is absolutely intriguing. In 2014, workers dredging the seabed at Long Island channel near Leamcon discovered the wreck of a seventeenth-century ship. Uniquely preserved in the sludge, it still contained a cargo of coconuts from the Caribbean, all bearing the planter's stamp. According to a report in the *Irish Examiner*, 'the ship was believed to be *en route* from the tropics when it was commandeered by the Dutch pirate Claus Campane, who operated in the Schull area. Records show that Campane indeed captured a ship which later sank in 1625 in the Long Island Channel.'

Was this the ship whose contents were auctioned off at Leamcon in 1625? If so, it would be a unique monument to the pirate era – and particularly to the fearless freebooter from Holland who dominated our coasts from Cork to Killybegs.

13

PIRATE PILGRIMAGE THE THIRTEENTH

Dunfanaghy, Achill Island

I am driving northwest from Donegal's biggest town, Letterkenny, through green, hilly countryside, past villages and hamlets whose names ring out as pleasingly as tenor and bass church bells: Kilmacrennan, Termon, Terlin, Creeslough, Portnablagh. As I catch my first glimpse of Sheephaven Bay (originally 'ship haven'), I know I am almost at my destination, the little harbour town of Dunfanaghy. I've always had a soft spot for this corner of Donegal – years ago, I used to enjoy summer holidays here with my young children. Its people are unusually friendly and warm-hearted. Dunfanaghy itself is as quaint a seaside village as you could ask for, but it also acts as a gateway to such natural wonders as Horn Head, a wild and exhilarating seabird sanctuary; the seemingly endless Tramore Beach; and the explosive sea-spout known as MacSwiney's Gun. Lying to the northwest is Tory Island, whose very name means 'Pirate Island' (it featured briefly in Pirate Pilgrimage the Fourth).

Even among Donegal towns, Dunfanaghy is different. It feels more like a Scottish village than an Irish one, and the local accent has traces of a Scots burr. Through various quirks of history, it has always enjoyed closer links with Scotland than it has with, say, Dublin, and this has left clear traces on its atmosphere and streetscape.

These days, its quayside is relatively quiet, and it is hard to imagine that the town was once a bustling, prosperous commercial port. Throughout the 1700s and early 1800s, it was a main supply base for Scots fishing vessels, but in 1818, a savage northwest gale all but wiped out one of these fleets. Only one ship out of 100 was saved, and Dunfanaghy's beaches were littered with washed-up bodies. The final blow to the town's career as a commercial port came in the early 1900s, when another high wind scooped hundreds of tons of loose sand from a sand-dune and dumped it straight into Dunfanaghy Bay, irredeemably silting up its sea approaches and sculpting an entirely new lake.

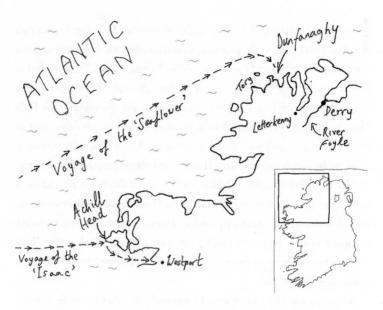

Today, the town is a vibrant tourist centre: in July and August, it buzzes with Belfast accents, as holidaymakers from Northern Ireland migrate here in droves. At other times of the year though, it takes on a more sedate and contemplative atmosphere. The air is magically pure and clear, yet strangely cool in its light-temperature. If you come here on a midsummer evening, and gaze around the sea and the mountains, you could easily imagine yourself somewhere much further north, in one of the lands of the midnight sun.

And it was on exactly that sort of day, more than three centuries ago, that 'Long Ben' Avery, then the world's most wanted pirate, paid a visit to sleepy Dunfanaghy.

The World's Most
Wanted Man

On a midsummer day in June 1696, a strange ship sails into Dunfanaghy Harbour, wind-battered, wave-pounded and its hull thick with marine growth after a long and arduous voyage across the Atlantic Ocean from the West Indies.

Along the quayside, the merchants and fishermen pause in their tasks and regard the unexpected vessel with suspicion. The fifty-ton sloop *Seaflower* is carrying four guns, and a glance at the hard-bitten crew shows that they are not men to be messed with. Some onlookers think it's a merchant ship; others guess that it's a privateer; but no-one in his wildest dreams could imagine the astonishing truth about the *Seaflower*: that it is a pirate treasure ship, laden down with plundered silver and gold from the exotic east.

The *Seaflower* offloads its crew and passengers: nineteen men and one woman, their legs unsteady after weeks at sea. There is the Captain, a tall figure with an English West Country drawl, who introduces himself as Captain Bridgeman. There is a mariner named John Dan, who seems curiously weighted down under an exceptionally heavy coat. There is a young man named Philip Middleton, who clearly harbours a serious grudge against a fourth seaman, John Sparkes – justifiably so, because any money that Middleton has earned from the perilous voyage, Sparkes has stolen. The sole female, who sticks close to Bridgeman, is a Mrs Adams. She is the wife of the Quartermaster, but currently the Captain's lover.

These pirates have travelled from the far side of the world, from the hot and steamy Indian Ocean, via the Cape of Good Hope, past the coast of Brazil and the palm-fringed sands of the Bahamas, to arrive at this little County Donegal village. They are carrying a fortune in Spanish pieces of eight and Venetian gold coins, all stolen with sickening ultra-violence from a ship of India carrying Islamic pilgrims home from Mecca.

The most wanted man in the world: A drawing from the 1700s shows Captain Henry 'Long Ben' Avery after his attack on a richly-laden pilgrim ship (shown in background). He landed much of his haul of gold and silver in the sleepy port of Dunfanaghy, Donegal.

'Captain Bridgeman' is actually the infamous pirate Captain Henry Avery, who is wanted on three continents for masterminding one of the most lucrative sea heists in history. His hijacking of the pilgrim ship, and his needlessly brutal treatment of the female passengers on board, has outraged the civilised world, created a major diplomatic crisis in India, sparked riots in the streets, and disrupted commerce on a huge scale on the subcontinent. A lot of wealthy people in England have lost a lot of money thanks to Captain Avery. The English Government has sworn to catch the pirate at all costs, and has put out an alert at all ports. But ever since the heist, Avery has seemingly vanished into thin air.

Until now.

These brutal buccaneers have survived mutinies, pirate in-fighting, sea attacks and fair and foul weather to haul their loot to Ireland. They are on the final stretch of their long journey, almost home. Only one man presents a potential obstacle on their road to riches. He is the local customs agent, Maurice Cuttle, and he has the power to arrest them, seize their ship and confiscate their heavy bags if he is in any way suspicious. He has no idea that he is dealing with pirates so ruthless that they would happily skewer his small intestine and eat it for breakfast if they thought for a moment that he stood between them and their money.

Four weeks earlier, a separate band of pirates had moored their Bahamas sloop in the chilly Atlantic waters off Achill Head on Ireland's west coast and waded on to the beach, each man bent double under the weight of stolen silver and gold.

A flabbergasted revenue official later testified that the group was carrying thirty-two large bags and a giant cask, each packed solidly with precious coins and 'each [weighing] as much as a man could well lift off the ground'.

Alone and undisturbed on this deserted shoreline on the far westerly fringe of Achill Island, they spread their haul across the strand and proceeded, painstakingly, to divide it out between them.

For these pirates, too, it was the final stage of a long and exhausting global journey. They were part of Avery's gang. After they had ferried their stolen gold and silver from the Indian Ocean to the Bahamas, the band had split up into three units before sailing eastwards across the Atlantic to separate destinations in Ireland. While Captain Avery's *Seaflower* had headed for Donegal in the far north, this particular ship, the *Isaac*, had aimed to make separate landfalls along the country's wild and unpoliced west coast. The *Isaac* alone was burdened down with an estimated twenty thousand pounds' worth of stolen gold, silver and coinage. Here in Achill, they put ashore ten or twelve members of their crew, who intended to make their way to their various homes in Ireland, Scotland and England. The remaining pirates would stay on the *Isaac*, head south, and disembark at points further down the coast.

In the half-light of the June evening, the pirates swatted away the constant attacks from Achill's notorious clouds of summer midges as they expertly divvied up their spoil. They worked quickly, with no attempts to hide the origin of their treasure – some witnesses later found evidence of muslin cloth, which was available only in the Middle East, and exotic coins from Asia. Speed was more important than discretion, because each man had a high price on his head.

But in Ireland, a secret does not remain secret for long. Within hours, the landing was the talk of the district. Some believed, wrongly, that the nocturnal visitors were political assassins on their way to kill the King. As the *Isaac* sailed away into the night, the new arrivals fanned out across country, offering crazy sums for horses to help them carry their heavy loot. '[They] gave great cause for suspicion,' said one report, '[because] they offered any rate for horses – £10 for a garron [a cheap workhorse] not worth £2.'

Desperate to cut down on weight, the men approached moneychangers and offered to swap bags of heavy silver 'pieces of eight' for lighter gold guinea coins at ridiculously generous rates of exchange.

Meanwhile, by 7 June, the *Isaac* had berthed in the busy harbour of Westport, declaring itself to be a merchant trader returning from New Providence in the Bahamas. No-one paid it any attention until 14 June. By the time the local sheriff had identified it with the reports from Achill, the *Isaac* had been sold to two Galway merchants, who had taken it home. The two merchants were found to have forty pounds' worth of exotic eastern coinage, 'not passable in this Kingdom'. Two of the fleeing pirates were arrested in Mayo with £200 in their pockets.

The *Isaac*'s captain, Thomas Hollingsworth, remained on board the ship in Galway and brazened it out. He claimed to be a merchant who had arrived from the Bahamas with a few tons of timber, duty paid at source. Apart from that, his ship carried only money, and 'money carries no duty'. Eventually released, he set off back to the Bahamas, but soon did a secret U-turn and ended up in Dublin.

Hollingsworth had got away with it. And he owed it all to the dark genius of his boss, the pirate mastermind Henry Avery.

Henry Avery was born into a seafaring family in Plymouth in England's West Country, so he might genuinely have had the Long John Silver drawl that we associate with pirates today. He was 'bred to the sea', and began his career as a ship's mate. But he had grand ambitions, and when he found himself stuck for a long period in La Coruña harbour on board the forty-gun warship *Charles II*, he hatched a grand plan to seize the vessel and make his fortune as a pirate. The bored crew were easily persuaded. Charles Gibson, the captain, was confined to his cabin with a high fever, and woke up to feel the unmistakeable motion of a ship at sea. Assuming the *Charles II* had slipped her anchor, he called for his first mate. Avery walked coolly into the cabin and assured the captain that all was well with the ship. However:

'I'll let you into a secret,' he said. 'I am the captain now, and this is my cabin. Therefore you must get out. I am a man of fortune, and must seek my fortune.'

With those few words, Henry Avery had transformed himself into a pirate captain in command of a forty-gun warship worth £1,000. It was May 1694. His new crew of eager volunteers comprised eighty-five men, including a significant number of Irish mutineers. Renaming his stolen vessel as the *Fancy*, he set course for Africa. After taking a number of ships, and obtaining some African slaves through trickery, he ended up in the Red Sea, with his crew doubled to 170. They tried to trade in one coastal town. However, 'the people would not trade with us,' recalled one seaman, John Dan, 'so we burned it'.

Avery had gone to the Red Sea with a definite purpose: he had his mind set on the heist to end all heists. Every year, wealthy Islamic pilgrims would sail to Mecca from Surat on India's west coast. They travelled in around two dozen ships, protected by the fleet's owner, the powerful Mogul Emperor Aurangazeb. The mission doubled as a trading operation: after making the pilgrimage and selling their wares in the Middle East, the ships would come back laden down with cash. Since the risk of pirate attack was obvious, the ships were bristling with heavy cannon and guarded by expert musketeers.

Avery was not deterred. His first tactic was to assemble all the disparate pirates, privateers and general thugs in the area, and to form them into one cohesive attack force. Some had travelled from as far away as America. For five weeks, they lay in wait for the Emperor's returning fleet to sail past. Nothing happened. Finally, the bored pirates seized a small vessel, whose crew gave them very bad news: the fleet's twenty-five ships had already sneaked past them in the darkness, and were well out of sight.

'We followed them,' John Dan testified later, 'and about three days … we came up with one of them, about 200–300 tons. We fired a broadside at her, and small shot, and took her.'

When they searched the ship, *Fath Mahmamadi*, the delighted pirates discovered £50,000 to £60,000 worth of gold and silver. They offloaded the treasure and returned to land, thinking their mission was over. However, Avery had his sights set on higher things. From his captives, he learned that there was a much larger ship – the *Ganj-i sawái* – in the fleet further ahead.

This was on a different scale of difficulty. The imperial ship *Ganj-i sawái* was the largest ship in Surat and, with eighty guns and 400 musketeers, it outgunned and outmanned the *Fancy* several times over. (According to John Dan, the *Ganj-i sawái* had forty guns and 800 fighting men.) Under its captain, Ibrahim Khan, it was carrying not only pilgrims, but 5,200,000 rupees in silver and gold, the result of a spectacularly successful trading mission.

Avery did not hesitate. 'We weighed anchor,' Dan recalled, 'and found her in about two hours.'

An Indian diplomat named Khafi Khan takes up the story. '[Our fleet] had come within eight or nine days of Surat, when an English ship came in sight, of much smaller size, and not having a third or fourth part of the armament of the *Ganj-i sawái*,' he wrote.

To have any chance at all, Avery needed not only courage and audacity, but a large dollop of good luck. On that day, he had all three. As the pirates closed in, the Emperor's gunners aimed their most powerful cannon directly at the *Fancy*, in a shot that should have smashed the English ship to matchwood. Instead, the gun itself exploded in one deafening, ignominious blast. As Khafi Khan reported, 'By ill luck, the gun burst, and three or four men were killed by its fragments.'

Henry Avery's pirates attack the treasure ship of an Indian emperor. The vessel carried gold, silver and jewels worth more than €20 million in today's money, but Avery lost it all and died a pauper.

Taking advantage of the confusion, Avery's gunner took aim at the Indian ship's mainmast – a difficult target with both craft in violent motion. The cannon roared and belched smoke, and the pirates cheered in disbelief as the mast came crashing down. It was a direct hit, and brought down the sails and rigging on to the heads of the defenders.

'[It] damaged the mainmast, on which the safety of the vessel depends,' reported Khafi Khan. 'The Englishmen perceived this, and being encouraged by it, bore down to attack and, drawing their swords, jumped on board their opponent.'

The fight wasn't over yet. The two sides locked in on each other in an ugly, close-quarters scrimmage on deck. 'She stood a fight of three hours [before she] yielded,' said Dan. Another seaman, Philip Middleton, reported that 'several men' on the Emperor's ship were killed in the action.

As the smoke cleared, the pirates found that the prize exceeded their wildest expectations. The flagship contained more than £120,000 worth of treasure, on top of the £60,000 they'd taken from the first ship – a total of £180,000, or perhaps €24 million by today's values. 'We took from her in money and plate enough gold and silver to make up each man's share to £1,000, [with] 180 men sharing in all,' Dan testified.

And that was not all. The 2,000 passengers on board both ships included some of Surat's wealthiest citizens, who were carrying their own jewellery as well as presents for their families. (The most extravagant was a saddle and bridle studded with rubies – a gift for the Emperor himself.) After ransacking all the cabins, the pirates were convinced the pilgrims had still more stashed away. The crews of several pirate ships took turns at boarding the prize vessel, each bunch of thugs equally enthusiastic about finding the secret hoard, but 'though they put several to the torture, they would not confess where the rest of the treasure lay', Middleton said chillingly. The English Governor at Mumbai was later to concede that the pirates 'did do very barbarously to the people of the [ships] to make them confess where their money was'.

Avery had made his fortune, many times over. But he was not content to let the passengers sail on. Instead, he took his prize ships to a safe coast where he allowed his men to rampage freely among the women passengers for a full week. Years later, he tried to justify the ensuing outrage by claiming that he had protected the high-born female passengers from his crew's clutches. However, the 200 females of low rank were a different matter:

'As for … the women of inferior rank … I cannot answer for what might happen in the first heat,' he wrote. 'But after the first heat of our men was over, what was done, was done quietly … there was not a woman among them but what was lain with four or five times over, that is to say, by several men.'

Khafi Khan, drawing on eyewitness accounts, said they 'dishonour[ed] the women, both old and young … several honourable women, when they found an opportunity, threw themselves into the sea to preserve their chastity, and some others killed themselves with knives and daggers.'

According to the English Governor, one husband committed suicide along with his wife and their nurse in order to avoid the ordeal. Even the elderly were violated, he reported. One of the victims was the aged wife of a prominent courtier, 'related to the King, returning from her pilgrimage to Mecca, in old age,' the Governor wrote later. 'She they abused very much, and forced several other women.'

John Dan wraps up the episode: 'When we had done as much as we thought convenient,' he said blandly, 'we sent her to Surat with the people in her.'

Back home in England, the ugly story was to become sanitised – and even sentimentalised. There were tall tales that Avery had fallen in love with an Indian princess, whom he married, and that his crewmen had romantically married her maidservants. The sordid truth eventually emerged, but the myth never died.

As the *Ganj-i sawái* limped home, the pirates divided up the spoil among themselves, according to their rank and the part they'd played in the action. 'Some had £1000, some £500, others £300,' said Dan. Young Philip Middleton was given just £100, which he intended to save to set himself up as an apprentice at home. Even that niggardly amount was stolen from him next morning by his shipmate Joseph Sparkes, who later had cause to regret his actions.

Inevitably, the thieves fell out among themselves, with allegations that some were cheating by shaving the edges off their gold coins before exchanging them with comrades. They split up and headed off in various directions. Avery knew exactly where he was going. To the Atlantic Ocean's wild west – New Providence Island in the Bahamas.

Emperor Aurangazeb had a close relative on board the robbed ship, and took the matter extremely personally. For the East India Company of traders, which was backed by powerful interests in London, the attack was a disaster. In Surat, 150 miles north of present-day Mumbai, the furious citizens rioted in the street.

According to the English Governor, 'there was a great noise in town, and the rabble very much incensed against the English ... [They] clapped all our people in irons.'

In Mumbai, the English blocked all the roads leading to their trading base and fortified the walls. '[They] made the place quite impregnable,' reported Khafi Khan.

Khafi Khan went in to the English fortress as a negotiator. The Governor, all charm and innocence, asked him for an explanation for the riots. Khafi Khan hit back indignantly: 'Although you do not acknowledge that shameful action ... which was perpetrated by your wicked men, this question you have put to me is as if a wise man should ask where the sun is when all the world is filled with its rays.'

The Governor had a ready answer. The attackers may have been English, but they were renegades, 'now serving as pirates'. He had no control over them.

Eventually the Emperor decided – with great reluctance – that, as Khafi Khan put it, 'a struggle with the English would result only in heavy loss to customs revenue'. A deal was reached: the Company agreed to provide security for the Emperor's ships, and the English King promised to bring the offenders to justice. He put a price of £500 on Henry Avery's head, with the Company agreeing to bankroll the reward. All ports were warned to be on the alert for the *Fancy*, pointing out that the wanted men 'may be probably known and discovered by the great quantities of ... Indian gold and silver they have with them'.

It was 18 August 1696, and Henry Avery had become the most wanted man in the world.

The Bahamas, April 1696.

The long journey around the African Cape and across the Atlantic to America had left the crew fractious, and Avery had to face down a mutiny and ditch some malcontents before finally reaching the Caribbean. He wrote to the Governor, Nicholas Trott, asking for safe passage in return for a substantial bribe. 'We made a collection of twenty pieces of eight a man, and forty from the captain, as a present to the Governor, besides elephants' teeth and other things to the value of £1,000,' recalled John Dan.

'[The Governor replied] that they would be welcome, and come and go again when they pleased,' said Middleton. Trott even entertained the pirates to a party at his own home, although he stingily charged one of them for breaking a drinking-glass.

An arrangement was made whereby the *Fancy* – by now a liability to Avery – was 'accidentally' run aground on the island for Trott to salvage. When Trott's men boarded the empty ship, they found a scene straight out of a modern Disney pirate fantasy: 'fifty tons of elephants' teeth, forty-six guns mounted, 100 barrels of gunpowder [and] several chests of buccaneer guns'.

The pirates headed off in different directions: some to the American mainland and others towards Europe. Avery invested £600 in a new sloop, the *Seaflower*, and put on board nineteen male crewmen and his new lover, Mrs Adams. Meanwhile, the *Isaac* was manned by twenty-three sailors and captained by Hollingsworth. The two captains pointed their prows towards the rising sun and steered a course for Ireland and home.

At Dunfanaghy harbour on that June day, the tension hangs as heavy as the mists over Muckish Mountain as the crew disembarks. A man with an obvious air of authority leaves the *Seaflower* and stalks down the quayside. He is probably wearing his usual land-gear: a tricorn hat covering a long wig, a three-quarter-length tunic, and by his side a threatening sword. He introduces himself as Captain Bridgeman, and asks to speak to the port's 'landwaiter' or customs official.

That would be Mr Maurice Cuttle, who duly appears, dusting down his coat and apologising: it's not every day he gets gentlemen like Captain Bridgeman honouring his small village. How can he be of assistance? The two men huddle briefly and reach a gentlemen's understanding. Bridgeman reveals that he has just sailed from the privateering haven of New Providence: ask no questions, Mr Cuttle, and I will tell you no lies. It would be extremely helpful if Mr Cuttle would let Bridgeman and his crew disembark and continue their journey by land without the need for any bothersome paperwork. They would also require passes to travel freely: he himself is about to head eastwards across the north of Ireland towards Scotland, and eight others will travel separately, southeast towards Dublin. Perhaps Mr Cuttle might even provide an escort. In return, Captain Bridgeman would show his appreciation with a generous consideration.

Mr Cuttle considers and agrees. Perhaps he is motivated by simple greed. On the other hand, perhaps he is working out a more Machiavellian tactic. Watching the nineteen sea-thugs in the background – seeing how they eye him up and down, how their fingers play on the butts of their muskets, how they edgily stroke the hand-grips of their cutlasses – he must realise that he has no chance of survival if he refuses this offer. Maurice Cuttle is essentially being offered a stark choice of *plata o plomo* – a bribe of silver, or a bullet of lead.

Cuttle accepts the *plata*. A handshake seals the deal. But as the customs man glances warily at the sun-baked, bearded faces of the crewmen, he realises that they do not trust him. They have been betrayed too many times before. And deep in his heart, Cuttle knows that they are right – because even as he writes out the safe-passes for Avery and his buccaneers, he is already plotting to turn them in.

The pirates waste no time bagging up their haul of gold and silver and taking to the road. Around half of them disperse independently. Once loaded up on horseback, the remaining nine-strong party forms what is virtually a travelling bank. Captain Avery is carrying £2,000 worth of treasure – a sum that must, quite literally, have been staggering. Seaman John Dan, still wearing his heavy coat on this June day, has over £1,000 stashed away. Sparkes and the other men have an average of £500 to £600. Young Philip Middleton has nothing left, and smoulders with resentment.

The obliging Maurice Cuttle escorts them for the first part of their journey, along the winding Donegal road between the mountains and the ocean. Six miles outside Dunfanaghy, Avery abruptly bids his farewell. He and Mrs Adams spur their horses down a side-road and are soon lost in the hills.

As the others reach the town of Letterkenny, Cuttle begins to breathe a little more easily. The scary 'Captain Bridgeman' is now out of the picture. He waits until he feels safe in the centre of town, then drops his bombshell.

—In the name of the King, I am detaining you and confiscating your money, he announces.

Two of the pirates bluff it out. Indignantly protesting their innocence, they tell him they can clear their names if they can meet a witness in the nearby city of Derry. Cuttle weakens. Could these men actually be telling the truth? He escorts them as far as the River Foyle, where suddenly the tables are turned once more.

Realising that the customs man is again vulnerable, out in the open countryside, John Dan puts another *plata o plomo* ultimatum. Cuttle can either accept an incredibly generous bribe of three pounds' *weight* in gold, or else suffer the consequences. The landwaiter agrees, this time without mental reservation. They have made him an offer he cannot refuse.

The aftermath of the Achill–Dunfanaghy episode would later emerge during a celebrated trial. The remaining pirates reached Dublin, where they split up. John Dan sailed to Holyhead and travelled overland to Rochester, where his luck ran out.

A maid was tidying his room when she lifted his ubiquitous jacket and gasped when it proved to be as heavy as a sack of potatoes. Her deft fingers felt in the lining and discovered more than a thousand Venetian gold coins, worth £1,045. She alerted the authorities, who swooped on the inn immediately. It was an ignominious end to Dan's globetrotting career – he had survived attacks in Africa, the blistering fire of imperial musketeers in the Indian Ocean, a shipboard revolt off Brazil, a hazardous Atlantic voyage, and a double-cross by a customs man in Ireland … only to be laid low by a curious maidservant in boring old England.

That autumn, six of Avery's henchmen were arrested and brought before London's Old Bailey court, charged with felony and piracy. Among the accused was John Sparkes, who had stolen young Philip Middleton's £100 share – not such a good idea, it turned out, as the irate Middleton now opted to turn King's evidence. However, the star prosecution witness was John Dan, who had swapped sides in return for immunity.

The first trial centred on the piracy of the two pilgrim ships. But despite the damning evidence of Middleton and Dan, the English jury somehow decided that an assault on the Islamic Great Mogul was not a crime.

'The jury, contrary to the expectation of the court, brought in all the prisoners not guilty,' said the dismayed prosecutor.

The theft of the solidly English ship *Charles II* in Spain was a different matter. After a lively trial, featuring some sparky arguments between the pirates, all six were found guilty. The judge said they had committed 'detestable crimes', and added: 'The law, for the heinousness of your crime, hath appointed a severe punishment by an ignominious death.'

On Wednesday, 25 November 1696, the six men were taken across London Bridge in a solemn procession, led by an Admiralty official carrying a symbolic silver oar. At Wapping, a scaffold had been erected at the low-tide mark. The hanging of pirates was intentionally 'ignominious', in order to deter future offenders. A ladder was removed, or a wagon wheeled away, to leave the victim suspended on the end of a rope. As the force of gravity slowly garrotted them, their feet would kick frantically in a gruesome jig known as 'doing the marshal's dance'. The corpses were either left to rot in the tide or suspended in chains further downriver.

Captain Henry Avery made it safely to England and was never brought to justice – although, as we'll see when we catch up with him again in Pirate Pilgrimage the Sixteenth, he may never have actually enjoyed the benefit of his stolen riches.

And Maurice Cuttle? His bribe-taking was eventually exposed, but in an era of endemic corruption, that in itself was not enough to ruin his career. (Nineteen years later, he was recorded as receiving a substantial State payment of more than £21 'for seizing seditious papers'.) However, we can be sure that his reputation as a law enforcer never recovered from the revelation that, on that June day in Dunfanaghy, Cuttle had encountered the world's most wanted fugitive – Henry Avery, sometimes dubbed 'the most successful pirate in history' – and let him slip clean through his fingers.

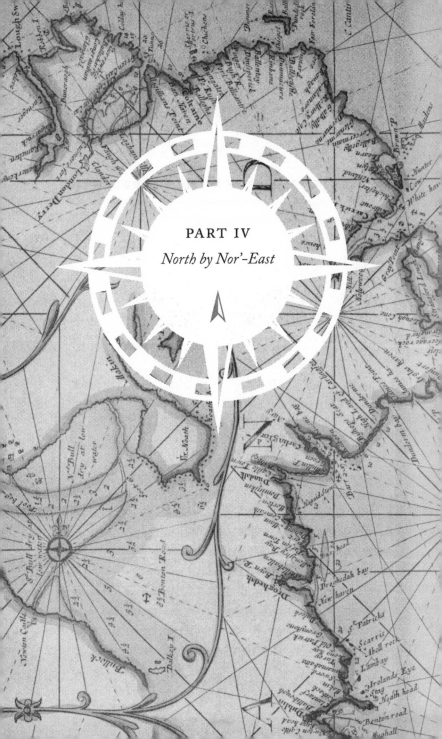

PART IV

North by Nor'-East

14

PIRATE PILGRIMAGE THE FOURTEENTH

Portrush

From Dunfanaghy, I drive back to Letterkenny and then northeast towards Derry, retracing the route taken by Cuttle and the pirates of the *Seaflower*. The sky is leaden and it is threatening rain as I drive through Donegal's northerly Inishowen Peninsula. I pass the lonely and enigmatic ringfort known as the Grianán of Aileach, which will feature in Pirate Pilgrimage the Seventeenth, before leaving the Republic and crossing the bridge over the River Foyle. For the next few days – and the next few chapters – I will be chasing pirates in Northern Ireland.

Heading further east, I cross the Bann – the river that will play a prominent part in this next story – at Coleraine. It is raining heavily as I adjust course northeast towards Portrush.

'A place where legends are made,' proclaims a poster as I enter the outskirts of town. It's promoting a motorcycle race, but the statement is true in a much deeper sense, for this town is at the epicentre of one of the island's most intriguing myths of piracy and buried treasure. From time to time, the streets of Portrush will come alive with a pirate festival, celebrating the life and career of a buccaneering icon.

I stop for a sandwich in the local yacht club, overlooking the busy harbour and the golden beach beyond. They have a TV display shuffling pictures of bygone Portrush, a pleasantly undeveloped village of quiet streets and whitewashed cottages. The 1800s craze for ocean bathing transformed this haven into a bustling seaside resort, and every summer these days, it is dense with crowds of day-trippers. As a youngster, I would have been among them. I know how cheerful this town can be in the sunshine, so today – as I watch locals scurrying home under umbrellas, and visitors standing in pub doorways staring out into the rain – I know I am not seeing Portrush at its best.

After a brief wander around the harbour and along the seafront, I return to my car and head a couple of miles further east along the Antrim Coast Road, to the ruins of Dunluce Castle. I am a wordsmith by trade, but all I could say when I walked down towards the sea and saw this wild and jagged clifftop fortress was: Wow.

Resembling some fantasy palace from a Tolkien epic, the castle is perched precariously – and pugnaciously – on a grassy basalt outcrop projecting into the sea. Round towers seem to burst out of the solid rock and rise upwards from sheer cliffs, the whole structure culminating in triangular gable walls that point defiantly skywards. This is the fortress that inspired *Narnia* author C.S. Lewis to dream up the castle of Cair Paravel.

It has also become famous internationally in its guise as the House of Greyjoy in the TV fantasy series *Game of Thrones*.

In real life, it was here that the Scots-Irish MacDonnells, ferocious sea-raiders, set up their Irish base. Belligerent by nature, rebellious in their politics and Catholic by religion, they were the worst nightmare of the English colonists in Ulster. In Elizabethan times, they had dispatched huge raiding forces from Scotland to Ireland. One expedition, from the Isle of Islay to Antrim, consisted of two thousand pirates in two dozen ships. After capturing Dunluce in 1584, they dug in to this almost impregnable fortress and harassed shipping all around the north coast.

The piracy didn't stop when the MacDonnells went legit. In 1614, an official in Derry complained that the *Lark*, a ship he had just sold, had been captured on its way to Coleraine – 'stolen away by pirates and soldiers from Portrush'.

However, my next story dates much further back in history – to the violent mediaeval era. Looking westward from Dunluce, back towards Portrush, I can see a group of islands lying low and dark on the horizon, ragged and uneven in profile: the Skerries. The easternmost of these seventeen islands is – at least according to legend – the burial place of an infamous pirate, and many locals will tell you that his treasure is buried there. Truth or fantasy? Read the remarkable story of the wonderfully named 'Black Tom, the Scummer of the Sea', and judge for yourself.

Black Tom, the Scummer of the Sea

The foes were entrapped in a deep swampy fen,
Like a huge salmon shoal in the fisher's close den …
But Thomas of Down, that 'strong theefe' of the sea,
Ploughed the Bann with his ships, and again set them free.

> – Poem describing the dramatic rescue of an entrapped army by the fourteenth-century pirate Thomas of Down, a.k.a. Black Tom

The movie *Braveheart* thrilled cinema audiences with its vivid dramatization of Scotland's first struggle for national independence. But it did not include one of the most extraordinary and thrilling episodes of that bloody war – the dramatic rescue of an entrapped Scots expeditionary force in Ireland by a daring Irish pirate named Black Tom.

Irish buccaneers don't usually have the sort of exotic names we associate with pirate captains. There are few juicy monikers to rival those of Calico Jack Rackham, Blackbeard, Long Ben or the fictional Long John Silver. However, one man stands out as an exception. He is Black Tom, nicknamed by his contemporaries 'the Scummer of the Sea'.

Although he commanded a fleet of only four galleys, this 'cruel pirate' presented a formidable threat to the English in the era of the rebel hero William (Braveheart) Wallace. He paralysed their shipping, supported the famous Scots insurgents Robert and Edward Bruce against them, launched a devastating raid on the Welsh port of Holyhead, and – most famously – sailed many miles inland into the heartland of Ulster to rescue a beleaguered Scots army that had become hopelessly stranded and pinned down by its English enemies in 1315. In short, he more than lived up to the annalists' description of 'a perpetrator of depredations on the sea'.

In an age where people were illiterate in multiple languages, it's no surprise that Tom had a host of aliases. To the Scottish, and to the townsfolk in present-day Portrush who still celebrate him, he is known as *Tavish Dhu* – Scots Gaelic for 'Black Tom'. In contemporary records, he is 'Thomas of Down' or 'Thomas of *Dun*'. At least two experts have interpreted this to mean that he may have come from Downpatrick (once called *Dún*, or *Duno*) in south County Down. Later, he was to become so closely associated with the Scots cause that he was referred to as a Scottish pirate, but in an age when communities in Ireland and Scotland were tightly intermarried and interlinked, the distinction between nationalities was not very clear-cut.

Little is known of Black Tom's childhood and background. In true Hollywood style, he simply bursts into the pages of history as a fully formed pirate, harassing and seizing merchant ships off the northeast of Ireland, to the great enragement of local aristocrats.

The early 1300s were a boom time for pirates in Irish waters. Unchallenged by any co-ordinated royal navy, they roamed free in their *birlinns* – single-masted, clinker-built, oar-driven galleys that were modelled on the Viking longships and had the same advantages of speed, sturdiness and adaptability.

Black Tom might have remained as just one more small-time pirate if he hadn't become swept up in the turmoil of Scotland's First War of Independence. This early struggle for national identity reached its peak of success against King Edward II of England in 1314, at Bannockburn Stream near Stirling Castle. Here, as every modern rugby fan knows, the Scots rebels defeated 'proud Edward's army'. Flexing his muscles after his victory, the Scots leader Robert Bruce decided to expand westwards, and despatched his brother Edward Bruce to conquer Ireland. His motives are still debated, but he probably wanted to distract his enemies and, in the longer term, to create an armed alliance of Scots, Irish and Welsh. He had the support of one powerful Irish king.

It was a sound plan, but they were short on logistics. How were they to spirit thousands of troops from Scotland to Antrim? That's where Black Tom came in. He offered to carry the troops in his four vessels, which some say were stolen from the English. And so, in April 1315, some 6,000 soldiers landed safely on the Antrim shore. They bulldozed over the opposition and set up their base at Carrickfergus. Edward Bruce declared himself King of Ireland, and blazed a trail of destruction southwards to Dundalk. At this stage, he posed a real threat to England's only secure zone – Dublin and the Pale. The English and their Irish allies hit back with a two-pronged counter-offensive. Edward Bruce was forced back northwards and westwards to Coleraine, where he crossed the River Bann, the north's largest river, and destroyed the only bridge behind him.

The Scots army halted, eyeballing their enemies across this wide and unfordable river, and took stock of their position. They were now on the western side of this natural boundary, cut off from their base at Carrickfergus on the east coast. To their rear, further west, lay another river, the Foyle. Their only hope lay in securing help from local Irish chieftains.

The commander of the English troops, the Earl of Ulster, was equally stymied. According to one Irish annalist, he was 'waiting for the water level to fall, or a shortage of food among his foes. One of these came about … in the Scottish camp four quarters of a sheep fetched two shillings sterling.' Both armies took out their frustration on the landscape. They left 'neither wood nor lea nor corn nor crop nor steading nor barn nor church, but fired and burned them all,' another annalist recorded.

Edward Bruce approached a local chieftain named O'Dempsey, a nominal ally, who promised to provide a safe campsite with plenty of food. 'In a very fair place, down by a burn [stream], O'Dempsey told them to make camp, and said he would go to get his men to bring them victuals,' wrote the contemporary chronicler John Barbour. 'He didn't stay any longer than he had to, because in his heart he was betraying them.'

Contrary to his pledge to provide food, the Irish chief withheld supplies until Bruce's exhausted troops were further worn down by hunger. The final stage of O'Dempsey's betrayal was the most dramatic. The 'very fair place' he had provided as a campsite was actually a flood zone. The small stream had originally been a lake, its waters held back by a dam upstream. It was the work of a few minutes for O'Dempsey's men to remove the water barrier in the middle of the night and to inundate the Scottish base.

The sleeping Scots didn't know what hit them as a torrent of icy water swept through their tents. 'The false traitor … let the water out in the night,' writes Barbour. 'The deluge came down on Sir Edward's men with such mighty force that they were in peril of drowning. Before they knew what was happening, they were afloat in water.'

The Scots struggled and swam to the surface, coughing and spluttering, frantically throwing off their heavy armour to prevent it dragging them down to their deaths. 'They had a lot of trouble in escaping,' Barbour wrote. 'Although they lost their armour, they kept their lives through the grace of God.' He added with black humour that the Irish chieftain had kept his promise to feed them, because they had been well filled up … with water.

The beleaguered Scots were now not only tired and hungry, but also 'good and wet' and deprived of shelter. Their situation seemed hopeless. 'They were in great distress,' wrote Barbour, 'for not only did they have no meat, but they were also stranded between two impassable rivers. The Bann, an arm of the sea, could not be forded even by men on horseback. It lay between them and [their base in] Ulster.'

A later poet colourfully described their predicament, aptly comparing the Scots to fish that had been lured into a backwater and were awaiting certain slaughter. '[They] were entrapped in a deep swampy fen,' he wrote, 'like a huge salmon shoal in the fisher's close den'.

Just when all seemed lost, four sails appeared on the horizon of the Bann estuary. It was the pirate Black Tom, who had learned of their dire predicament and had taken the enormous risk of sailing inland to rescue his beleaguered comrades.

We can imagine the lusty cheers from the weary soldiers as the Irish freebooter carefully negotiated his four vessels through the waterlogged fen, mooring as close as he dared to the stranded army. 'They knew him well,' Barbour recalled, 'and were greatly heartened.'

Black Tom ferried the Scotsmen in stages across the Bann until they were able to satisfy their hunger with 'victuals and meat enough' and enjoy the sensation of having sound, dry land under their feet.

The poet was not so impressed. 'Thomas of Down, that "strong theefe" of the sea, ploughed the Bann with his ships and set them all free,' he wrote. 'Would that nine maids with salt foam for their vest, had him clasped with his crew to their cold marble breast.'

The beauty of the rescue was that it had all been done stealthily – as far as their enemies knew, they were still safely stranded across the river. They were able to 'relax and have good cheer' as they recuperated. Black Tom's audacious rescue restored their good spirits as well as their good health, and before long, they were able to turn the tables on their enemies. They intercepted a supply column that was carrying victuals to the English. By swapping clothes with the supply unit, they were able to ride unchallenged into the heart of the English camp, where they launched straight into an attack and slaughtered 1,000 men. The English swore vengeance, but when they regrouped and rode to assault what they believed was the Scottish camp – Bruce had left banners flying to deceive them – they rode straight into an ambush from a concealed Scots force.

This defeat at Connor, County Antrim, in September 1315 was one of the greatest setbacks suffered by English forces in Ireland, and none of it would have been possible but for the bravery and brass neck of Thomas of Down and his piratical band of 'scummers of the sea'.

Emboldened by his success and by the growing legend surrounding him, Black Tom began to behave less like a pirate and more like an admiral of an unofficial Scots insurgent navy. As he relentlessly ravaged their shipping, the exasperated English described him as 'a perpetrator of depredations', 'a strong thief' and 'a cruel pirate'. Barbour's contemptuous term 'scummer of the sea' – written later that same century – would have reflected the views of many long-suffering merchants and sea captains.

In September 1315, Black Tom stunned the English authorities by launching a lightning raid on the Welsh port of Holyhead. His flotilla of four warships – one of them commanded by another Irish pirate – seized a valuable ship named the *James*. The vessel's aggrieved captain had his suspicions about the ease with which Black Tom had gained access to the harbour, and the lack of any retaliation, and suspected that the raid was an inside job involving a corrupt local official.

We can get some idea of the seriousness of the threat posed by Black Tom from an incident later that year. When a top English general sailed to Ireland, he had to be protected by a small army 'because Thomas Dun and divers other enemies ... are doing much mischief and daily perpetrate evil'.

Their tormentor continued his ravages at sea for two more years, until the English King, Edward II, was forced into action. He commandeered a number of merchant ships in Ireland and ordered their unfortunate captains to scour the seas for Black Tom. Meanwhile, he instructed his shipbuilders to create what amounted to a super-ship, a 140-oar galley that outclassed by far anything the pirates could muster.

On 2 July, Thomas of Down met his match when he came up against a fellow Irishman, an expert naval strategist named John of Athy. The two veteran seamen clashed in a decisive battle, in which more than three dozen pirates were killed before the notorious Black Tom was finally captured. The seventeenth-century historian William Camden recorded that Thomas, 'a resolute pirate, was taken in a sea fight by the Lord John de Athy, and 40 of his men or thereabouts cut off; and his head was brought by him to Dublin'. The officer responsible for the capture was hailed as a hero and given a substantial reward.

There was major rejoicing in Dublin, and in ports on both sides of the Irish Sea, when the arch-pirate's severed head was ferried to the Irish capital and, presumably, displayed to the public in the customary manner. His career as a pirate had been quite spectacular, and his audacious naval operations had kept the English Navy cowed for more than three years, allowing his Scots allies to penetrate deep into Ireland's heartland and come close to conquering the island.

In the end, the Scots were driven out of Ireland not by military force, but by horrendous weather and the dreadful famine that resulted. When Edward Bruce was killed in battle in 1318, and his body quartered, the Scots' military invasion was essentially over.

Black Tom has been largely forgotten today – except in Portrush, near the scene of his dramatic river rescue, where he continues to be remembered and celebrated under his Scots name of *Tavish Dhu*. Local legend claims that his base was on the Skerries, a small group of seventeen islands off Portrush. One writer recorded in 1923: 'The islet furthest east is called Island Dubh. It is probable that it was named after Tavish Dubh, a pirate who once frequented the Skerries, and died on his ship here, and was buried on the island, but the place of his grave is unknown.'

This leaves a lot of scope for fanciful speculation. What if the English tale of Black Tom's capture had been propaganda? What if the real Tom escaped to the Skerries and maintained a low profile until he died a natural death and was buried on these desolate islets? And above all, what if local tradition is correct and he buried his treasure – 'three bullock skins of silver' according to one local website – alongside him? Bullocks or not, the story lives on.

Whatever happened, and wherever he is buried, Black Tom's ghost is probably looking down on it all, quite happy that his legend is still being celebrated after seven centuries.

15

PIRATE PILGRIMAGE THE FIFTEENTH

Carrickfergus

From Dunluce, I continue along the coast to Ballycastle, stopping off at the Giant's Causeway – nothing to do with pirates, you understand, but you just have to – before heading southeast along one of the world's most scenic drives towards Carrickfergus. I've driven the famous Antrim Coast Road so often, I could almost do it with my eyes closed, but with such corkscrewing hills and dizzying drops, it wouldn't be advisable.

After passing agreeable little villages like Cushendall, Carnlough and Glenarm, I reach the ancient port of Carrickfergus. The sun has reappeared, and the reflected light off the wavelets glitters like a million diamonds, as I drive towards the harbour and the iconic Norman castle that has dominated this shoreline for more than eight centuries.

Carrickfergus, lying some eleven miles from Belfast, once overshadowed its larger neighbour. Today, it is a busy commuter town, and is perhaps best known from the folk song 'Carrickfergus' – although whether the homesick emigrant was referring to this town or to an area near Kilkenny is hotly debated among those who hotly debate such things.

I gaze out into the waters of the harbour, thinking about the night of 21 April 1778, when an American 'privateer' captain attempted a daring midnight attack on the British warship *Drake* under the very shadow of the

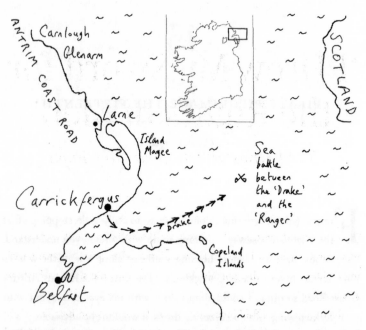

well-fortified castle and its big guns. Here's how the incident was described in the shipping-news section of one Irish newspaper, before the identity of the attacker became known:

'On Monday last a vessel supposed to be an American privateer of between 200–300 tons entered [Carrickfergus] harbour ... she sailed around the *Drake* sloop of war and sailed off again. A gun was fired by the sloop in consequence of her hail not being returned.'

The full story of this abortive attack was much more dramatic than that, and we can tell it in the words of the American captain who didn't give up at that point, but persisted until he finally ran the *Drake* to ground. The attack ship was called the *Ranger* ... and the captain's name was John Paul Jones.

'I Drew My Sword for the Rights of Men'

The Extraordinary John Paul Jones

It was after midnight, and the air was sharp with frost. The strengthening west wind cut like a knife, and the darkened skies were pregnant with impending snow as the gunship *Ranger* stole into the sleeping harbour at Carrickfergus.

Its captain, John Paul Jones, had never planned to be in Belfast Lough: his aim had been to launch a land raid on England's west coast. But he had been frustrated by an onshore wind, so instead he had crossed the channel to try his luck in Ireland. Just outside Carrickfergus Harbour, he signalled for a pilot to guide him in, just as any regular merchant ship would have done. He didn't really want a pilot. He wanted information.

He was soon rewarded by the sight of a fishing boat emerging from the darkness towards him. It was manned by half a dozen fishermen, who knew these waters intimately. They were able to tell him that the vessel riding at the harbour entrance was the heavily armed British naval patrol ship *Drake*.

John Paul Jones had not expected such luck. His task was to capture British ships, and in this case he had the rare advantage of surprise. He decided to sneak up on the *Drake*'s bow and trap her by sailing directly over her anchor cable. The British captain would probably react by cutting the cable, but by that stage the *Ranger* would be close enough to hurl grappling irons on board and close in. His musketeers would give covering fire as their Revolutionary comrades stormed on board.

He gave the order to drop anchor beside the *Drake*, but the action was delayed by a few crucial seconds. (In one version of events, Jones blames his mate for having 'drunk too much brandy'.) At the precise moment the anchor took hold, the wind freshened and swung the *Ranger* around, so that instead of approaching the *Drake's* forepeak, it ended up nearly alongside the target vessel, hopelessly exposed to half a dozen of its twenty big guns. For a few terrifying moments, everyone on the *Ranger* held his breath, awaiting the roar of cannon. But aboard the *Drake*, there was not a stir. John Paul Jones quietly cut his own anchor cable to free the *Ranger*, and slipped out of the harbour, determined to circle, return and try again.

It was not to be. The wind escalated into a howling gale, and the *Ranger* hurtled out into the open lough. 'I with difficulty weathered the [Copeland Islands] lighthouse on the lee side of the Lough as the gale increased,' he wrote.

However, John Paul Jones was not a man who gave up at the first setback. He would capture the *Drake*, he swore to himself. It just wouldn't be tonight.

John Paul Jones was a fascinating figure. Today, if you do an internet search on his name, you'll probably get results for the similarly named bass player with Led Zeppelin. This is hardly fair, because the two men have little in common. One of them was a hellraiser who changed his commonplace name to 'John Paul Jones' in order to sound grander; who was lusted after by an army of devoted female fans; and who toured England in the 'seventies, trashing every venue, to a soundtrack of deafening, destructive noise. And the other, of course, played bass on 'Stairway to Heaven'.

The naval commander John Paul Jones was born in Kirkcudbright, Scotland, in July 1747, and began life as plain 'John Paul'. (Much later, he added the 'Jones' part as a patronymic – Jones meaning 'John's son' – to give his name a classical ring.) From his earliest childhood, he was hoisting flags on imaginary vessels and barking orders to a fantasy crew. After learning about manoeuvring techniques from sailors on shore leave, the youngster would stand on the shoreline shouting out instructions – correct ones – to vessels entering the Solway Firth. By age twelve, he had already travelled to America as an apprentice on a merchant ship, and by seventeen he was Third Mate on a slaving vessel. Two years later, he was forced to take command of a ship after both its officers died of fever, and handled that job so well that he soon became a captain in his own right.

John Paul Jones, the fascinatingly complex character who is now revered as a founder of the American Navy. But when he chalked up his game-changing victory over the British naval ship *Drake* off the Copeland Islands, he thought of himself more as a freedom fighter without national ties.

Jones was a harsh disciplinarian, and was once arrested for the murder of a crewman. Although he was acquitted, the scandal affected his career and he retired as a landlubber in Virginia. But when the Revolutionary War erupted, he wrote to Thomas Jefferson asking for a commission, and in 1775, became a lieutenant in the fledgling US Navy. Two years later, after capturing several British ships off the Americas, he was despatched to France in the newly built *Ranger*, and was instructed by the US consul Benjamin Franklin to harass the enemy in the Irish Sea. Which is why he ended up in Carrickfergus.

Now, purists will argue that Jones, as a commissioned US officer and a father of the American Navy, should not be included in a book about pirates and privateers. They have a point. Although the English regarded him at the time as 'a privateer', and even as 'a plunderer, a pirate, cruel and unprincipled', he had actually been appointed as First Lieutenant by the US Congress three years beforehand. However, things were not nearly as clear-cut in 1778 as they appear in historical hindsight. The crew of the *Ranger* included many civilian volunteers, who had been lured by the promise that the expedition would 'make their fortunes'. Jones's restless seamen certainly behaved more like privateers than disciplined Navy men: they demanded a democratic say in decisions, and insisted on plundering treasure as the only way they could be certain of being paid. For his part, Jones thought of himself more as an international freedom-fighter, without national ties, than an American officer. 'Though I have drawn my sword in the present generous struggle for the rights of men, yet I am not in arms as an American,' he wrote just after the Carrickfergus incident. '… I profess myself a citizen of the world, totally unfettered by the little, mean distinctions of climate or of country.' The reality was that the early American Navy was of necessity an ad hoc organisation, relying heavily on privateers for help in Europe. There were many grey areas among the patriotic red, white and blue.

Having said all that, Jones is rightly revered today as a pioneer of the American Navy: the first to raise the Grand Union flag on a warship, and the first to have the flag recognised with a gun salute by a foreign power. He was highly praised for his courage and daring. Once, when he was coming off worse in a sea battle and the enemy called upon him to surrender, he famously replied: 'I have not yet begun to fight!'

Portraits show a pale man with a long nose, arched eyebrows, and a misleadingly gentle appearance: he could easily be taken for a small-town lawyer who volunteers for Sunday School on weekends. 'He appeared to be very well bred, and a man of few words,' wrote one witness. Another described him in Paris in 1780, surrounded by a fan club of breathless female admirers, 'who are all wild for love of him, as he for them'. He was described as 'a smart man of 36 … an extraordinary genius, a poet as well as a hero'. Asked to compose a poem on the spot, Jones tossed off a verse beginning:

Insulted, freedom bled; I felt her cause
And drew my sword to vindicate her laws.

In the thick of action, he cut a totally different figure. One account depicts him in the heat of battle, 'dressed in a short jacket and long trousers, with about twelve charged pistols slung in a belt around his middle, with a cutlass in his hand'. The writer claims he shot seven of his crewmen for deserting their posts.

It was in this guise, as the fearless sea warrior, that he finally caught up with his nemesis in Belfast Lough, three days after his humiliation in Carrickfergus. And this time, he swore, he would not let the *Drake* escape.

The officer in charge of the *Drake*, Captain Burdon, had known better days. He was advanced in years and nearing the end of his naval career. At this particular time, he was 'very ill' and relied heavily upon his officers. Unfortunately, two of them had just died, and a newly appointed lieutenant had just been drafted in as an emergency replacement. 'No time could have been so unfortunate,' lamented one English report.

Despite these drawbacks, there was a general agreement that the powerful naval vessel would soon capture and humiliate this cheeky American upstart called the *Ranger*. The *Drake*, which had just taken on soldiers and had impressed 'volunteers' from Belfast, comfortably outmanned Jones's ship. So many people wanted to see the *Ranger* get its come-uppance that pleasure boats were already cruising Belfast Lough, packed with sightseers who wanted a close-up seat for the big event.

Since that night in Carrickfergus, Jones had ridden the gale across the channel to Whitehaven on the English coast, where he'd raided the port at midnight in an attempt to torch the hundreds of ships at anchor there. Although he burned only one vessel, his audacity in spiking and disabling the port's thirty-six defence guns had humiliated the British Navy and exposed the coast's vulnerability. The result was widespread panic – some

'I drew my sword for the rights of men': John Paul Jones, poet and patriot.

citizens were said to have gone almost insane with terror – and an instant quadrupling of insurance costs. Meanwhile, Jones had landed in Scotland, where he attempted to kidnap the Earl of Selkirk. The Earl was not at home, and the raiders found themselves dealing with the nobleman's beautiful and defiant young wife. Later, Jones would write to Lady Selkirk, explaining the purity of his motives and asking for her help in ending the war, 'as the feelings of your gentle bosom cannot but be congenial to mine'. After hostilities had ended, he would personally repurchase and return some silverware that his men had stolen from her.

Unseasonal snow lay deep across Scotland, England and Ireland 'as far as the eye could see', as Jones re-crossed the channel to Belfast Lough on 24 April, to hunt out his quarry the *Drake*. He was closing in on Carrickfergus when he saw the navy ship dispatch a small boat to check him out. He was in luck – the English hadn't yet recognised him. Jones turned his back on the *Drake* in order to prolong the mystery. The British officer boarded what he thought was a merchant ship, and was 'greatly surprised to find himself a prisoner'. When Jones disclosed his identity, the officer told him they had retrieved the anchor that he had lost at Carrickfergus.

As alarm fires were lit all along the coast of the lough, Jones found his movements hampered by five boatloads of sightseers, all 'led by curiosity to see an engagement'. But when the *Drake* – still unaware of the *Ranger*'s identity – sailed out from harbour to investigate, the spectators wisely retreated.

'What ship are you?' the *Drake* hailed as it drew close.

'The American Continental ship *Ranger*,' Jones replied, hoisting the starry flag. 'We are waiting for you. It is one hour from sunset, and time to begin.'

He underlined the point with a blast of cannon fire. The *Drake* came alongside and shot back at close quarters. 'The action was warm, close and obstinate,' Jones reported later.

The two ships were closely matched in firepower, with the *Ranger*'s eighteen guns facing the *Drake*'s twenty guns, but the Americans were better marksmen. 'Every shot told, and they gave the *Drake* three broadsides for [every] two,' Jones reported. 'The result of the action was due entirely to the superb gunnery of my crew ... The enemy's fire was spirited, but, for a King's Ship, very ineffective.' In contrast, the *Ranger*'s quartergunner – the wonderfully named Owen Starbuck from Nantucket – kept a cool head and forensically timed his shots to strike the *Drake* under the waterline each time the British ship's underbelly was exposed by the rolling sea.

As the two sea-giants swung at each other, grappling and blasting and cursing, the roar of cannon was joined by the sound of the cracking and splintering of the *Drake*'s masts. The American sharpshooters had skilfully demolished the vital yards and gaffs that controlled the sails. The canvas itself was shot to ribbons, with the main sails cut away and the jib trailing into the water. 'The *Drake* was almost wrecked,' Jones reported, '... [but] it was not my policy to sink the *Drake* ... I wished to take her alive.' Soon the British ship was totally disabled. 'The *Drake* was unmanageable,' says one English report, 'so that the privateer raked her as she pleased.'

—Strike! yelled the Americans, in the classic demand for a surrender.

—I never will, Captain Burdon hollered back from the bloodstained decks of the *Drake*.

Seconds later, a musket ball killed him on the spot. His new lieutenant took over, but he, too, was mortally wounded. Exactly one minute after the captain's death – and sixty-five minutes after the first shot in the engagement – the crippled *Drake* was forced to surrender. It had sustained 127 gunshot holes, including thirty-six below the waterline. While the *Ranger* had lost only three men, the *Drake* had already lost nineteen, including her captain and lieutenant. Jones buried them at sea with full honours. He later regretted the deaths of such brave men in this 'dreadful carnage'.

Emergency repairs enabled the captured *Drake* to be escorted safely to France. Before he left Belfast Lough, however, Jones wanted to settle with the six fishermen he had seized at Carrickfergus on the first night. Their boat had sunk in the bad weather, leaving them without any means of livelihood. '[I gave] them the necessary sum to purchase everything new,' Jones reported, '… and a good boat to transport themselves ashore.' The fishermen paid tribute to their captor with three loud cheers as they rowed away.

When the *Drake* finally arrived in Brest, it caused a sensation. Although it was a rich prize in itself, the shot-blasted vessel was also a potent symbol of the Americans' growing naval prowess. The myth of British naval invincibility had been shattered, just as dramatically as the pulverised spars and rigging on her once-glorious fighting ship.

As one writer put it: 'Paul Jones had done the impossible, and had lived to tell the tale … His fame was unassailable: he had earned for himself a permanent place in the history of France and of the world.'

16

PIRATE PILGRIMAGE THE SIXTEENTH

Belfast, Holywood, Bangor, Donaghadee

Jonathan Swift's Sleeping Giant still dozes above Belfast as I revisit the city that used to be my home, a few decades and a peace process ago. Cave Hill, the basalt rock formation that has been compared to a slumbering colossus, is supposedly the feature that inspired Swift to dream up the best-known image from his fantasy *Gulliver's Travels*. When I lived there during the worst of the Troubles, Belfast did indeed seem like a sleeping giant, a heroic city nightmarishly tied down by tiny, small-minded figures with guns. But when peace came and Belfast finally awoke to find its true potential, there was no holding it back.

From the top of Cave Hill, you are rewarded with a unique, bird's-eye view of the wide, muddy estuary that the ancients named Calf Lough, the Elizabethans relabelled as Carrickfergus Bay, and the modern world knows as Belfast Lough. To your left is the Antrim coast, and to your right, County Down. Carrickfergus, on the Antrim shore, used to be the Lough's main harbour. Belfast, where the River Lagan flowed sluggishly into the estuary and created what was then a messy sea-swamp of mudflats and slobland, was for many centuries not worth the effort for shipping. Vessels had to anchor a few miles out from Belfast, at a deeper spot near Holywood known as the Pool of Garmoyle, and offload their cargoes into barges. It wasn't until the Victorian era that a proper channel was gouged out through the mudflats.

The success of its linen industry in the 1700s made Belfast shipping a prime target for pirates. 'This place is full of privateers, the greater part of their crews English and Irish,' one disgruntled captain was quoted in the *Belfast News Letter* in 1781. 'They hope to make their fortunes by taking some of our linen ships.'

Belfast's mayor became so frustrated that he wrote to Parliament in passive-aggressive terms that stopped just short of attacking the King: 'When we see our coasts insulted and our trade plundered by pirates and hostile privateers, we lament that the present situation ... [has] incapacitated our Gracious Sovereign from affording his faithful subjects that protection which we are confident he wishes to grant.'

Belfast Lough is extraordinarily rich in tales of buccaneering and freebooting. So follow me as I do a piratical pilgrimage around the southern shore of the estuary, from Belfast itself, through Holywood and Bangor, to Donaghadee at its extreme eastern entrance. And first, to whet your appetite, a remarkable true story involving a Belfast ship-boy and his dramatic escape from his pirate captors off the coast of Virginia.

Pirates and Belfast Lough

The astonishing story of young Robert McClelland's spectacular escape from pirate captivity in 1778 reads like something from a *Boys' Own* comic, with two youngsters daringly turning the tables on the buccaneers who'd seized them. While Robert Louis Stevenson might have got away with this sort of tale in fiction, any other writer would firmly be told by his editors to tone down his imagination. Yet this particular story happens to be true: it was recorded in the shipping-news columns of several Irish and English newspapers in July that year.

That March, while still a boy, Robert McClelland from Belfast signed up with a Captain Campbell for a voyage to the West Indies aboard a merchant vessel called the *Loyalty*. The *Loyalty*, registered here in Belfast, was a two-masted, square-rigged ship of the type known as a 'brig'. We're not told whether this was Robert's first sea trip, but during the voyage he wrote letters home to his mother, telling her of his experiences in the exotic Caribbean.

It was just another sailing day, and Robert was no doubt taking his turn at the dozens of mundane jobs assigned to young lads at sea, when a strange ship appeared on the horizon. The veterans on board rapidly identified her as a French privateer.

After carefully checking out their victim, the privateers closed in and ordered Captain Campbell to surrender. Outnumbered, he had no choice but to capitulate. The pirates adopted the usual routine of removing the Belfast crew to the French ship and installing their own 'prize crew' of thirteen men on the *Loyalty*. However, they were short on space and didn't think it worthwhile to remove Robert McClelland and another boy, Robert Horseman.

Both ships headed for the safety of the French colony of Martinique in the Lesser Antilles. On board the *Loyalty*, the thirteen Frenchmen relaxed their guard. After a long day's sailing, they convinced themselves that they were owed a drink or two to celebrate their success.

They checked out the captain's cabin and found a treasure trove of hard liquor. Bottles were passed around. One cry of '*à votre santé!*' led to another, and the party roared on until late that night. By midnight, the two young Roberts were the only sober people on board.

At dawn next morning – day two after the capture – the two boys looked around them and saw only semi-comatose and hungover wretches. They glanced at each other and nodded. It was now or never. They grabbed a couple of unguarded weapons, primed them to fire and ordered those Frenchmen still on deck to join their suffering comrades down below. Once the last privateer had gone down, they slammed the hatch and locked it.

'The French sailors on board had intoxicated themselves with the captain's wine,' Robert McClelland later wrote to his mother. '[We] had the boldness to seize the arms and ordered the French under hatches, which they submitted to.'

The boys could not afford to waste time in self-congratulation. They knew that the pirates would soon rouse their sleeping comrades and smash their way through the hatch. They took control of the sails and, between them summoning up all the skills they'd learned since leaving Belfast, steered towards a mystery ship they spotted, far off on the horizon.

They were lucky. The ship turned out to be another privateer, but this time a British one from Antigua. The British privateers put their own crew on board the *Loyalty*, clapped the still-hungover Frenchmen in irons, and changed course for their own base in the Leeward Islands. On 30 March, the *Loyalty* arrived safe and sound in friendly territory, to be joined three days later by the captain and the rest of the hands. (Presumably they had been ransomed.) The thirteen Frenchmen were treated to a spell of involuntary rehab in an Antiguan jailhouse.

Captain Campbell must have done a double-take when he saw the *Loyalty*, the vessel he'd given up for lost, securely anchored and safe. I like to think – though in that heartless day and age it's by no means certain – that he rewarded the two courageous youngsters for saving his ship and his cargo. I would bet, too, that when the news broke back home, Mrs McClelland was the proudest mother in Belfast.

I drive past the gantries of the shipyard that built many a sound and seaworthy vessel, but which these days, perversely, is most famous for the ill-fated *Titanic*. The Lagan waterfront would have been unrecognisable three centuries ago. You would have to mentally erase nearly all of its familiar features, including most of the riverside quays and the entire Titanic Quarter. Instead, you had a wide, sluggish, heavily silted river, passable by a ford at low tide.

Imagine the scene in late February 1758, when a merchant ship named the *Blakeney* sailed to Belfast, carrying another strange tale of pirate attack and freedom regained. She was a snow, a square-rigged vessel with two principal masts, and an auxiliary third mast right behind the mainmast. The *Blakeney*'s master, William Smith, told the authorities that he had been sailing from Philadelphia with a cargo of flax seed for the linen industry, when a French privateer swooped. With ten carriage guns, the aggressor outgunned the Blakeney, so the captain was forced to surrender. A prize crew of ten Frenchmen took over the ship. '[They] plundered the vessel,' reported the *Belfast News Letter*, '… and took Captain Smith aboard the privateer with all his hands except James McKesnie the mate, the carpenter, and three small boys.'

On 11 December 1757, twelve days after the attack, a squall struck in the mid-Atlantic, and six of the French crew were forced to climb high on the rigging to adjust the topsail. Taking advantage of this unique opportunity, McKesnie and the carpenter attacked the two privateers who were guarding them in the cabin, and seized their guns. They tied up the two guards, and surprised the remaining two Frenchmen – the captain and the helmsman – who were on the quarterdeck, lost in concentration as they navigated the heaving, bucking ship through the storm. '[All this] was effected before any of the rest were got down from the shrouds,' reported the *Shipping News*. 'They took these one by one and secured them in the hatchway.'

The Irish crew were back in charge, but they still faced a battle against the Atlantic weather. An enormous wave swept over the *Blakeney*, snapping off every mast 'except the stump of the top foremast,' the report says. Heroically, the men fought their way through the gales with a jury-rig on their single remaining half-mast. It wasn't until 29 January, nearly fifty days after their escape, that they limped into Lewis in the Hebrides, where they were able to carry out rudimentary repairs and continue their journey.

Amazingly, all the crew – including the three boys – seem to have made it home safe and sound. The privateers were not so fortunate. 'Seven of the Frenchmen are dead,' the report ends flatly, without further explanation, '[and] the other three are now on board.'

The fatalistic comment of the captor to the captive: 'It is the fortune of war: today for you, tomorrow for me,' crops up again and again in pirate narratives. Reading the reports, you can understand why. Ships were regularly taken, captured back, and sometimes even retaken.

Belfast ships were no exception. An early victim of the American Revolutionary War was the snow *Jenny*, which sailed into its home port at the mouth of the Lagan in December 1776, after a heart-stopping journey from Barbados. The captain, William McNeilly, had been carrying a cargo of rum from the West Indies to Ireland, but ended up instead in Long Island, New York. The *Jenny* was intercepted by privateers from the infant nation of the USA, which had declared independence only a few months earlier. The attackers removed nearly all the crew and posted their own men on board. They set course for Providence, Rhode Island, but on the way they encountered a Royal Navy frigate, which had no difficulty in retaking the ship. Captain McNeilly and a young boy who had also been allowed to remain on the *Jenny* were rescued, and the rum-run finally went ahead as planned.

In May 1781, another Belfast ship, the *Eleanor*, set sail for Barbados from Cobh in Cork, only to be captured by the US privateer *Junius Brutus* just off Clear Island. The master was put into a small boat with three other captive captains, and released just off Crookhaven.

The Belfast captain whose sloop *Douglas* was captured by the Salem privateer *Oliver Cromwell* in 1777, was luckier. 'The privateer plundered him of his money, sails and rigging,' reported the *News Letter*, 'and afterwards gave the sloop to the captain on condition that he would land sixteen prisoners in some English or Irish port.'

American privateers often had a soft spot for the Irish. In 1776, Captain Weekes of the privateer *Surprisal* seized the Belfast ship *Duchess of Leinster* on its way from Antigua to Dublin. Its master, Captain Carthrew, was summoned on board Weekes's ship.

—Your ship is from Ireland? Weekes asked.

—Yes.

—And your cargo of rum is Irish property?

—It is.

Weekes tossed the papers back to his captive.

—On your way, he said. We will not distress the Irish, because we know the Irish would not distress us. Have a safe passage home.

Following the southern coast of Belfast Lough eastwards, I pause briefly in the village of Holywood (spelled with one L, because it's one L of a town) to break for coffee in a café near its unique central maypole. Historic Holywood, built around a seventh-century abbey, is the only town in Ireland to maintain a maypole, in a tradition dating back to the 1600s. Today, it is best known as the birthplace of golfer Rory McIlroy. But it has a special place in my heart, because it is the town where I met, romanced and married my wife.

It also warrants an entry in the history of piracy because one of its townspeople, a mariner named John Brown, had the experience of being captured by Spanish privateers, and then recaptured by British freebooters. That in itself was not so unusual. What makes this story special was that Brown set off in an empty ship and ended up in a *full* one, laden down with stolen pirate booty. This unexpected bonanza had a downside, as Brown was immediately suspected of having been a pirate himself.

According to *The Deposition of John Brown of Holywood*, he was hired by a Larne captain to serve as first mate aboard the ship *Apollo*, bound for Virginia, in the spring of 1745. The vessel, owned by Scots merchant Richard Oswald, set sail from Belfast Lough in March, empty except for ballast. By 16 June, the vessel was just forty miles from its destination when it was attacked and overwhelmed by Spanish privateers in a fast, highly manoeuvrable snow, impressively named *Nuestra Señora de los Dolores y de las Animas* (Our Lady of Sorrows and Souls). With eighty fighting men on board, the Spaniards easily outnumbered the Irish mariners.

'The commander of the privateer … brought over into his own vessel the master and all the men [of our ship] except [myself] and a boy,' Brown told his suspicious interrogators later. '[He] put on board her sixteen mariners.'

It turned out that a few days earlier, the Spaniards had taken and ransacked an English merchant ship, and were laden down with the spoils. The Spanish captain, Don Carlos Francisco de Bissava, decided to offload a large portion of his haul into his empty captive ship *Apollo*, before heading for a friendly port in Caracas.

British and Spanish ships clash during the wars of the 1700s. This period was to be the backdrop to some of the most colourful pirate tales featuring ships from Belfast.

For four days, Brown and the boy watched as the Spanish privateers passed the booty across and stowed it in the hold, until the formerly empty ship was laden deep in the water. The task completed, both ships set course for Venezuela. They sailed southward for nearly four weeks, with Brown continuing to work the decks.

Just east of Bermuda, they spotted an ominous vessel bearing down upon them. It turned out to be the English privateer *Trembleur* (Quaker), a high-speed Bermuda sloop with fourteen cannon and twenty swivel guns. The commander, a then-famous freebooter named Captain Obadiah Bowne, challenged the Spaniards, who surrendered without resistance, and so the whole process began all over again. The Spaniards were slammed in the brig, a dozen of Bowne's mariners took over, and the *Apollo* altered course for Pennsylvania. John Brown stayed on board, working as usual – his actual role had hardly changed throughout the entire affair.

The *Pennsylvania Gazette* recorded the arrival of the two ships in Philadelphia. 'Yesterday [31 July] arrived the privateer *Trembleur* ... and brought in the Scotch ship taken some weeks since by the Spanish privateer snow off the Capes of Virginia.'

The customs authorities searched *Apollo*'s hold and discovered the treasure trove of stolen goods. They were understandably suspicious of the Holywood man – after all, John Brown had been on deck alongside the Spanish privateers when he was captured. There was no reason to believe he had not been complicit.

Brown was no doubt sweating in the summer heat as he was put through the mill in a lengthy interrogation. In the end, however, his questioners were convinced by his detailed account of his appointment in Larne, and his experiences on board the *Apollo*, and he was released. I can find no record of what happened to the recaptured haul: the Spaniards could not remember the name of the vessel they'd taken it from, so it was probably never returned. And Brown himself presumably went home none the richer.

I leave Holywood behind and journey on to Bangor, a seaside resort that remained, for the most part, a haven of quietude throughout the thirty years of the Troubles. It wasn't always so peaceful. In the early 820s, the walls of its ancient abbey echoed to the sounds of Nordic war-cries, screams and crackling flames, as Viking sea-robbers made one of their most devastating and demoralising land raids. 'Bangor was spoiled and ransacked by the Danes, together with St Cowgall's church yard,' records one annalist. Its shrines were shattered, and its clerics brutally murdered. The following year, just as the monks were picking up the pieces and rebuilding their centre of learning, Norsemen swooped again to repeat the atrocity.

I continue further east. In the early 1600s, when Belfast was still a marshy backwater, one of the main seaports of Belfast Lough lay on its eastern approaches, on the southern shore. Donaghadee, famous today for the distinctive white lighthouse that gently ushers shipping towards the estuary, was one of the Lough's three main commercial harbours, and for a long time the main ferry link to Scotland. I have bittersweet memories of this town. It was here that I met my first girlfriend, and experienced all the soaring highs and devastating lows that romance and breakup bring at age seventeen. Later, in my twenties, I bought a part-share in a beautiful clinker-built boat – traditionally built, all shining brasswork and varnished teak. During a seemingly endless summer of Riviera-style heatwaves, I spent long, blissful days sailing around these waters, either fishing or swimming and picnicking at deserted coves in the nearby Copeland Islands. During this heatwave, I noticed that I had suddenly become very attractive to young women who had never seemed interested in me before. For some inexplicable reason, they went cool on me as soon as the temperatures did.

In those days I had no idea, as I dropped anchor in some clear bay on the Copeland Islands, that generations of pirates and privateers had done exactly the same thing. The Copelands had always made an ideal ambush point for buccaneers, targeting merchant vessels headed for Carrickfergus or Bangor.

For instance, one day in September 1779, Dublin privateer Patrick Dowlin (we met him in Pirate Pilgrimage the Fourth) lay in wait between these islands, preparing an ambush strategy that he had perfected off Wexford's Saltee Islands. When a Larne-bound sloop passed by, he streaked out and pounced on it. The ship was ransacked, and then ransomed back to its owners for 200 guineas.

Another ship, the *Industry*, arrived in Belfast the same day, its captain still smarting from an encounter with Dowlin somewhere between Strangford and Donaghadee. '[The victim] was boarded by a boat belonging to the American privateer *Black Prince* [with] 130 men,' reported the *Belfast News Letter*. 'After plundering [him] of ten guineas gold and some silver [and] all his spare wearing apparel, watch and buckles, he carried him aboard the privateer.' Dowlin later moved further north to target the seaport of Larne.

Dowlin dominated Belfast Lough, on and off, for the best part of three years. In 1780, the *News Letter* warned that Dowlin had returned in the American privateer *Black Princess*, 'master and crew mostly Irish'. And in 1781, when he captured the brig *Bell* on its way out from Belfast to Bristol, and ransomed the vessel for a jaw-dropping four thousand guineas, Dowlin had no fewer than seven other captured captains on board.

Donaghadee was also the last Irish port of call of Captain Henry Avery, whom we met in Pirate Pilgrimage the Thirteenth. You'll recall that the world's most wanted man arrived in Donegal from the Bahamas, laden down with gold and silver stolen from an Indian pilgrim ship. He vanished along with his lover Mrs Adams somewhere on the road from Dunfanaghy to Letterkenny, just in time to avoid betrayal by the double-dealing customs officer Maurice Cuttle.

I wander along Donaghadee's ancient High Street, and I know exactly where I'm headed: to one of my favourite pubs, the 400-year-old tavern that is today known as Grace Neill's, but for most of its venerable life was called the King's Arms. First opened in 1611, it is often described as the oldest pub in Northern Ireland. (In the Republic, a bar in Athlone beats it by some 700 years.) This was the main roadhouse for travellers in the 1600s, and it is probable that when Avery and Mrs Adams passed through in 1696, they sat in this very same dark, low-ceilinged room where I am seated right now, quenching their thirst and enjoying a break from the rigours of the road. Had they arrived just one year later, they could have encountered a dashing, moustachioed figure – Peter the Great of Russia, who stayed in this pub during a grand tour in 1697.

Avery and his mistress were about to take a boat for Scotland, on the final leg of their long, long journey from the Indian Ocean, via the Caribbean, back to Avery's home in England. His former seaman John Dan later testified that 'the wife of Adams, who was their quartermaster … was with Captain Avery at Donaghadee and … they went over [to Scotland] together'.

Once across the North Channel, Avery vanished, along with his money. John Dan never saw him again, although, by sheer coincidence, he did bump into Mrs Adams once, as she climbed on to a stagecoach in St Alban's. She said she was on her way to see Avery, but sensibly refused to tell Dan where he was.

Sensibly because, unlike most of his shipmates, Avery escaped the scaffold. There were many fanciful stories about his final years. One legend claims he established a pirate kingdom in Madagascar. However, his biographer Captain Charles Johnson pours cold water on that myth. Rather than living it up in Madagascar, he writes, Avery was 'starving in England'.

According to Johnson, Avery settled under another false name in the Devon town of Bideford. With no way of turning his fortune of plundered 'diamonds and vessels of gold' into hard cash, he was forced to rely on a shadowy group of Bristol merchants who agreed to take the jewellery and fence it, piece by piece. After a while, however, the flow of money dried up, until Avery was staring penury in the face. When he travelled to Bristol to confront the merchants, they laughed in his face.

—What are you going to do about it? they jeered. Go to the law?

The penniless pirate fled back to Ireland, where he was 'reduced to beggary', and had to work his passage back to Devon as a basic seaman. When he died shortly afterwards, there was not even enough money to buy him a coffin.

The white-collar criminals of Bristol had stolen the Great Mogul's treasure in much the same way as Avery had. Or, to use Johnson's apt phrase, 'The merchants [were] as good pirates at land as he was at sea.'

17

PIRATE PILGRIMAGE THE SEVENTEENTH

Rathlin, Inishowen, Howth, Strangford, Dublin

Through the mist and the salt spume on the ferry's cabin window, Rathlin Island looms up to starboard like some post-impressionist painting, its already muted colours soft-focused and fragmented into a thousand *pointilliste* brush-daubs. As we approach the pier at Church Bay on this drizzly day, Northern Ireland's only inhabited island seems strangely solemn, brooding and melancholy, as though hopelessly weighted down by its painful history.

Although it is only six miles long, Rathlin has experienced more than its fair share of bloodshed. Its position, two miles from the Antrim Coast and sixteen miles from Scotland, has made it an ideal stepping stone for armies headed in both directions. And like most stepping stones, it has been soundly and repeatedly trampled underfoot: atrocities were horrifically commonplace. I have returned here, to the far north coast of Antrim, because Rathlin was the scene of the first attack on Ireland by those sea raiders who were, far and away, the most ruthless, well-organised and successful pirates ever to operate in Ireland – the Vikings.

So buckle your seatbelts and fasten your lifejackets. This chapter will be a fast and bumpy trip, taking us from wind-battered Rathlin Island, and Inishowen in Donegal, through Strangford Lough in County Down, to the ancient Viking settlement of Dyflin (Dublin to you and me).

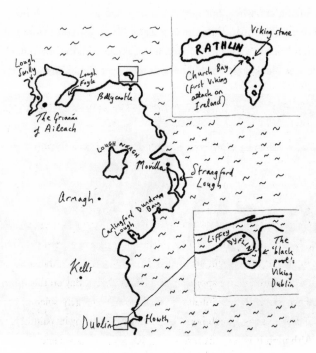

It'll be a hectic, high-speed race through the two centuries that have become known as the Viking Age. In this era of sheer, naked terror, thousands of civilians were murdered, robbed and enslaved by a new breed of sea robbers, whose advanced seafaring skills and ferociously efficient blitzkrieg tactics were matched only by their fearlessness in battle.

Today, as we disembark, Church Bay is serene and graceful in the diffused light. The only predator in sight is a grey seal, splashing around in the harbour in search of fish. To the left is a steep and rugged escarpment, with tumbling gorse. To the right, a harbour and a sandy beach.

We walk around for a while, along beautifully desolate boreens with vivid yellow gorse and rush-filled tarns, until a friendly local woman directs us to the monument I'm looking for. It is a remarkable standing stone from the Viking era, white, but speckled orange and green by centuries' growth of lichen, which marks the site of a major Norse graveyard from the ninth century. It seems a suitable touchstone to connect with the Scandinavian sea-raiders, as I look down the hill towards the target of their first Irish invasion.

A Viking fleet in action. From a base in Strangford Lough, County Down, the Norsemen tried to establish a colony in Ireland's northeast, but they met with stiff resistance from Irish chieftains, and were ultimately driven out of the area.

It was here at Church Bay, in 795 AD, that the Vikings first appeared in Ireland. The sheer speed of their seaborne attack took the monks at Rechru monastery completely by surprise. The wild-looking warriors dragged their longboats on to the sand and ran ashore, brandishing swords and battleaxes and howling war-cries. One Irish writer summed up the drama of a typical Viking raid: 'Foreign, barbarous cries were raised, and the noise of many war trumpets ... then many arrows were loosed ... and short spears, and finally they took to their heavy and hard-smiting swords.'

The attack would have followed a similar pattern to earlier church raids in England, where 'they miserably ravaged and pillaged everything ... they plundered all the treasures of the church. Some brethren they slew, others they carried off in chains.'

On Rathlin, the invaders smashed a shrine and sacked the church of any gold or silver they could find. Finally, they set fire to the church and the surrounding houses. Describing a similar raid on a Scottish island very much like Rathlin, a Norse poet gave the Viking perspective: 'Tongues of fire playfully licked the sky,' he wrote. 'People fled from their blazing homes ... [The Viking leader], his sword steeped in blood, ravaged the island with fire ... [and] caused many a young maid to weep.'

Another Norse account of a typical attack went: 'They slew fifteen or sixteen men. Some escaped by running away. They plundered the place, destroying what they could not take with them.'

The Rathlin raiders, who had probably sailed down from the Orkney Islands, had no idea that they had just stumbled upon the northern extreme of a pillager's paradise: a large and fertile island called Ireland, whose multitude of monasteries were stocked with unbelievable wealth. In time, they were to discover dozens of abbeys, far greater than Rechru, rich with silver crosses and gold ornaments. The day they discovered Ireland, they hit the jackpot. They would keep coming back for two centuries, and in the end, they would simply stop going away.

I return to the mainland and follow the lowering sun until I reach another prominent landmark – the Inishowen Peninsula, between loughs Foyle and Swilly. Stretching out defiantly like an upraised fist, it contains Ireland's most northerly point, Malin Head. At the entrance to this promontory stands a desolate and brooding Irish fortress known as the Grianán of Aileach.

Turning off the main Derry–Letterkenny highway, I drive up a narrow, twisting road to the top of an 800-foot hill. The giant, three-terraced circular ringfort looms on the heather-covered hilltop, majestic and imposing, its weathered grey stone mottled white, green and brown with lichen and moss. Its sheer bulk is intimidating, even for a modern visitor, as you walk through the narrow portal, beneath tons of stone, into the enclosed central rotunda.

This fortress, seventy-seven feet across, was built in the late 700s or early 800s AD – around the same time as the first Viking raid – as the epicentre of the mediaeval Irish kingdom of Aileach. One of its kings, Murtough Leathercloak, was compared to the Trojan hero Hector because of his tireless fight against the Norse invaders.

From the ramparts, you can usually see out across the two sea-loughs, but today is so drizzly that the Foyle is completely obscured and Lough Swilly keeps dissolving into swirls of mist. This is excellent for my purposes – it is easier to imagine a similarly misty morning, more than a thousand years ago, when the Aileach sentinels looked out from their hilltop to see that a lone Viking longboat had lost its way and become grounded on an estuary sandbank.

The King ordered his troops to investigate. What happened next was the climax of an extraordinary, yet historically documented, story, rivalling Alex Haley's book *Roots* as an epic tale of an exiled slave and an heroic bid to reconnect with estranged kinfolk at home. It is the saga of an Irish princess named Melcorca, who was abducted by Vikings – probably here in Aileach in the early 900s – and enslaved in Iceland. It tells how she succeeded after many years, and against all the odds, in making contact with her royal father back home in this rugged, windswept corner of Donegal.

The Viking Pirates, the Irish Slavemaster and the Captive Princess

Olaf the Viking was hopelessly lost. He had sailed his longboat all the way from his home in Iceland to Ireland, without any trouble. But now the dense sea-mist had left him disorientated – 'sea-bewildered', as his thirteenth-century biographer later put it. Olaf was only eighteen. This was his first command. And already he knew he was rapidly losing the confidence of his men.

Things got even worse. The longboat nearly foundered when a rocky coast loomed out from the mist, just a few feet ahead. When the oarsmen rowed backwards in panic, they found reefs right behind them. They dropped anchor and waited for the fog to lift.

Eventually the mist cleared, to show that these Norse raiders were in shallow water – and deep trouble. The tide was ebbing, leaving the boat to settle on the seabed. Their stranded ship would be an easy target for the local Irish clansmen. The predators would become the prey.

Olaf acted quickly. He ordered his men to drag the ship into a deep sea-pool, where it could remain afloat. Minutes later, a band of Irish fighters appeared. They waded into the water in a bid to drag the ship ashore. But the pool was too deep for them.

The Vikings closed ranks and prepared to defend their vessel. '[They] stood with shield overlapping shield,' says the biographer, 'and a spear-point at the lower end of every shield.' Standing on the prow, Olaf wore 'a coat of mail, and a gold-reddened helmet'. He carried 'a sword with gold inlaid hilt; and a barbed spear'.

The Irish warriors retreated and informed their King, who led a large army down to the shore. Olaf still stood fearlessly on the prow. When he learned the King's name, he astonished everyone by addressing him in perfect Irish. 'My mother is called Melcorca,' Olaf declared, 'and she is your daughter.'

How we've always imagined the Vikings: A Norse longboat prepares to land on a pillaging mission, as depicted by an artist in 1909. But the winged and horned helmets of myth were never worn in reality.

Nearly twenty years previously, the King's daughter – fifteen-year-old Princess Melcorca – had been kidnapped and enslaved by Viking pirates. In Norway, she had been sold to an Icelandic trader, who fathered a child by her. That child was Olaf and now, by incredible coincidence, he was about to be reunited with the royal grandfather he had never known. Olaf and his Viking warriors would later join the King in fighting his enemies, both Irish and Norse. Back home in Iceland, Olaf would rise to become a heroic figure and a very wealthy man – and the enslaved Irish princess would once again rise in power and status, as the matriarch of a powerful Icelandic dynasty.

This is the story of Melcorca and her son Olaf, as told in the thirteenth-century *Laxdaela Saga*. It is difficult to know how much of it is true, but it is probable that some of the people depicted in it are real historical figures.

But before we tell Melcorca's own spellbinding story, let's try to trace how the opportunistic eighth-century slashers-and-burners who raided Rathlin matured over the following 150 years into the ruthlessly efficient human trafficking network that was the Viking empire in Melcorca's day.

When the first raids came in the late 700s and the early 800s, the Irish clans weren't especially worried. Raiding and hostage-taking had always been a regular feature of life in Ireland, and these were just new kids on the block. One Irish king said he 'was not surprised that they did what they did, because they were entitled to it'. Feuding tribes would ally with the newcomers to defeat their neighbours. 'Alas,' wrote one contemporary annalist, 'it is a pity for the Irish that they have the bad habit of fighting among themselves, and that they do not rise [against the Vikings] together.'

The Rathlin raid in 795 was followed by attacks on Skerries, near Dublin, and then Sligo, Galway and Mayo. These were all hit-and-run raids, with captive-taking as a side benefit. But all that changed in the year 821, when the Vikings realised that they could make far more money from selling and ransoming human beings.

On the next stage of my Viking expedition, I head for Howth, a sizeable fishing port to the northeast of Dublin. This time I approach it by sea, sailing across Dublin Bay in a thirty-six-foot sailboat. As we pass close by wild and rocky Howth Head ('Howth' is Norse for 'headland'), I try to get inside the minds of the Vikings who made this same journey in longships that weren't much bigger. From this angle, the steep escarpment looks enormous, with the tiny figures of hikers far above us serving only to emphasise the distance. At first a few houses cling to the scrubby flanks of the slope, but as we get to the end of the headland, even they disappear and Howth Head assumes an ancient, jagged grandeur. Guillemots, fulmars and seagulls cry desolately as they circle the sea-angling boats. We pass the Baily Lighthouse, negotiate around the point, and get our first glimpse of the marina and the commercial fishing harbour.

Finally standing on shore, I try to imagine how terrifying it must have been for the townsfolk of Howth when, one night in 821, the Norse slavers suddenly appeared from nowhere – probably rounding the headland without warning, just as we have done – and stormed on to the beach, determined to capture as many women as they could for sale on the slave markets.

For the Irish, the raid on Howth was something new and devastatingly unexpected. The attacks of the past decade had been smash and grab raids. At Howth in 821, they shifted up a gear. The Vikings now wanted to steal human beings – and especially women.

'[Howth] was plundered by the heathens,' says *The Annals of Ulster*. 'They carried off a great number of women into captivity.' Another annalist talks of the 'plundering of [Howth] by the foreigners', and says they abducted 'a great prey of women'.

It was the beginning of two centuries of attacks, in which the toll of enslavement steadily increased. One mediaeval historian recorded:

'As many women as they could lay hands on, noble or ignoble, young or old, married or unmarried, whatsoever birth or age … were by them abused, most beastly and filthily.' He said the most attractive were exported as concubines: 'Such of them as they liked best were sent overseas into their own countries, there to be kept by them to use their unlawful lusts.'

Sixteen years after the first raid on Howth, the Vikings once again raised the stakes. The despairing Irish looked out to sea and saw two enormous fleets, each consisting of sixty ships, sail into the Boyne and Liffey rivers. The Norsemen were bent on establishing permanent *longphorts*, or sea-forts, on the coast. From here, they would use the arteries of rivers to strike deep into the Irish heartland. Soon they were swooping on remote monasteries and townships far inland, and dragging off hundreds of slaves.

The numbers involved were staggering, at least in an Irish context. At Armagh, at least 1,710 people were either killed or captured. In the Forth area of County Carlow, 1,200 slaves were abducted. Kildare was plundered by Vikings, 'who carried off with them fourteen score persons into captivity in their ships'. In Duleek, 'a great number of persons were carried off into captivity', and in a single slave raid on the Kells region, a Viking lord named Gothfrith captured 'three thousand men or more … and a great spoil of cattle, horses, gold and silver'.

The captives were sold on the slave market and then put to work – the males as manual workers or craftsmen, and the females as concubines, servants, or both. Such was the fate of Melcorca.

According to the *Laxdaela Saga*, Melcorca was in her mid-teens when she was captured in a Viking pirate raid – probably during the attack on Aileach that is recorded by Irish annals in the early 900s. Determined to hide her identity, the terrified captive pretended to be deaf and dumb. Eventually, she ended up in a batch of slaves bought by Gilli The *Rus*.

The shadowy figure of 'Gilli The *Rus*' in the Saga is especially intriguing. We are told nothing of his background, but we're told he was an extremely wealthy and successful trafficker. Both his nickname and his penchant for wearing Russian-style fur hats suggest that his slave-dealing empire extended to the Vikings' Eastern European trading route. This stretched from Scandinavia down the Volga to present-day Russia, Ukraine and beyond, as far as Constantinople. Yet, according to three of my scholarly source-books, Gilli was actually Irish. His name is Gaelic, meaning 'servant', in the sense of a religious devotee. (The name survives today in surnames like Gilpatrick, or 'follower of Patrick', and Gilchrist.) Gilli was typical of a class of Irish entrepreneurs who exploited the Viking raids by literally selling out their own countryfolk.

Gilli's miserable captives were shipped to Norway, presumably under horrendous conditions, and separated into categories for sale at a large fair. Most were sold openly, but Gilli selected twelve of his highest-value female captives, keeping them aside in a curtained alcove where they could be viewed only by the wealthiest patrons. Melcorca was among the selected dozen.

A wealthy Icelander named Hoskuld visited Gilli's discreet salesroom, 'a stately tent far away from the other booths'. Gilli, resplendent in expensive velvet and a fur hat, introduced himself. Hoskuld realised he was talking to 'the richest of men [in] the guild of merchants'.

Seller and buyer indulged in some guarded dialogue. Gilli's joshing, slagging tone is immediately recognisable to Irish ears and does nothing to dispel the idea that he was indeed from Ireland.

'You must have things to sell that a man might wish to buy,' said Hoskuld.

'It depends,' said the Irishman. 'What do you wish to buy?'

Hoskuld looked around the apparently empty tent and said he wanted a female slave. The Irish trader laughed.

—You're trying to catch me out by asking for what I haven't got, he said. But you might be wrong.

Gilli dramatically drew back a curtain to reveal the dozen women.

Hoskult selected a dishevelled young woman who was 'fair to look upon', and was quoted a price of three marks – triple the usual rate. When Hoskult protested, Gilli shrugged: 'Choose any of the others, and pay me one mark.'

Hoskuld shook his head and produced the three marks, but Gilli insisted on full disclosure: 'She is dumb,' he warned. 'I have tried in many ways to get her to talk, but never got a word out of her.'

When Hoskuld returned home to Iceland with his beautiful concubine, his wife Jorunn was not impressed. The atmosphere in the marital home must have cooled further when Melcorca became pregnant with Hoskuld's child. 'That woman must do some work,' Jorunn stipulated, 'or else go away.' Melcorca was demoted to the status of kitchenmaid.

Two years later, after she gave birth to little Olaf, Melcorca's cover was blown. Out walking one morning, Hoskuld surprised Melcorca in the act of chattering happily to her child. The 'dumb' princess had to own up. 'I am Melcorca,' she admitted. 'My father is a king in Ireland.'

Hoskuld's wife Jorunn was furious at the disclosure. She attacked Melcorca, who retaliated by punching her on the nose. After that, Hoskuld was forced to move his mistress to a new home further upriver.

When Olaf turned eighteen, Hoskuld abandoned Melcorca. She decided to gamble everything on a desperate bid to re-connect with her Irish family. 'I cannot bear your being called the son of a slave woman,' she told Olaf. She urged him to set sail and find his royal relations. As proof of her identity, she gave Olaf a gold ring she had received as a baby.

Olaf agreed and set off to Ireland, where – as we heard earlier – he met his royal grandfather. Fortunately, the King recognised the ring and agreed that Olaf was the image of his missing daughter. The two men joined forces, and 'those who came against them thought this was indeed a grim alliance'.

Back in Iceland, Olaf's status soared when his royal background was revealed. He and his wife became the forebears of a long and honoured Icelandic-Viking dynasty, with Melcorca as the matriarch. Meanwhile, Melcorca married, had another child, and enjoyed a long and peaceful life. She never saw her father, her Irish family or her beloved homeland again.

Who was Princess Melcorca? The woman known in Iceland as *Melkorka Myrkjartansdottir* doesn't appear in any Irish historical records. The *Laxdaela Saga* names her royal father as 'Myrkjartan', a translation of the Irish name Muirchertach or Murtough. The most promising candidate is Murtough Leathercloak, who ruled Aileach in the early 900s. His territory was indeed raided by Vikings, and he did spend most of his life fighting them – more of that later. However, there are other candidates, including a southern Irish king named Cerball, whose daughters really did end up in Iceland around that time and produced an important Icelandic dynasty. Whatever the truth, her son Olaf was a real historical figure, and the extraordinary tale of Princess Melcorca may indeed be based on fact.

Whether or not Melcorca was a real person who left Ireland as a slave and ended up in Iceland, it is a proven fact that many, many Irishwomen did exactly that. Between around 800 and 1000 AD, an uncounted, yet undoubtedly huge, number of slaves were abducted from Ireland and sent abroad. DNA evidence has revealed that modern Icelanders can trace most of their *male* forebears to Scandinavia, but most of their *female* ancestors to Ireland. This is easily explained: when Scandinavian males first colonised Iceland in the late 800s, they had no womenfolk, and relied upon an influx of female slaves captured in Ireland – slaves exactly like Princess Melcorca.

The fates of these female slaves varied widely. Melcorca's experience of being first an object of physical attraction, then a secondary wife and mother, then a drudge, and, finally as she grew older, an embarrassment to be hidden away, was probably typical. At the gentler end of the scale, slave women joined families as cooks and childminders. But at the other, extreme, end of the spectrum, there were documented cases of horrific treatment, especially among the *Rus* – the Vikings who traded in Eastern Europe and Asia and who went on to found modern Russia. These Norsemen and their collaborators, such as Gilli, ferried hundreds of Irish captives down along the Volga River, and sold them to Middle Eastern buyers in exchange for silver, jewellery and silks. Ibn Fadlan, a diplomat from Baghdad, was disgusted by the Viking slavers. 'They are the filthiest race God ever created,' he said. They disdained the most basic toilet hygiene, and shared a single bowl of water for washing, each man spitting and blowing his nose into the water before passing it on.

Ten or twenty Vikings would share a house. 'Each man has a couch where he sits with the most beautiful girls he has for sale.' They would become intimate with the slave women in public: 'At times several of them will be thus engaged, each in full view of the others.'

When a rich Viking died, one of his female slaves was selected to be burned with his corpse aboard his ship. She was drugged and then assaulted, until finally her ordeal was ended by an old woman known as the Angel of Death, who stabbed her while the dead man's friends ritually strangled her with a rope. 'The men beat on their shields to drown out her cries,' Ibn Fadlan says chillingly, 'which might deter other girls.'

In other Viking territories, rich men were buried alongside females – presumably slaves – who had been ritually despatched with a battleaxe. To put it mildly, these were not nice people.

There was always the possibility – however remote – of escape. An intrepid Irish captive named Findan, a member of a prominent Leinster family, managed to get away from Norse raiders on two occasions. During one raid on his village, the Norsemen pursued Findan through the narrow streets. Findan ducked into a house and hid behind a door, holding his breath. We can only imagine his terror as the leaping torch-flames cast giant shadows of the helmeted warriors and their battleaxes on the wattled walls. Somehow, they missed him.

Findan's next escape was even more dramatic. Betrayed to the Vikings by a rival clan, he ended up on a slave ship bound for Norway. When the Vikings landed on a small Scottish island for supplies, he slipped away and ducked into a hollow beneath a large shore-rock. As he hid there, shivering with cold and fear, the tide crept closer and closer. 'On one side the sea hemmed him in, and on the other [was] the enemy, running to and fro, even walking over the rock, calling his name.'

Findan's cave began to fill with water. As darkness fell, he snuck out on his elbows and knees, inching between the heather bushes. When the Norsemen finally sailed off, he swam to the mainland. 'Saint Findan' – as he eventually became – went on to establish a monastery in Switzerland. Safe in his landlocked sanctuary, he would probably have echoed the view of a fellow Irish monk who once wrote gratefully: 'The wind blows wildly tonight, tossing the silver hair of the ocean. I have no fear of ferocious Vikings sailing across the sea.'

Very occasionally, Irish slaves would be freed *en masse* by a relieving army. In 866, an Irish force defeated Viking slavers. 'A few of the Norwegians escaped, naked and wounded,' writes one annalist. 'Great quantities of gold and silver and beautiful women were left behind.' Later, an Irish King named Mael Sechlainn attacked the Viking stronghold of Fingal and released a 'very great number' of Irish slaves.

If you believe one annalist, Ireland actually imported slaves from Africa. In the late 800s, two Norse brothers sailed into an unnamed Irish port with 'a great host' of slaves from the sub-Saharan region of Mauritania. As the distinctive captives filed off the Viking ships, they were a source of great wonder to the locals, who dubbed them 'the blue men'.

Questioned, the two brothers explained that they had gone to Spain 'destroying and plundering', before crossing the Straits to North Africa and ending up in Mauritania, where they devastated the countryside and enslaved many locals. 'They brought a great host of them captive with them to Ireland,' says the annalist. '… These black men remained in Ireland for a long time.' Despite much speculation, the fate of these mysterious Africans remains an intriguing mystery.

Who exactly were the Vikings – these piratical raiders who caused such havoc? The first wave of raiders came from Norway, usually via Scots islands. Later, large armies of Danes would come from England and Wales and fight against the original Norwegians.

While some Vikings were forced away from home because of dwindling resources, many others went raiding for more basic reasons: the lure of easy wealth, the search for adventure, a rite of passage to adulthood, an escape from stultifying authority. 'Harrying' – raiding and pillaging – was not only a legitimate profession, but also a worthy and manly activity.

In those early days, a routine raiding mission in Ireland would begin with a captain who had overwintered on a Scottish island gathering recruits and preparing his ships for plunder. 'He let it be known that he meant to go freebooting,' reads one typical account. 'He made ready in the Spring three warships, all large, and 300 men.'

Viking longboats were brilliantly designed and constructed. Built with overlapping planks of wood, they proved not only light enough to carry, but also supple enough to flex with the ocean waves. A standard longship had a raised prow and a square sail that made the most of the wind. They didn't waste an inch of space: the twenty warriors on a typical small craft had to sleep on deck and share space with supplies, captured booty and captives, and sometimes livestock. That shortage of space was one good reason why they didn't really wear the horned helmets of Hollywood fantasy.

But what really put the Vikings sea-miles ahead of the opposition was their navigation skills. They ventured fearlessly out into the open ocean, and became expert at navigating by sun and stars, even under cloudy skies.

The Vikings' legendary fearlessness was rooted not only in the prospect of an afterlife in Valhalla, but by a fatalism dictating that you were destined either to live or die; therefore, caution was pointless. Bizarrely, they felt they were doing their victims a service by forcing a violent death upon them. In one saga, a Viking raider loots a house while the householder is asleep. Halfway back to the ship, he pauses, filled with shame. 'Our going is all wrong, and not warlike,' he says. 'We have stolen the owner's property without him knowing.' He goes back to the house, sets it ablaze, and kills the occupants as they flee. This was regarded as a noble act.

That story is relevant here, because the Vikings regularly used fire as a weapon in Ireland. Burnings of innocent civilians were commonplace. In Drumrainey monastery in western Meath, they torched a church with 150 people inside. In nearby Dunshaughlin, three oratories, containing 320 people, were burned.

Forced drownings were also common, and there are curious accounts of Irish chieftains being captured, dragged all the way to the *longphort*, and then 'killed at the ships', presumably either for ritual or propaganda purposes.

The Vikings' treatment of their dead foes' corpses was gruesome. They took the head of one Irish chief, 'stuck it on a pole, and took turns shooting at it'. After another battle, the victors used the heaped-up corpses of their enemies as stands for cooking pots and spits. Asked why, they shrugged: They would have done the same to us.

As Norse invaders bred with the local Irish, there arose a new ethnic group known as *Gall-Gaedil*, who the annalists claimed were 'much worse' than the original Vikings. One lot achieved notoriety under the wonderfully biker-gang name of the Sons of Death.

The Vikings could never conquer Ireland, because there was no central authority to conquer: every new region contained a different army, requiring a new war. While the locals scored many significant victories, there was no single decisive battle. (Brian Boru did not drive out the Vikings by defeating the Dublin warlord Sitric at Clontarf in 1014. Sitric, who was actually half-Irish and a Christian, stayed in control of Dublin and founded Christ Church Cathedral.)

But if there was one single theatre of war where the Vikings' most determined advance was held back and turned … it was in Ireland's northeast.

The peaceful county of Down, with its rolling green drumlin hills and hauntingly beautiful silver estuaries, doesn't leap to mind when you think of conflict. Most of it remained relatively quiet during the Troubles of the late twentieth century. As you walk on the eastern shore of Strangford Lough on a tranquil spring evening, listening to the mournful cries of terns and oystercatchers as they swoop over seaweed-strewn rocks and islands, it is difficult to imagine that this lough was once the backdrop for 'the shrieking of the javelins, and the crashing blows of swords, and the hammering of shields being struck, and the cries of soldiers being overcome'.

In fact, this entire region was once the cockpit of a bitter and decisive war between Norse and Irish. Strangford Lough itself was a major base for Viking invaders from Scotland, bent on establishing a colony in east Ulster.

The military struggle for control of the northeast was to last more than a century, until the Strangford Lough Vikings were ultimately vanquished. The foreign invaders retreated, their noses bloodied, to concentrate their base on the River Liffey instead. It's strange to think that, but for this heroic resistance, the Vikings would have put down their roots here instead of further south. The largest city on this island could easily have been located somewhere around Newtownards, at the head of Strangford Lough, instead of Dublin.

One of the first major episodes in this conflict was the sacking and burning of Movilla Abbey in Newtownards, in the year 825. Viking longboats sailed up Strangford Lough and moored at its northern end. Shouldering their shields and battleaxes, the warriors stormed up the hill towards the monastery and fell upon the unsuspecting monks like ferocious, baying wolves.

After sacking the abbey and killing its Abbot, Flannabhra, the Vikings smashed a shrine and set the entire complex ablaze. Then they triumphantly marched back to their longboats, laden down with silver, gold and bejewelled treasures, herding their slaves before them. The long war in the northeast had begun.

The Vikings also set up a base in Lough Neagh, and Armagh became a regular target for plunder. It was sacked three times in a single month. An army of warrior-monks from Armagh confronted the Vikings in South Down, but they were soundly defeated and 'great numbers were taken captive'. After a battle between rival Viking navies in Carlingford Lough, the raids resumed. In 867, Armagh was 'plundered and burned', and 1,000 people were either killed or captured. A decade later, 710 people from the city were enslaved.

Locals began to despair. A contemporary poem lamented:

Saint Patrick, you can pray and pray
And cast your holy hex:
It won't protect your churches
From the Viking battleaxe.

Still, the local Irish scored some significant victories. 'A slaughter was made of [the Vikings],' an annalist records of one battle in 864. 'Their heads were collected to one place ... and twelve score heads were reckoned.'

When the Strangford Vikings sailed into Dundrum Bay, a fierce storm sank most of their ships, drowning up to 1,200 warriors. Undaunted, the survivors sailed north and sacked the Antrim coast.

The Viking advance in the northeast was stalled by the king we met earlier – Murtough Leathercloak, Melcorca's father, who won major victories before he was killed in battle at Ardee. Murtough's sons avenged their father by clearing the Viking fleet out of Lough Neagh. Meanwhile, Irish forces had descended on Strangford Lough and demolished the Norse base there. The Vikings' bid to conquer the northeast was over. However, they have left their legacy in the name of the lough – Strang Fjord, the estuary of strong currents.

For the final stop of my Viking trip, I return to Dublin to pore over the vast treasure trove of Viking exhibits in the National Museum. Dozens of graves and excavation sites have yielded not only swords, shields and spears, but brooches and arm-rings, tongs, pincers and weighing scales. One particular item sticks in my mind, nagging at my soul like the memory of a nightmare.

From the National Museum, I wander to Dublin Castle and relax in a small park just outside the Chester Beatty Library. This was the site of the Vikings' anchorage, the *Dyflin* or black pool that gave Dublin its name. Although they were ejected by the Irish for a few decades in the early 900s, they soon returned and merged into the population.

Their legacy is everywhere. Much of the Ireland we know today originated with the Vikings, from our major cities to many of our surnames. If you are a McAuliff, you are a descendant of Olaf. McManus means son of Magnus. Paul Hewson, better known as Bono of U2, has a Viking surname. As I write this, our President is Michael D Higgins, whose surname means '*uiginn*' or 'Viking'. It is a mistake to think of the Vikings as a story of 'us' and 'them'. To a large extent, we *are* 'them'.

What did the Vikings ever do for us? They gave us our first trading economy, and our first minted money. They influenced some of our most distinctive art. One of their most surprising legacies – and I would never have guessed this in a million years – lay in the realm of clothes fashion design. Among other things, they gave us trousers and the first properly constructed shoes.

Above all, they gave us our capital city, Dublin. This great city, birthplace of Swift and Yeats and Joyce and Beckett, would not exist in its present form if those settlers had not liked the look of that 'black pool', and built it up into an international trading centre. However, one of the main things they traded was people.

Sitting in that park, I think of the human misery that must have been concentrated in this small area. I imagine the lines of weeping female captives from Howth and Armagh, waiting to be transported in foul-smelling ships from the Black Pool to the Black Sea, to be traded for silks and silver dirhams at some sweltering eastern market; I imagine the olive-skinned Mediterranean captives headed for Scandinavia; the Africans, the Franks, the Saxons, all being processed through this riverside slave market. Yes, this was a black place indeed, and in more ways than one.

I suddenly remember the disturbing item I saw earlier in the National Museum. It was a Viking slave-shackle, a vicious human dog-collar complete with a long, heavy iron chain. It is a dreadful symbol of the slave trade that gave Dublin its first economy. Sitting by the former black pool, I close my eyes and hear the clank of iron chains, the moans of the slaves, and the groan of the hawsers on the slaving ships, and I come to the chilling realisation that my home town of Dublin – just as surely as Kingston, Jamaica, or Charleston, South Carolina – is a city that was built on slavery.

18·

PIRATE PILGRIMAGE THE EIGHTEENTH

Ringsend

From the city centre I take a southbound Dart commuter train to Dún Laoghaire. My Pirate Pilgrimage is almost at an end: I have gone full circle around Ireland's coastline, east, south, west and north, to end up at the same Dublin seascape where I began my journey.

I have learned so much along the way. I have met a representative selection of Ireland's buccaneers: I have encountered male pirates and female pirates; depraved pirates and principled political pirates; successful pirates and bungling pirates; sociopathic pirates and soft-hearted pirates. And I understand, for the first time, their complex and often symbiotic relationship with the land-based community.

I have one last locale to visit. It is the setting for a story like no other in this book. The seamen who feature in this tale were either (a) brilliant pirates, who brought back one of the most lavish hauls of treasure in Irish buccaneering history, or else (b) not pirates at all.

I hitch a ride on a yacht travelling from Dún Laoghaire and up the River Liffey, as far as Ringsend in Dublin. This ancient harbour is the setting for the city's greatest piratical puzzler: The mystery of the *Ouzel Galley*.

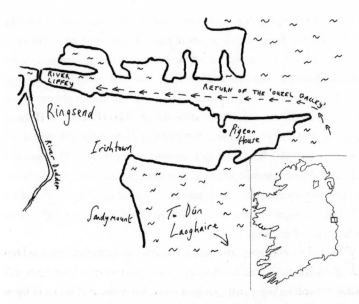

The sky is a grim mix of lead and pewter as we cast off from Dún Laoghaire and sail out through the embracing arms of the mighty granite piers, mindful of the generations of emigrants who left through this port in the hungry years. Carefully picking our way through the myriad of dayglo sailing dinghies – blasts of Sergeant Pepper psychedelic colour against the 'fifties-grey of the sea – we reach open water and head towards the twin candy-cane chimneys that dominate the entrance to Dublin port. Seagulls holler raucously as we round the South Wall and enter the Liffey.

Way back in 1448, the Lord Mayor decided the eastern boundary of Dublin port by entering the water on horseback 'as far as a man might ride' and then casting a spear as far as he could. In recent years, killjoy politicians have defined the boundary in more practical terms (a chart-line from Howth's Baily lighthouse to Sorrento Point in Dalkey), but the ancient ceremony has survived, with a tugboat taking the place of the horse. The spear-throwing part remains unchanged.

To our left, families stroll along the South Wall, now thankfully unbothered by decomposing pirates in cages. To our right, across the estuary to the north, looms Bull Island, now a wildlife haven. Strange to think that we have the notorious William Bligh, the hard-nosed commander of the *Bounty*, to thank for this amenity. Long after the famous mutiny aboard his ship, Bligh was called in to solve the problem of silting in Dublin's harbour entrance. He recommended building a new stone wall that would constrict the tide's flow, creating a scouring action that would deepen the channel almost threefold. Bligh's plan worked like a dream, with the unintended consequence that the displaced silt shifted up and became today's Bull Island. So let's toast Captain Bligh: perhaps history has not given him a fair crack of the whip.

As we travel deeper into the estuary, the city unfolds. Ahead, we can see the futuristic Convention Centre, a thick glass cylinder tilted back rakishly. It has been compared to a glass drum, but to me it looks more like a Jameson whiskey tumbler tilted to a perfect drinking angle. Which, when you think of it, is not a bad way to welcome the 1.3 million tourists who arrive here annually by sea. Right beside it is the gracile Samuel Beckett Bridge, whose name seems oddly fitting today since, far away to our right, a group of motionless surfers sit astride their boards on Dollymount Strand, staring eerily out to sea, awaiting the perfect wave. Since there's no wind and the water is flat-calm, the patient watchers seem like characters from an aquatic production of *Waiting for Godot*. They're actually waiting for the car ferry, which is guaranteed to send an exhilarating wake across the estuary. But in the meantime … they do not move.

As we pass Dublin Port, giant Terminator-style machines shunt truck-sized containers. Ships with flags we don't recognise and homeports we've never heard of sit brooding by the wharf. Now we're nearing my destination: Ringsend, the peninsula village that was once the country's busiest seaport. People here have always had a fiercely independent outlook, which is not surprising: it was originally populated by Irish who were banished outside the city walls by the English.

In this final chapter, I want to time-travel back to the year 1700, when much of this industrialised seafront was still under water, and Ringsend was known as 'a clean, healthy and beautiful village', with vine-covered houses, raucous taverns, and ships filled with tough men who were not above indulging in a little piracy.

The Puzzle of the *Ouzel*

Imagine an ordinary day in 1700s Ringsend, with mariners preparing ships for sea, crewmen caulking hulls on beached vessels, and dockers hefting bags of cargo off the ships on the quayside. Then, one by one, they stop what they're doing and stare out to sea in open-mouthed astonishment.

Sailing homewards up the river, with 'flags flying at her mast-heads and mizzen-peak' is a ship named *Ouzel Galley*. She has been away for five years and has long since been given up for lost. Merchants have already been compensated for her lost cargo, and some of the assumed 'widows' of the crewmen have since remarried and borne children with their new husbands. Now the *Ouzel Galley* has returned out of the mists like some seafaring Rip Van Winkle, with a crew that is very obviously alive and hollering out sea-shanties as though their return is nothing out of the ordinary. Her cargo, however, is far from ordinary. She left Ringsend with farming produce, hides and timber, but she has returned laden down with pirate treasure.

What happened to the *Ouzel Galley*? Where has she been for five years? Were the crew held captive or did they vanish willingly? Were they the victims of pirates – or had they been pirates themselves?

After three centuries, these questions remain as tantalisingly unresolved as they were on the day of the *Ouzel Galley*'s return to Ringsend.

Before we judge the facts, let's start by recounting the classic tale as it is told over many a pint in pubs like the Oarsman or the Windjammer. And bear in mind that this version has just as much right as any other to be regarded as true.

When the *Ouzel Galley* left Ringsend in 1695, wives and sweethearts hugged their menfolk goodbye, hoping that they would see them again within a year or so. Their trading mission to the Turkish city of Izmir (then Smyrna) was relatively straightforward. Irish foodstuffs and hides would be exchanged for spices and exotic Mediterranean wares, and the crew of thirty-seven men and three officers would be back home by the following summer.

Of course, every sea voyage was dangerous by definition. The men on the *Ouzel Galley* would have to take their chances with the equinox storms in the Atlantic; and once she had survived the Bay of Biscay, she would have to run the gauntlet of the dreaded Barbary corsairs, pirates who preyed on European ships from their bases in Algiers, Tunis and Tripoli. Many a wife had waited in vain for her husband, only to learn that he was confined in an Algiers bagnio prison, working as a slave and awaiting a ransom she could never afford to pay.

However, they had a sound ship and their captain – an anonymous mariner, but named by most sources as Captain Eoghan Massey from Waterford – was an experienced sailor. The firm of Messrs Ferris, Twigg and Cash, backers of the enterprise, were not overly anxious, but had prudently laid off the risk with a company of insurers.

The wharf echoed with the lusty roar of work-songs as the crew cast off and headed downriver to the open sea. Once past the mouth of the Liffey, they hoisted the sails on her three masts. The *Ouzel Galley* caught the breeze and heeled over, her keel digging in against the grey wall of water to convert the sideways energy of the wind into a brisk forward movement. Watching from the furthest embankment, families followed her until she disappeared over the horizon, leaving cold, grey and drizzly Ireland for the lands of sunshine.

The mysterious *Ouzel Galley*, as depicted in W.H.G. Kingston's influential book in the 1870s. Were her long-lost crewmen captured by Barbary corsairs – or were they pirates themselves?

The journey did not go as planned. According to the captain's later account, they survived the ocean winds, but fell victim to the second great hazard: the notorious corsairs. We have no contemporary account of how it happened. But if it were a typical corsair attack, the pirate ship would have stalked them like a cat stalks a mouse, observing from a distance as the predators carefully gauged the risk and the rewards. The corsair captain would have noted that the *Ouzel Galley* was too laden down with cargo to outrun a pirate ship built for speed, and that her crew was too small to mount a realistic defence. The attack ship would have moved steadily closer, perhaps displaying a false flag to buy a little more time. Once within clear view, the captain would have lined up his fighting men on deck to demonstrate that any resistance would simply prolong the agony and cause needless bloodshed. When the two vessels were within hailing distance, the Barbary captain would order the ship's officers to launch a boat and row across to the corsair ship. Only when the officers were in irons would the pirates actually board their target. There were exceptions, but in most cases, the whole business was transacted as smoothly and as bloodlessly as a company takeover.

Typically, the captive crew would have been taken to Algiers, where they were declared as slaves of the Turkish Ottoman Sultan and sold at auction. But it was common practice for skilled seamen to be put back to work at what they did best, rowing the Barbary galleys or working before the mast on oceangoing ships.

According to the most often-told account of the *Ouzel Galley* saga, the crew was kept intact to work their own ship, under new management. The *Ouzel Galley* was refitted as a pirate vessel and the Ringsend men were forced to become pirates.

Years passed by as the men sweated under the Mediterranean sun, pulling oars and hauling sheets as their new masters hunted down their prey, the cargo ships of Christian Europe. After a while, tensions between masters and slaves began to ease. The captors lowered their guard and gave the Irishmen more responsibility. Familiarity led to greater freedom.

The crew bided their time, waiting for the perfect opportunity. It came one night when the North Africans captured a lucrative prize. They stowed their treasure in the hold of the *Ouzel Galley* and began celebrating. Perhaps, as was the religious custom, they even gave a small portion of their loot to the Irish slaves who had helped them win it.

When the victors tired of their celebrations, the Irishmen kept working on deck. The pirates were happy to let them. The prisoners waited for an opportunity, and jumped the unsuspecting corsairs. The Ringsend men were notoriously tough, and handy with their fists and blades. The fight was probably fast and dirty. Soon the captors had become the captives.

What happened to the corsairs is not recorded. Perhaps they were killed, but more likely they were set adrift or put ashore. Either way, the newly freed *Ouzel Galley* set course for home, carrying the pirates' haul of stolen treasure.

Meanwhile, back at home, the ship had been given up for lost. The legal situation – which became a case study in arbitration law, and remains so to this day – was summed up by Ireland's Law Reform Commission in a 2008 consultation paper.

'When a third year passed without any sign of her or her crew, it was generally assumed by the people of Dublin that she had been lost at sea,' wrote the Commission. 'In 1698 a panel comprising the city's most distinguished merchants was established to settle the question of insurance. The panel's ruling was that the ship had been lost and that its owners and insurers should receive their due compensation. The galley's complement of 37 crew and three officers were declared dead and the insurance was paid out.'

So it was a Lazarus moment when in the autumn of 1700, five years after their departure, the silhouette of the *Ouzel Galley* loomed out of the grey shroud of the Liffey mists like a spectral vision. Men ran from house to house with the unbelievable news. Wives blessed themselves and hurried to the wharf. But one woman's delight was another woman's despair. Some 'widows' had remarried and had borne babies with their new partners. A single moment had turned them into bigamists and made their children's status legally problematic. It is said that, ever since then, children from unconventional relationships were known as 'ouzellers' in Ringsend slang.

The writer James Joyce picks up on that point in *Finnegans Wake*. At one point the narrator questions his birth origins, 'to inquire whether I, draggedasunder, be the forced generation of group marriage, holocryptogam, of my essenes, *or carried of cloud from land of locust, in ouzel galley borne ...*' [My italics.]

The scene in Ringsend on the day of the ship's return was once summed up by Bertie Ahern, then Taoiseach (prime minister) of Ireland and a proud inner-city Dubliner from just across the river. 'One can only begin to imagine the consternation surrounding the return of the *Ouzel Galley* to Dublin in 1700,' he said in one public address. '[The ship] having long been considered lost at sea, the ship's owners had received their insurance payouts, not to mention the sea-merchants' wives who had turned elsewhere for comfort.'

There was also the thorny issue of the pirate treasure. If the *Ouzel Galley* had returned bearing the original cargo, it would clearly have belonged to the insurers, who had already paid up. However, those original goods had been taken by corsairs, so the insurers' payout was justifiable. The problem lay with the *new* cargo of pirated treasure. Who did it belong to? Only one fact stood out clearly. The poor captain and crew didn't have a look-in. They could not legally profit from piracy.

The legal disputes continued for years, until all the parties appointed a panel of arbiters to fast-track the case and decide. They did their job well. According to one account in 1818, their 'luminous decision was highly approved of, and a satisfactory decision cheerfully acquiesced in, by all parties.'

In fact, the process worked so smoothly that, in 1705, a group of arbiters was permanently established to deal with such disputes in the future. It was called the Ouzel Galley Society. It reached its peak of influence in the late 1700s and early 1800s, and eventually it morphed into the most powerful business organisation in the capital: the Dublin Chamber of Commerce.

And that, essentially, is how the story goes. However, there is another, darker, version. It has been claimed that Massey and his crew were not the captives of pirates, but active and willing pirates themselves. They had never had any intention of going to the Mediterranean on a legitimate trading expedition – that was just a cover story. Instead, they had taken a right-turn and headed to the Caribbean to ply their trade there. More of this theory later.

I first became intrigued by the *Ouzel Galley* mystery in 2005, when the Dublin Port Company celebrated the three-hundredth anniversary of the Ouzel Galley Society with the then Taoiseach, Bertie Ahern, as guest of honour. He summed up the story in the quote I've cited above. In 2008, much the same version was given by the Law Reform Society, and then, two years later, by the Dublin Lord Mayor and the Dublin Port Company (who added that, even in 1700, the story of corsair capture was considered 'far-fetched'). So clearly, the *Ouzel Galley* story has deep roots in Dublin tradition and is kept alive by some very imposing and influential figures.

But is it actually true? That's what I need to find out.

From the wharf at Ringsend I wander to the library, determined to solve the mystery by mining down into the original sources. Hours later, I have worked through a stack of books and articles – and I'm no nearer a solution.

Sadly, there are no primary sources for the tale and, so far as I know, no contemporary accounts in state papers, journals or newspapers. The first records of the 1705 Ouzel Galley Society have, in the words of one historian, 'long been irrevocably lost'.

I think we can be reasonably certain of one thing: that a ship that set out from Ringsend in 1695 went missing, was declared lost, and then returned in 1700 to a legal wrangle over its unexpectedly valuable cargo. This much was stated in the 1818 account, and three decades later a newspaper identified that ship as the *Ouzel Galley*.

Apart from a brief record of 1748, and that vague reference from 1818, the first reliable non-fiction account of the *Ouzel Galley*'s voyage was published as late as 1904, in a book by the impressively named Caesar Litton Falkiner. He was a historian, a barrister and a former president of the Trinity College Philosophical Society, so he was a level-headed sort of chap. He recounts how the *Ouzel Galley* returned 'to the astonishment of all concerned', and goes on: 'The captain had a strange tale to tell. Proceeding in her eastern course down the Mediterranean, the *Ouzel* had fallen a victim to the Algerine corsairs, who, in those days, and indeed for long after, were still the scourge of the mercantile marine.' He relates the story of the crew's capture, and tells how 'by some fortunate chance the crew were able to turn the tables on their conquerors, to repossess themselves of their ship and cargo, and to return in safety to the port from whence they had sailed … The *Ouzel* brought home in her hold … the piratical spoils of her sometime Algerine masters. This loot was of a value far exceeding that of the legitimate cargo.'

There is nothing sceptical in Falkiner's tone. He states as fact that the ship returned with a lucrative haul of pirate booty, and there is nothing to indicate that he discounts the tale of Barbary capture – in fact, he supports it with his comment on the corsair menace. Was he simply drawing on traditional accounts? Or accessing some now-vanished legal records? We will never know, as he cites no sources.

At the very least, Falkiner's book shows that the *Ouzel Galley* story was well known long before the appearance of the next factual book in my research pile – *The Ouzel Galley* by George Aloysius Little. Writing in 1940, Little gives an ostensibly non-fiction account of the saga. However, it soon transforms into a rip-roaring adventure yarn in which many new elements appear: for instance, the ship is captured through the treachery of some newly-enlisted Moorish crewmen. The Dubliners escape in a fracas in which their tough Irish daggers overwhelm the Syrian sabres of the corsairs. It's all wonderfully readable, and it brought the legend into mainstream consciousness for the first time.

In 1983, Trinity College academician Professor Louis Cullen published a history of Dublin Chamber of Commerce, entitled *Pirates and Princes*. The blurb on the jacket said that the *Ouzel Galley* was 'presumed lost, only to reappear in her home port in 1700 laden with pirate loot'. However, the book itself devotes only a couple of paragraphs to the episode. Professor Cullen says that the story of the voyage is obscure and that some attempts to describe it have been 'fanciful'. He does not elaborate on the pirate element.

None of these factual books had anything like the same influence as an earlier work of fiction: *The Missing Ship, or The Log of the Ouzel*, a Victorian thriller by W.H.G. Kingston, author of boys' adventure stories. He claimed that he had attended a dinner of the Ouzel Galley Society in Dublin, where he'd been granted access to the *Ouzel Galley's* long-vanished log. Although this is a common device in fiction, many readers in the 1870s seem to have taken it as true.

In Kingston's version, the ship left Dublin, but became embroiled in a war, and ended up in the Caribbean. She was assumed lost, but when her backers went to find her, they found she had been taken over by a rapacious buccaneer (an Irish pirate, not a North African corsair) while on her way home from Montego Bay. Captain Massey and his men escaped in a canoe to Cuba, but were recaptured. After many adventures, the *Ouzel Galley* was re-taken by the Royal Navy, and Massey regained his vessel, complete with a 'large amount of treasure ... pillaged from some Spanish ship'. However, the pirate hoard was not an important element in Kingston's story. In this version, it was immediately surrendered to the English authorities in Jamaica, leaving the *Ouzel Galley* to return to Dublin empty of cargo: 'On a bright morning, the *Ouzel Galley* sailed into the Bay of Dublin, with flags flying at her mast-heads and mizzen peak. She was quickly recognised as she ran up the Liffey.'

One modern theory holds that there would have been no pirate dimension to the *Ouzel Galley* story had it not been for Kingston, who embellished a simple tale of a vanished and returned vessel with a new buccaneering element. I am not convinced. For a start, people were referring to 'pirates' in connection with the *Ouzel Galley* as far back as 1754, nearly 120 years before Kingston's book: the word appears in the oath taken by the captain, or chairman, of the Ouzel Galley Society.

In an article in the *Irish Times* a few years ago, the writer John Moran revealed an intriguing new angle to this debate. He wrote that Kingston had genuinely attended a dinner of the Ouzel Galley Society, probably in 1856, and that Kingston's cousin had been a stalwart of the society. John Moran speculated that this cousin – who had business interests in the Caribbean – may have given inside information to the author, possibly from the society's now-vanished first records.

There have been many persuasive theories about the *Ouzel Galley* saga.

First, let's examine the theory I mentioned earlier: that the crew of the real *Ouzel Galley* were actually pirates themselves, right from the very beginning. In this alternative version, the Ringsend men wanted to go to the Caribbean as privateers, but since the law forbade them, they pretended to set off to the Mediterranean on a trading mission. After five years of successful privateering in the Americas, they returned home laden with loot, without realising they had been given up as lost.

Some strong arguments have been advanced in support of this theory. We are told (for example, by the Dublin Port Company) that this was heavily rumoured at the time – the proverbial 'sea-dogs in the street' knew the real story. The Ringsend mariners were natural outcasts, and it would have come as no surprise if they'd got around the legal ban on privateering by laying a false trail.

In my view, this theory has an inbuilt problem. Having gone to such lengths to conceal their pirate trip, why should these secret privateers sail right up into Dublin's main harbour to openly declare a haul of treasure that nobody knew they had? Such resourceful outlaws would surely have sold or hidden their treasure before returning home.

A second theory is that the *Ouzel Galley* story is pure fairytale: no more than a mishmash of various seafaring stories that had excited the public imagination throughout the years.

Yet a third possibility is that the story was deliberately invented, long after the fact, to give an excuse to some Dublin bons-viveurs in the 1700s and 1800s to get away from their wives and attend 'convivial' drinking sessions in an atmosphere of quasi-naval tomfoolery, at meetings of the Ouzel Galley Society.

In the form that it took two centuries ago – and none of this applies to a modern charitable group with the same name – the Ouzel Galley Society (O.G.S.) did seem a rather unusual organisation. It was supposedly a high-minded legal body, yet in 1748, you'd have found the members discussing business in the Phoenix Tavern; in 1751 at the Ship Tavern; and in 1765 at the Rose & Bottle. It also held lavish dinners. 'Most of the business of the society was transacted at or after dinner,' writes Litton Falkiner drily, 'except at the November meeting, which held immediately before dinner.'

New members were inducted with a drinking test that any modern frat-house beer guzzler would immediately recognise. It involved 'the draining, in a single draught, of a bumper of claret'. A bumper is an 'enormous cup' filled right to the brim.

Members of the O.G.S. pretended to be on board an actual ship. Officials were given ship's ranks (from captain right down to carpenter's mate), and were piped 'aboard' by a bo'sun. There were dark warnings against 'mutiny' as the captain swore: '[In] this galley, entrusted to my command, I will, to the best of my power, defend against all pirates either by sea or land; the rules and orders established on board I will see observed to the utmost of my power, and justice administered to the crew ...'

Yet the O.G.S. was far from a ship of fools. This was an achingly exclusive society, whose forty members were carefully selected from the top echelons of Dublin society. Litton Falkiner wrote that the Society in the late 1700s had outgrown its earlier role. It 'became highly popular among the merchants of Dublin as a convivial association'.

In 2011, historian Dr Lisa Marie Griffith wrote an academic article entitled 'The Ouzel Galley Society in the Eighteenth Century: Arbitration Body or Drinking Club?' Her article sought to prove 'that the account of the origins of the society, the *Ouzel Galley* ship, is a nineteenth century invention; that the society's original importance came from arbitration rather than a true-to-life adventure tale, and that the eighteenth century society was more a convivial drinking and dining club than arbitration body'.

I would agree that the society was an exclusive drinking club, but I'd actually go further. In my opinion, it's possible that the O.G.S. in the mid- to late 1700s may actually have been a secret political society, designed to protect the Protestant Anglican ruling caste from an increasing threat posed by a growing Catholic middle class of merchants and intellectuals who were beginning to flex their muscles. Also – and just as importantly

– the threat from the moderate Protestants who wanted to show greater tolerance to the Catholics. The naval tomfoolery may have been a cover for some deadly serious political meetings. Seen from this viewpoint, the seemingly farcical oath taken by the O.G.S. captain takes on a new and darker meaning. He warned the members against 'mutiny' and pledged 'to the best of my power, defend against all pirates either by sea or land'. Could this have been code for the very real threats faced by the conservative establishment – not only from the 'pirates' who endangered their comfortable supremacy, but also from the 'mutineers'?

I emerge from the library and seek fresh air in the grounds of beautiful Trinity College, my head reeling with facts and myths and conspiracy theories.

I have to admit that the *Ouzel Galley* puzzle has left me stumped. With little or no hard evidence to support any of the main theories, we are left stumbling in the dark. But as I stroll past the cricket green of Trinity College in the fading light, my head begins to clear.

Mentally reviewing all the commentaries, I realise that the most common objection to the corsair-capture story is that it was too unbelievable to be taken seriously. As the Dublin Port Company's press release put it in 2010: 'The tall story of Algerian corsairs and a five-year captivity in North Africa, not to mention the fortuitous escape of the entire crew, was considered too far-fetched to be true.'

But was this story really so incredible? We tend to forget the astonishing scale of the Barbary slave trade in that era. One calculation claims that, over three centuries, up to a million Europeans were captured and enslaved by North African pirates. This was a frighteningly common occurrence and a risk mariners faced on every voyage.

In some well-documented cases, the captives did indeed gain the upper hand over their captors. I have spent years studying accounts of capture by the Barbary corsairs, and I can immediately think of several similar cases in the 1600s alone. Just three decades beforehand, an English Quaker sea captain named Thomas Lurting had his ship taken over by Algerine pirates. When the corsairs sheltered below decks during a ferocious rainstorm, he locked them in and his crew regained command. Another example, from the 1630s, features an English captive named William Okeley, who not only escaped from slavery in Algiers, but also managed to smuggle home a fortune in the false bottom of a trunk.

So, really, I don't find the story of Barbary capture and escape in this case *intrinsically* unbelievable. If we apply Occam's Razor – the principle that the simplest solution is probably correct – I can see absolutely no reason to prefer the more elaborate 'Caribbean' version to the traditional story that the ship was taken by Algerine corsairs. Until we get better information, it seems likely to me that the most commonly told story of Barbary capture is actually ... the true one.

Meanwhile, the name of the Ouzel Galley Society lives on. The original O.G.S. was dissolved in 1889, but in 1988 it was revived as a fundraising and charitable group. The modern O.G.S. is a society of decent folk doing much good work, and I want to stress that none of the things I have said about the 'old' Society of the 1700s and 1800s applies to the O.G.S. in its post-1988 version.

As I wander out through the arched portal of Trinity College, I give a nod to the ghost of Caesar Litton Falkiner, the man whose account remains the most believable. I cross the crowded street and steer towards my last port of call on this particular pilgrimage – College Green, the former hub of city politics and banking. I pause outside Commercial Buildings, one of the locations where the 1700s Ouzel Galley Society used to meet. And there, above an arched doorway, resplendent against the dull red brickwork, is a circular white plaque, centuries old, showing a relief image of a glorious three-masted ship under full sail on a turbulent ocean, a flag fluttering proudly from her stern. Here, in the very heart of the metropolis, totally unnoticed by the tens of thousands of passers-by, the *Ouzel Galley* sails on eternally.

ACKNOWLEDGEMENTS

Travelling around the coast of Ireland in search of pirate stories was the most enormous fun, but don't tell that to my publishers, because I'm trying to pretend that it was hard work. I want to thank everyone who helped make this 'pirate pilgrimage' one of the great experiences of my life.

For the southern part of my trip, I made two journeys, the first by land and the second by sea, sailing from Dublin via Wicklow, Wexford, Waterford, Cork Harbour and Roaring Water Bay to Bantry Bay in West Cork. The book gained immeasurably from that maritime perspective, and I want to thank my friends Peter and Marian, without whom it would never have been possible.

Special thanks, too, to my travelling companions at various points on land and sea: Pete, Marian, Matt, Thecla, Jo and, of course, my wife Sally.

My deep gratitude to publisher Michael O'Brien, for his positivity and encouragement and faith in my writing ability. To my editor Eoin O'Brien, who made this book much better. Thirdly, to graphic designers Emma Byrne and Helene Pertl, for adding an extra dimension of visual zest and sparkle to my writings.

For facilitating my researches, I am indebted to the patient and helpful staff at the National Library of Ireland; to the custodians of the Irish Collection at the Dublin City Library and Archive; to the libraries at Trinity College, Dublin; to the British Library; to the UK National Archives; to the Killybegs Maritime and Heritage Centre; and the National Maritime Museum of Ireland.

I also want to pay tribute to all those writers who have tackled the subject of piracy in Ireland before me, but with the sort of academic rigour that leaves me in awe. I recommend their writings at various points in the text and in the source notes.

My friends from my days in journalism were, as always, an unfailing font of morale-boosting support. Special thanks to Colin McAlpin, for his gift of a source-book of whose existence I was unaware.

I could not have done this without the support of my family: my grown-up children Chris, Sarah and Gráinne (who is delighted that I finally got around to writing about her pirate namesake Gráinne O'Malley), and my brother and sister. Special love to my ever-patient, ever-encouraging wife Sally, who has become used to sitting across a dinner table from a husband who is present in body, but whose soul is roaming some ancient ocean and whose inner eye is fixed on the horizon of some distant piratical seascape. That's my roundabout way of saying that I know I can be a real pain in the neck when I'm in the middle of writing a book. Thank you.

Finally, my apologies that, for space reasons, I was unable to include pirate stories from every coastal county I visited. This does not mean that the counties omitted didn't *have* pirates, or, worse, that I didn't think that they were worth including – it was just that I didn't have room in one book to do them justice. Maybe in Volume Two ...?

SOURCE NOTES

Where possible, I have used eyewitness reports, courtroom testimonies, contemporary documents, official despatches, annals and newspaper reports compiled at the time. Where that was not possible, I used books written during the pirate era (mostly 1500s, 1600s, 1700s and early 1800s). As I am interested in historiography (for example, in my attempt to trace the fascinating evolution of the Granuaile myths), I have also cited books from the Victorian and Edwardian eras. However, I have benefitted from the analysis of modern writers and have identified 'recommended reading' with the abbreviation 'rec'. Works that are already clearly referenced in the text will not be further referenced here.

PIRATE PILGRIMAGE THE FIRST

'Narrative of a Horrid Murder on the High Seas', from *The Gentleman's Magazine* (1765), Vol 35, p.545; 'Mutiny & Murders on board ship Earl of Sandwich', from *Shipping News*, 13 December 1765, *PRONI* D document no. 9808135; 'Peter McKinlie [etc] Executed for Piracy and Murder', 19 December 1765, in *The Newgate Calendar*, with thanks to the National Maritime Museum of Ireland archive; *Wanderings in West Africa* (1863), by Sir Richard Francis Burton, p.79.

Rec, *The 18th Century Pirates of the Muglins* (1989), by Pádraig Laffan, Foxrock Local History Society; *When the Battle of the Atlantic Was a Different Affair* (1941), by RH Davis, in *PRONI* D document no 9804413; *Dollar Bay* from www.eoceanic.com.

PIRATE PILGRIMAGE THE SECOND

The Grand Pyrate, or The Life and Death of Capt. George Cusack, the Great Sea-Robber (1676) by 'Impartial Hand'. Also rec, Amanda Ruggeri (2016), in BBC Britain: 'The London Gallows Where Pirates Were Hanged'.

PIRATE PILGRIMAGE THE THIRD

Wexford generally:

Philip Hore (1900), *History of the Town and County of Wexford* and (1911) *Journal of the Waterford & South-East of Ireland Archaeological Society*, Vol XIV.

Rec, Billy Colfer (2004), *The Hook Peninsula* (Cork University Press).

Cromwell quote: in Charles Knight (1880), *Popular History of England* v4, p.123.

Lampart:

Life story, background and quotes: WL's own testimony to the Mexican Inquisition; also, Luis González Obrogón (1906), *Los Precursores de la Independencia Mexicana* and (1908) *D Guillén de Lampart, La Inquisición y la Independencia en el Siglo XVII;* GRG Conway (1927), *An Englishman and the Mexican Inquisition 1556–1560.*

Guillén de Lampart, aka William Lampart (1640–42), *Proclama por la liberación de la Nueva España,* available at www.bdmx.mx/detalle/?id_cod=25.

Rec: José Ortiz Monasterio (1993), *Historia y Ficción* (Universidad Iberoamericana).

Fabio Troncarelli (2001), 'The Man Behind the Mask of Zorro' in *History Ireland* Vol 9.

Gerard Ronan (2004), *'The Irish Zorro'* (Brandon).

Andrew Philip Konove (2004), *The Devil and the Irish King* (thesis, Haverford College).

Dominic Crewe Ryan (2007), 'William Lampart' in *Irish Migration Studies in Latin America,* pp.74–76.

Concepción Moreno (2010), 'La Increíble y Triste Historia del Primer Independentista de México' in *El Economista,* 11 August 2010.

Pirates' tactics: Henry Mainwaring (1586–1653). *Discourse on Pirates.*

Two victims' quotes: ie, John Foss and Thomas Pellow.

Dutch patrol: rec, Ronan.

Fever of activity: Anon (1659), *Claes G Compaen of Oostzanen.*

Pirate battle quote: John Smith in Mainwaring, *Discourse.*

1870s writer: Vicente Riva Palacio (1872), *Memorias de un Impostor.*

Bob Kane: Moreno.

PIRATE PILGRIMAGE THE FOURTH

Most of this chapter is based on the letters exchanged between Franklin, Ryan and Macatter; Dowlin, Coffyn and Torris (US National Archives); and contemporary newspaper accounts of the privateers' attacks and activities, and the two trials. All facts and all quotes from the main characters are from the Franklin Letters, except where otherwise referenced. Other works:

'American Privateers at Dunkerque' in United States Naval Institute (1911), *Proceedings* v37, p.949.

Gardner W Allen (1913), *A Naval History of the American Revolution Vol 2*, p.592+.

Vincent Morley (2002), *Irish Opinion and the American Revolution 1760–1783* (Cambridge University Press).

Michael J O'Brien (1919), *A Hidden Phase of American History: Ireland's Part in America's Struggle for Liberty.*

Modern analyses: I can thoroughly recommend a rare and very enjoyable US book: William Ben Clark (1956), *Ben Franklin's Privateers* (Greenwood, New York): in my opinion, the definitive account. Also recommended, Luke Ryan chapter in Joe O'Shea (2012), *Murder, Mutiny and Mayhem* (O'Brien Press).

Dowlin at Saltees: Letter from J Gahan, Customs House, Waterford, 13 August 1781.

Black Dog prison: JT Gilbert (1861), *History of the City of Dublin*, p.262+.

Escape and 'old smuggler' quote: Franklin, cited by Allen.

Typical contract: Naval *Proceedings*, p.949.

'Desperate' quote: Cited in Clark, p.8.

The trio's success compared in 'livres': Naval *Proceedings*, p.952.

'Bitters enough' encounter: Letter from captain published in *Saunders's News Letter*, Dublin, 11 August 1780, p.1.

Hiding places: Naval *Proceedings*, p.962.

Yates: Case of Yates v. Hall, 1785, in Durnford & East (1791), *Court of King's Bench 1785–1790*.

Mail ships: *Belfast News Letter*, 10 March 1780, PRONI 9808355.

'Small stature': cited in *Dublin Historical Record*, v23-26, p.36.

'I have sailed': cited in *American Neptune*, v55, p.194.

Captain Sinclair: *Newcastle Chronicle*, 22 April 1780, p.2; Clark, p.126.

'Fortune of war': Naval *Proceedings*, p.966.

Ryan and Derry shooting party: *Stamford Mercury*, 14 September 1780, p.1.

Daily attacks, uncontrolled: Eric J Graham, *A Maritime History of Scotland 1650–1790*; John Donald, p.270; *American Neptune* v55, p.194.

'You can no longer ...': Naval *Proceedings*, p.958.

Ryan capture: Robert Beatson, *Naval and Military Memoirs ... v5*, p.400; *Gentleman's Magazine* (1781, v51); James Ralfe, *Naval Biography of Great Britain*; 'wrung hands', *Universal Magazine* (1781) v68–69; 'Perfectly at ease': *Finn's Leinster Journal*, cited in Morley.

Trial, conviction, 'elegant': *Hibernian Magazine*, April 1782, and *Gentleman's Magazine* (1782, v52).

Marie Antoinette: Beatson, v6.

'He expected …' and debtor's prison: John D'Alton, *History of Drogheda* and *History of County of Dublin*, p.431.

Mystery lady: *Gentleman's Magazine*, June 1789.

'When he returned …' and Louis XVI: Naval *Proceedings*.

Ryan's death: *The Literary Magazine*, Jan–Jun 1789, and *Gentleman's Magazine*, v59 part one.

Dowlin's end: Clark, p.175.

Statistics: Clark, p.177.

PIRATE PILGRIMAGE THE FIFTH

Creadan Head and 'Road of Black Women': Patrick Power (1907), *The Place-names of Decies*, p.211; Billy Colfer, *The Hook Peninsula*, p.107; *Munster Express*, 10 November 2015, *Piracy Recalled*; www.eoceanic.com, *Creadan Head*.

Baltimore vs Waterford wars: John O'Donovan (ed.) (1849), *Miscellany of the Celtic Society*, pp.93–95; Daniel Donovan (1876), *Sketches in Carbery*, pp.47–49; Charles Gibson, *History of Cork*, p.519.

Rec: Bernie McCarthy (2012), *Pirates of Baltimore*, Baltimore Castle Publications, ch.1.

Raleigh: Edmund Gosse (1886), *Raleigh*, p.60.

Boyle and Lismore: www.lismorecastle.com.

Boyle and piracy: Dorothea Townshend (1904), *Life and Letters of the Great Earl of Cork*, pp.113, 116, 160, 215.

PIRATE PILGRIMAGE THE SIXTH

Thomas testimony and trial: Robert Baldwin (1721), *The Tryals of Captain John Rackam* (transcript of hearing in Jamaica), PRO CO 137.14.

Main biography: Charles Johnson (1724), *General History of the Pyrates*.

Childhood in Bullen's Bay: John Thuillier (2014), *Kinsale Harbour, a History* (Collins) p.149.

Aftermath: AB in *Oxford Dictionary of National Biography*.

PIRATE PILGRIMAGE THE SEVENTH

'Sea sharks', Danvers fear: *CSPI* 1608–10, p.100 and p.130; *CSPI* 1611–14, lxi.

Pirate flotilla Cork: CSPI 1608–10, p.130, p.273, p.277.

Dundanion Castle background: *Irish Examiner*, 17 May 2014; *Cork Independent*, 8 April 2014.

Gallwey, *Santa Maria Desaie*: E Keble Chatterton (1914), *The Romance of Piracy*, p.39.

'Since we do not ...': 18 November 1548, in Richard Caulfield (1876), *Council Book of Cork*, xv.

'Our haven ...': 16 April 1563, *ibid*, xv.

Blackrock Castle and pirates: *Journal of the Cork Historical and Archaeological Society* (1915), p.102; also rec, Kieran McCarthy (2016), 'Blackrock Castle' in *Cork City History Tour* (Amberley).

Peter Roach story based on courtroom evidence in (1704) *The Arraignment, Tryal and Condemnation of Captain John Quelch and Others*. 'Judicial murder' and execution quotes: rec, George Dow and John Edmonds (1923), *Pirates of the New England Coast* (Marine Research Society).

Philip Roche: Mostly from Charles Johnson, *General History*, but also rec, ET Fox (2014), 'The Examination of Philip Roche', in *Pirates in Their Own Words* (Lulu Press). Brief reference in Philip Gosse (1924), *The Pirates' Who's Who* (Burt Franklin).

PIRATE PILGRIMAGE THE EIGHTH

Mainly based on reports from the *Calendar of State Papers Ireland* (CSPI) and contemporary documents, with my own interpretations. However, I have been helped immensely by the analyses of John Appleby and Clive Senior in the following works:

John Appleby (1990), 'A Nursery of Pirates', in *International Journal of Maritime History*, v2.

John Appleby (1992), *A Calendar of Material relating to Ireland from the High Court of Admiralty Examinations 1536–1641* (Genealogical Office).

John Appleby (2001), 'Women and Piracy in Ireland', in CR Pennell, *Bandits at Sea* (NYU Press).

John Appleby (2006), 'The Problem of Piracy in Ireland 1570–1630', in Claire Jowitt, *Pirates? The Politics of Plunder* (Palgrave Macmillan).

Clive Senior (1976), *A Nation of Pirates* (David & Charles).

'Covering their vessels': In William Lindsay (1876), *History of Merchant Shipping*, v2.

Callis: 'Calles' entry in Gosse, *TPWW*.

'The young African woman': This is my subjective description of an incident that really did take place in 1615. Analysis, mine. For facts behind this and about Jobson generally, see (all rec) Senior, pp.39 and 139; Appleby, *Nursery*, p.21, and *Problem*, p.53; *Studia Hibernica*, vs 24–26, p.83; Jobson vs Hawkins, rec, Mark G Hanna (2015), *Pirate Nests*, p.55 (UNC Press).

Confederacy: Lords of Council, *CSPI* 1611–14, lxx; also *CSPI* 1608–10, p.278; admirals, *CSPI* 1608–11, p.273.

Up to 27 ships: i.e., John Nutt. See John Forster (1872), *Sir John Eliot*. Rec, Philip Gosse (1932), *History of Piracy* (Longman), p.134.

Tralee 1589: Basil Fuller, Ronald Leslie-Melville (1935), *Pirate Harbours* (Stanley Paul), p.169.

Lieutenant: Connie Kelleher quoted in *Live Science*, 26 February 2014.

Legal loophole: *CSPI* 1611–14, lxiii.

Routinely sold: i.e., Baugh, see below.

£2,000 fund: John Nutt, *CSPI* 1615–25, p.411; 'Examination of Hugh Baker' in the *Council Book of Youghal*, xlix.

Morat evangelist, zealot: De Vries, *Historie van Barbaryen*, pp.65–66, cited in M van Gelder (2015), 'The Republic's Renegades', in *Journal of Early Modern History* 19 (2–3); church, priest, *Letter by Klaus Eyjólffson*, 1627.

Boniton sweetener: Appleby, *Problem*, p.52; also see *CSPI* 1611–14, lxiv.

Williams: *CSPI* 1608–10, p.42+.

Baugh: *CSPI* 1611–14, pp.306 and 310.

Button: rec, Andrew Thrush, entry for B. in *Oxford Dict. Nat. Biog.*

Leamcon as pirate nest, Skipwith, hellhounds, financial zone, bury treasure: *CSPI* 1611–14, lxv and pp.95 and 99.

Jennings, Williams: *CSPI* 1608–10, p.42+.

Auction 1625: *CSPI* 1615–25, p.584.

Hull background: *Gentleman's Magazine*, July–Dec 1818, p.121; *Proceedings of the Royal Irish Academy 1913*, p.269; *Irish Historical Studies* 95–96 v1, pp.308–323; John Appleby (1989–90), 'A Profile of William Hull', in *Studia Hibernica* 25; *CSPI* 1608–10, p.397.

$7 million: Connie Kelleher, quoted in *Live Science*, 26 February 2014. Two centres: *CSPI* 1611–14, lxix and pp.238 and 301.

Juries: rec, Michael MacCarthy Morrough (1986), *The Munster Plantation*, and rec, Senior, p.57.

Gates of hell, and Spanish ship: *CSPI* 1608–10, p.100.

Alehouses: Richard Caulfield (1879), *Council Book of Kinsale*, 6 August 1610; *Council Book of Youghal* (1631), pp. 154, 171; Mainwaring, *op. cit.*

Riotous: rec, Senior, p.56.

Ingle and Orenge: Appleby, *Calendar*, pp.130, 132; and *Problem*, pp.52–53.

Forced into piracy: Rec, Senior, citing HCA report 18 August 1609; rec, Appleby, *Nursery*, pp.9–12.

Barbary gold: *Exam. of Hugh Baker.*

Magee: *Irish Times*, 8 December 2012.

Easton at Valentia: *CSPI* 1611–14, p.287; typical fleet size, *CSPI* 1608–10, p.277; *CSPI* 1611–14, p.89; rec, Appleby, *Nursery*.

Easton life: *CSPI* 1611–14, intro lxv and p.89; Richard Whitbourne (1620), *Discovery of Newfoundland*; rec, Gosse, *History*, p.129; Senior, p.35.

Sheila: Peter Edwards (2012), *Encyclopaedia of Canadian Organised Crime*, McClelland & Stewart, p.232; Gerald Hallowell (2004), *Oxford Companion to Canadian History*, p.424.

'Too weak' and 'overboard': *CSPI* 1608–10, p.495.

French ship: *CSPI* 1611–14, p.383.

David Burke: rec, Appleby, *Calendar*, pp.141–2.

John Nutt and quotes: Forster, *Eliot*; rec, Gosse, *History*, p.134.

Baker: *Exam. of Hugh Baker*.

Visit Crookhaven: George Bennett (1869), *History of Bandon*, ch.5.

Women in pirate society: For a full discussion of this topic, rec, Appleby, *Women and Piracy*.

Ward biog and his rules: Andrew Barker (1609), *Captain Ward's Piracies*, and Anon (1609), *Newes from Sea*. Also see *CSPI* 1608–10, pp.278–9.

Bishop, well manned, clamour, 21 ships [i.e., 11+10]: *CSPI* 1608–10, p.277; die poor, *CSPI* 1611–14, p.91.

Mainwaring: *Discourse, op. cit.*

Had 8 pirates hanged: rec, Patrick Hickey (2002), *Famine in West Cork* (Mercier).

Dutch and Myagh: rec, Appleby, *Nursery*, p.24, and Connie Kelleher, quoted in *Live Science, op. cit.*

Baltimore raid: Des Ekin (2006), *The Stolen Village* (O'Brien).

John Winthrop and Ireland: Robert Charles Winthrop (1867), *Life and Letters of John Winthrop* v1; rec, Nicholas Canny in William Louis *et al.* (2001), *Oxford History of the British Empire* v1 (Oxford University Press), p.6, etc; and Francis J Bremer (2005), *John Winthrop* (OUP).

Nutt treasure legend: Bennett, *History*, ch.5.

PIRATE PILGRIMAGE THE NINTH

Mainly based on the contemporary writings of Matthew Paris (1240–53), *Chron. Maj.* V3, 4, 6; Thomas Wikes (*c.*1304); Roger of Wendover (1242), *Flores Historiarum*; the writer known as 'Matthew of Westminster'; *The Annals of Waverley* (1242); Raphael Hollingshead (*c.*1587), *Chronicles of England*.

For the facts on Clement's murder, I'm indebted to Frederic William Maitland (1911), 'The Murder of Henry Clement', in his *Collected Papers,* and later Frederick Powicke (1941), 'The Murder of Henry Clement', in *Ways of Mediaeval Life and Thought* (Biblio & Tannen), ch.3: highly recommended.

Sabine Baring-Gould (1908), 'The Pirates of Lundy', in *Devonshire Characters*, p.224+.

Samuel Seyer (1823), *Memoirs Historical and Topographical of Bristol*, v2, p.12+.

'Irishman by nation': 'Matthew of Westminster' and the *Annals of Waverley*, cited in Seyer, p.13.

Geoffrey biog, Mareschal episode: *Dictionary of National Biography* (1896); Thomas Leland (1814), *History of Ireland v1*, p.211+; Goddard Henry Orpen (1911), *Ireland Under the Normans*.

Marsh family, Geoffrey kills 20,000; 'Forgetful of' and 'Geoffrey having crushed' quote; and Lundy under WM: Hervey de Montmorency-Morres (1817), *Genealogical Memoir* ... Clement affair: Leland v1; rec, Maitland, Powicke.

'He earned the contempt': *Encyclopaedia Britannica 1911*.

'It has only one ...': Thomas de la More, cited in *London Society* v14.

'After the jealous ...': in *The Spectator*, 18 August 1877.

Woodstock attack: Paris, 'Matthew of Westminster', *Annals of Waverley*.

'poor Bristol traders' and 'The king, fearful': John Page (1895), *The Coasts of Devon and Lundy Island*.

'To avoid ...': Richard Ayton, William Daniell (1823), *A Voyage Round Great Britain*.

'The evidence incriminating ...': Baring-Gould.

PIRATE PILGRIMAGE THE TENTH

Surprisingly, there are no contemporary accounts of GO'M from Irish sources in the 1500s, except for a brief reference to 'Grace of the Gamblers' from one Shane O'Dogherty. Primary sources mostly derive from (a) the highly critical reports, often exaggerated, from English colonial officials, as referenced below, and (b) the exchange of documents between GO'M and the London court in the 1590s. Except where otherwise indicated, all my quotes from GO'M and details of her life come from the latter. The main points of these exchanges have been accurately quoted by Victorian historians (see individual references), but transcripts can be read in Melissa Smith (2004), *Reading Early Modern Women* (London: Routledge), together with an excellent analysis.

Recommended reading: The best and most readable account of GO'M's career is Anne Chambers's classic *Granuaile* (Wolfhound) from 1979. I also enjoyed Judith Cook's (2004) *Pirate Queen* (Mercier).

Other sources:

Anthologia Hibernica v2 and *v3* (1793 and 1794) ['AH'].

E. Owens Blackburne (1877), *Illustrious Irishwomen* v2.

Dublin University Magazine v55 (April 1860) ['DUM'].

GO'M entry in (1878) *A Compendium of Irish Biography* ['CIB'].

John Healy (Archbishop) (1906), essay on GO'M in *Irish Essays: Literary and Historical*

Illustrated Dublin Journal (14 September 1861) ['IDJ'].

Hubert Knox (1908), *History of County of Mayo.*

William O'Brien (1892), *A Gem of Misgovernment in Ireland.*

John O'Donovan (ed.) (1838), *Ordnance Survey Letters Mayo v2.* Also introduction by Michael
    Herity in 2009 edition by Fourmasters Press.

Caesar Otway (1841), *Grace O'Mealey* in Coyne and Willis, *The Scenery and Antiquities of Ireland* v2.

Royal Irish Academy (1992–2009), *New Survey of Clare Island* ['NSoCI'].

'Affrighted': *AH.*

'A terror': Henry Sidney, *Oxford Handbook of Modern Irish History*, p.195.

'Ugliness remarkable': Blackburne, p.90.

'A dark lady': CIB; also DUM, p.393.

GO'M father and mother: GO'M cited in Healy.

'A good man …' and motto: DUM; Healy; Otway.

Protection racket, fishing boats: Malby in 1580; Knox, p.189.

'Dying like pigs': O'Donovan.

One chieftain … storm: NCoCI v5, p.18.

Prayer in stone: IDJ, Healy.

O'M, O'Flaherty wars: Roderick O'Flaherty (1684), *Chorographical Description of West
    Connaught*, edited by James Hardiman, p.382.

G and Donal: Healy, DUM.

'She ploughed …': Samuel Ferguson (1810–86).

Typical force: NCoCI v5, p.18+.

'They depended': GB O'Connor (1900), *Elizabethan Ireland*, p.66.

Number of galleys, scope of raids: Healy; rec John Appleby (2001), *Women and Piracy in Ireland*,
    in CR Pennell (ed.), *Bandits at Sea* (NYU Press), p.287.

'Surpassed': IDJ.

'Plundered': *AH.*

Various 'thread' and 'cable' stories: *AH*; *Irish Independent*, 13 November 2010.

Lighthouse: Gerard Moran *et al.* (eds.), *Mayo: History and Society* (Geography Publications),
    p.673.

'There came to me …': Sidney to Walsingham 1583, Carew Ms; cited in CIB and Knox, p.186.

Drury quotes, GO'M captured and jailed: Carew Ms; cited in CIB; Knox, p.186; James Froude
(1850), *History of England*, p.188.

Galway attack, 'so spirited': Healy; DUM; IDJ.

Malby quotes: DUM; Knox, p.196; Healy.

Rent, 'fought with me': Healy.

RB died, cows and mares: DUM; CIB; Healy.

'When G's son … very poor': DUM.

Raid on Arans: DUM; Healy; Knox, pp.232, 245.

Raid on Murrough, 'fire and sword': DUM.

Bingham's letter to London: Healy, CIB.

Elizabeth verdict: In letter to RB, Hist Ms Comm. Cited in Knox, p.254.

Three new warships, Donegal: DUM; CIB.

G death, legacy, burial: O'Donovan; DUM; also rec, www.opw.ie.

Toby's honours: Lodge's *Genealogy*; Healy.

Manning quote: *NSoCI Historical Outline*, p.20; Gosling quote, v5, p.30.

1753 song: *AH* v3, p.340; Henry Grattan, *Memoirs of Henry Grattan*, p.79; James Hardiman,
Irish Minstrelcy v2.

Historical background: *AH* v3, p.340; William Coxe (1829), *Memoirs of Henry Pelham*, v2,
p.284; 'Duke of Dorset' in *Dictionary of National Biography*.

GO'M as symbol of Ireland: John Marshall (1924), *Popular Rhymes of Ireland*, ch.2.

Roderic O'Flaherty: *op. cit.*

Religiosity: e.g., *Grainne Meal* by Sean MacDonnell (1691–1754).

'Silly stories': DUM.

SEVEN MYTHS

The haircut:

True origin of *Granuaile*: Healy.

Short hair a disgrace: *The Lamentable Cries of Prisoners* (1624).

Royal queen:

1872 writer: O'Brien.

PJ O'Rourke (1993), *Give War A Chance* (Grove Press).

'She was never …': *NSoCI, Historical Outline*, p.20, by Conleth Manning.

'I dismiss thee':

Legend: Otway.

Official documents: e.g., Sidney; Malby, *op. cit.*

Theresa Murray: in *History Ireland* Mar–Apr 2005.

Met Elizabeth:

Etching: In *AH*.

'Sister sovereign': K337; O'Brien.

'Patronised': O'Brien.

Raleigh, lapdog: Otway.

'No authentic …': Healy.

Chester versions: Otway; John O'Hart (1915), *Irish Pedigrees* v2.

Brady quote: Ciaran Brady (2014), 'Coming into the weigh-house: Elizabeth I and the government of Ireland', in Brendan Kane and Valerie McGowan-Doyle (2014), *Elizabeth I and Ireland*.

De Lacy:

All referenced in text except: reviews in *Irish Monthly Magazine* v3 and D.U.M.

Howth kidnap: 'I checked … twenty-one': Author's view based on facts in Lodge, John (1789), *The Peerage of Ireland* vol 3; and Cockayne, GE (1892), *Complete Peerage* vol 4.

1400s story: MacFirbis in *Book of Genealogies*; Knox, p.158; Healy.

Re-enactment: Healy.

Fitzgerald: in *Journal of the Royal Society of Antiquaries of Ireland* part 4, v37.

1830 version: John Timbs, *The Mirror of Literature* v15.

Algerine pirates:

Simon Danser: Gosse, *History*, pp.44 and 49.

London birth version accepted: eg Otway, DUM.

Refuted in early 1900s: Healy.

Hennelly's stories: O'Donovan v2 ms247. O'D and H relationship, O'D *passim*. 'Mayo character': Herity in intro to 2009 edition, xvi.

PIRATE PILGRIMAGE THE ELEVENTH

A Voyage by Sir William Monson … about England, Scotland and Ireland, 1614 in *Sir William Monson's Naval Tracts in Six Books* (1703) (London: Churchill), v2, p.246.

WM life: *Encyclopaedia Britannica* (1910–11); *Dictionary of National Biography*.

'Cormat' = 'Michael Cormick', and Compaen visit 1626: CSPI 1625–33, p.104. Thanks for background info to (rec) Roy Stokes (2015), *Between the Tides* (Amberley).

'Most barbarous': CSPI 1615–25, p.580.

'They put rushes …': M De la Boullaye le Gouz, 1644.

'No less than …': Cited in *Analecta Hibernica* No 2 (1931), p.52.

'Go up and …': Cited in Richard Berleth (2002), *The Twilight Lords* (Roberts Rinehart), p.76.

Woodcut: John Derricke, *Images of Ireland* (1581).

'Towards evening …': Letter from Edward Willes, *c.*1760.

PIRATE PILGRIMAGE THE TWELFTH

CC's arrival in Killybegs, Brooke's reports, CC's response and their meeting, see CSPI 1625–31, pp.231, 232, 236; Leamcon, CSPI 1615–25, p.584; CC's activities in Ireland from Oct 1624 to May 1625, CSPI 1615–25, pp.531, 549, 558–559; CC in Dublin, Broad Haven, Kerry, Donegal, CSPI 1625–33, pp.96, 104, 123; Cary's secret scheme to enlist pirates, CSPI 1615–25, p.480.

CC biog: Anon ('The Schoolmaster') (1659), *Claes G Compaen of Oostzanen*; Nicholas Wassenaer (*c.*1625), *Historic Account …*; rec, Stephen Snelders (2005), *The Devil's Anarchy* (Autonomedia); rec, Alex Ritsema (2008), *Pirates and Privateers from the Low Countries* (Lulu.com); rec, Virginia West Lunsford (2005), *Piracy and Privateering in the Golden Age Netherlands* (Palgrave Macmillan).

CC overnight with Hull: rec, Snelders, p.19, citing Wassenaer v13.

Devon cargo: rec, Ritsema, p.58.

Kidnap, pockets bulging, previous mutiny: rec, Snelders, pp.20, 27, 34, citing Anon, *CGCoO*.

Brooke biog: From numerous references in CSPI 1603–1625; *Illustrated Dublin Journal* v1 no 15, 1861; *Irish Penny Journal* v1, p.186; rec, Brian Barton (1988), *Brookeborough* (Queen's University Belfast).

Irish Examiner, 12 May 2014.

PIRATE PILGRIMAGE THE THIRTEENTH

This chapter mostly based on the eyewitness testimonies of Philip Middleton and John Dan, recorded in the *Calendar of State Papers Colonial, America and West Indies* v15 and v16, 1695–1697; and the trial transcript in (1696) *The Trial of Joseph Dawson and Others*.

Achill episode: 'Abstract of Letters relating to the Sloop *Isaac* June 16–July 7 1696', collected by John Jameson (1923), in *Privateering and Piracy in the Colonial Period*.

Avery background: Charles Johnson (1742), 'The Life of Captain Avery', in *A General and True History …*

Khafi Khan's memoirs and Mogul perspective: in *Capture of a Royal Ship by the English*, in HM Elliot (ed.) (1867–77), *History of India as Told by its Own Historians* v7 LXXIX.

'As for the women ...': Quoted in Daniel Defoe (1719), *The King of Pirates*.

Reaction in India, English Governor: *Letters from Bombay 12.10.1695* in Jameson, *op. cit.*;
Henry Briggs (1849), *The Cities of Gujaráshtra*.

Cuttle £21: Recorded on 9 July 1715.

PIRATE PILGRIMAGE THE FOURTEENTH

John Barbour (1375), *The Bruce, Being a Metrical History of Robert the Bruce*.

The Bruces in Ireland (1857), in *Ulster Journal of Archaeology* v5, pp.1–12.

Poem: William Drummond (1826), *Bruce's Invasion of Ireland* (useful for its extensive historical
footnotes).

John T Gilbert (1884), *Chartularies of St Mary's Abbey, Dublin*.

Annals of Innisfallen.

Annals of Lough Ce.

James Grace of Kilkenny (1539), *Annales Hiberniae*.

William Camden (1615 and 1617), *Annales* and (1596) *Britannia*.

Margaret Cusack (1868), *An Illustrated History of Ireland*.

Birlinns, naval background: rec, Spiers *et al.* (2012), *Military History of Scotland* (Edinburgh
University Press), pp.151–52.

Rec, Colm McNamee (1997), *The Wars of The Bruces* (Tuckwell Press) and (2012) *Robert Bruce,
Our Most Valiant Prince, King and Lord* (Birlinn).

Rec, Tim Hodkinson, *Mediaeval Pirates: The Tale of Tavish Dhu*, and *On the 700th Anniversary of
the Scottish Invasion of Ireland* in timhodkinson.blogspot.ie.

MacDonnells: rec, Appleby, *Problem, op. cit.*, p.44.

The Lark: *Ordnance Survey of Londonderry*, 1837.

Neither wood nor lea: *Annála Connacht*, 1315.

Black Tom and Skerries, burial: Hugh Forde (1923): *Sketches of Olden Days in Northern Ireland*
(Linenhall); tales of buried treasure, e.g., *Three-Day Myths and Legends Tour* at www.
causewaycampers.com; and www.facebook.com/PiratesOffPortrush.

PIRATE PILGRIMAGE THE FIFTEENTH

This chapter based on contemporary reports and on JPJ's own journals and letters. Other
analyses:

M MacDermot Crawford (1913), *The Sailor Whom England Feared*.

Edgar Stanton Maclay (1899), *A History of American Privateers*.

Don Seitz (1917), *Paul Jones, His Exploits in English Seas* [Collection of contemporary newspaper articles].

John Sherburne (1851), *The Life and Character of John Paul Jones*.

'On Monday last …': *Shipping News*, 21 April 1778, *PRONI* 9807964.

Childhood, patronymic, early career: Sherburne, p.9+; Crawford, p.9+.

Murder: *Morning Chronicle*, 8 May 1778; also see (1770) *Warrant for the Arrest of JPJ*.

'Pirate' and 'plunderer': *General Advertiser*, 28 September 1779; Sherburne, xvi.

Commission: Congress to JPJ, 10 October 1776.

'Make their fortunes': Recruiting poster for *Ranger*, 1777.

'Though I have drawn …' and 'as the feelings': *Letter to Lady Selkirk*, 8 May 1778.

'Not yet begun': 1779 battle against *Serapis*.

'He appeared …' and 'in action': Seitz, pp. 55, 158.

'Wild for love', smart man, poem: *Letters from Miss Edes at Versailles*.

Burdon, volunteers, sightseers: Sherburne, p.64; Seitz, pp. 10, 19.

Whitehaven, insane, Selkirk: Sherburne, p.45+; Seitz, p.17, Crawford, p.141.

Encounter with Drake: JPJ to Mr Hewes in Crawford, p.149+; *Report from The Cumberland Packet 28.4.78*; Sherburne, p.45+.

Strike: Seitz, p.19.

Carnage: Letter to Lady Selkirk.

Fishermen: Sherburne, p.50.

Brest and 'impossible' quote: Crawford, pp.158–159.

PIRATE PILGRIMAGE THE SIXTEENTH

'This place is full …' and 'When we see …': *Belfast News Letter*, 16 October 1781, in Public Record Office of Northern Ireland [*PRONI*] documents 9808366 and 9808325.

Robert McClelland: 'Capture of the brig *Loyalty*', *Saunders's News Letter*, Dublin, 10 July 1778; *Shipping News*, 3 July 1778, *PRONI* 9807970.

Snow *Blakeney*: *Shipping News*, 28 February 1758, *PRONI* 9808103.

Snow *Jenny*: *Shipping News*, 20 December 1776, *PRONI* 9808171.

Ship *Eleanor*: *Belfast News Letter*, 29 May 1781 *PRONI* 9808362.

Sloop *Douglas*: *Shipping News*, 29 August 1777, *PRONI* 9808184.

Duchess of Leinster: *Shipping News*, 6 September 1776, *PRONI* 9808168.

John Brown: *The Deposition of John Brown of Holywood*, in John Jameson (1923), *Privateering and Piracy in the Colonial Period*, Doc 174.

Bangor and Vikings: *Annals of Clonmacnoise*, 821 AD.

Dowlin at Copelands: *News Letter*, 10 September 1779, *PRONI* 9808346.

Dowlin, 'master and crew mostly Irish': *News Letter*, 28 July 1780, *PRONI* 9808354.

Brig *Bell*: *News Letter*, 14 September 1781, *PRONI* 9808363.

Avery in Donaghadee: *Testimony of John Dan* (Chapter 14).

Avery in England, lost fortune: Charles Johnson (1724), *General History*, p.54.

PIRATE PILGRIMAGE THE SEVENTEENTH

Overview: the stories of Melcorca, Olaf and Gilli are from the *Laxdaela Saga*. Findan from the *Life of the Holy Findan*. Irish annals quoted are the *Annals of the Four Masters* ['*AFM*'] *Clonmacnoise* ['*AC*'], *Ulster* ['*AU*'] and the *Fragmentary Annals* ['*FA*']. Unless otherwise stated, all individual Viking incidents are from these annals.

   I am indebted to the wonderful *Viking Ireland* exhibition at the National Museum of Ireland for an introduction to the subject, and to Lenore Fischer's *A County by County Reference List for Viking Activities in Ireland*, which proved an invaluable portal to the original sources.

Rec, Donnchadh Ó Corráin (1999), *Viking Ireland – Afterthoughts*, in HB Clarke *et al.* (eds.),
    Ireland and Scandinavia in the Early Viking Age (Four Courts).

Rathlin raid: *AU* 795. (Although some historians dispute the location.)

'Foreign, barbarous …': *FA* 338, 886.

'Miserably ravaged …': Symeon of Durham on Lindisfarne raid.

'Tongues of fire …': Viking bard on raid on Iona, *c*.1100.

'They slew 15 …': *Egil Saga*.

Aileach, Murtough: *AU*; Muircheartach d943 in (1885–1900) *Dictionary of National Biography*.

'Not surprised': *AFM* 864.

'Alas …': *FA*.

'Plundering of Howth by foreigners …': *AFM*.

'As many women …': *AC*.

Cerball and dynasty: Ó Corráin, p.17.

DNA evidence: Studies by Agnar Helgason.

Rus and Ibn Fadlan: Ahmad ibn-Fadlan, *Letter on the Vikings*.

'The wind blows …': Written *c*.850 AD by unnamed Irish monk, possibly from Down, now
    kept in Swiss monastery.

African slaves: *FA*; also see (rec) Ann Christys (2015), *Vikings in the South* (Bloomsbury), p.56.

'He let it be known'; 'Our going …': *Egil Saga*.

V bid to establish kingdom in northeast; cockpit of war; prevented by Murtough: rec, Ó Corráin, p.7.

'The shrieking …': *FA*.

Movilla 825: *AU*, *AFM*.

Poem: Free translation of verse in *AU* 895.

Surnames: *Irish Times*, 19 October 2015, *Irish Roots: Viking Surnames*.

What Vikings did for us: *Viking Ireland*, NMI.

Dublin centre of slave trade: rec, Desmond Keenan (2016), *The Social History of Ireland* (XLibris); Else Roesdahl (1998), *The Vikings* (Penguin).

PIRATE PILGRIMAGE THE EIGHTEENTH

Gentleman and Citizen's Almanack (January 1815), p.192.

John Warburton, James Whitelaw and Robert Walsh (1818), *History of the City of Dublin*

Thom's Irish Almanac (1857), p.966.

WHG Kingston (1875), *The Missing Ship, or The Log of the Ouzel Galley*.

C Litton Falkiner (1904), *Illustrations of Irish History and Topography*.

George A Little (1940), *The Ouzel Galley* (Old Dublin Society).

LM Cullen (1983), *Princes and Pirates: The Dublin Chamber of Commerce 1783–1983*.

Bertie Ahern (2005), speech at the 300th anniversary of the Ouzel Galley Society.

John Moran (2005), 'A Legend to Rival the *Marie Celeste*' in *The Irish Times*, 1 November 2005.

Dublin International Arbitration Centre (2005), *A History of Arbitration in Ireland*.

Irish Law Reform Commission (2008), consultation paper *Alternative Dispute Resolution*.

Emer Costello, then Lord Mayor of Dublin (21 June 2010), speech at Dublin Port; also Dublin Port Company (same date), *About the Dublin Port Company*.

Lisa Marie Griffith (2011), 'The Ouzel Galley Society in the 18th Century…' in Brown, M, and Donlan, SP (eds.), *The Laws and Other Legalities of Ireland, 1689–1850*; also her article '"Never Let The Facts Interfere with a Good Story": The Origin of the Ouzel Galley Society' in *History Ireland*.

RTÉ Radio One, *Seascapes*, 1 August 2014.

Roy Stokes, 'The Legend of the *Ouzel Galley*: A Fresh Look', in www.ouzelgalley.net.

Other books by Des Ekin

In June 1631, pirates from Algiers and armed troops of the Turkish Ottoman Empire, led by the notorious captain Morat Rais, stormed ashore at the little harbour village of Baltimore in West Cork. They captured almost all the villagers and bore them away to a life of slavery in North Africa.

The prisoners were destined for a variety of fates – some would live out their days chained to the oars as galley slaves, others in the scented seclusion of the harem or within the walls of the Sultan's palace. Only two of them ever saw Ireland again.

The Stolen Village is a fascinating tale of international piracy and culture clash nearly 400 years ago, and is the first book to cover this relatively unknown and under-researched incident in Irish history.

Shortlisted for the Argosy Irish Nonfiction Book of the Year Award

Kinsale, Ireland: Christmas Eve, 1601. As thunder crashes and lightning rakes the sky, three commanders line up for a battle that will decide the fate of a nation.

General Juan del Águila is in command of the last great Spanish Armada. Its mission: to seize a bridgehead in Queen Elizabeth's territory and hold it.

Facing him is Charles Blount, a brilliant English strategist whose affair with a married woman brought him to within a hair's breadth of the gallows.

Meanwhile, Irish insurgent Hugh O'Neill knows that this is his final chance to drive the English out of Ireland.

For each man, this is the last throw of the dice. Tomorrow they will be either heroes – or has-beens.

'Fascinating … lively and enthralling … Ekin is a wonderful guide through this engrossing tale.'
Sunday Times

THE
SOUTH-W[est]
COAST O[f]
IRELAN[d]
from Dungar[van]
to the River Shai[nnon]

Leagues 20 in a Degre[e]

Shannon mouth

Cape Lem
or Leghead

Old head

Casheen R.

Mary Cove

Killmesby

Tralli Bay

rt Trally

Finder I.

THE

COUNTY

OF KERRY

Castlemaine

Valkom

Dingle

Ballywacker
Mountains

C O

C O U

Cape Clear Cp.

Calves

Stakes